Praise for the 3<u>rd</u> Edition of *Email Marketing Rules*

"Chad is dead on with this book. Stop chasing the next new thing and get good at email."

> **—Joe Pulizzi**, Founder of the Content Marketing Institute; author of five books, including *Content Inc.* and *Epic Content Marketing*

"Email marketing is more critical than ever. *Email Marketing Rules* is timely, relevant, and necessary. Highly recommended!"

> **—Jay Baer**, President of Convince & Convert; author of *Hug Your Haters* and *Youtility*

"Chad is honestly one of the brightest minds in email marketing, and this book is the gold standard on email best practices."

> **—Mathew Sweezey**, Principal of Marketing Insights at Salesforce; author of *Marketing Automation for Dummies*

"Avoid leaving money on the table. *Email Marketing Rules* gives you a well-structured, easy-to-follow template for reviewing and improving your program."

> **—Dr. Dave Chaffey**, CEO & Publisher of SmartInsights.com; digital marketing author

"I train hundreds of email marketers and reference this book regularly. A must-have."

> **—Kristin Bond**, Sr. Email Marketing Manager at Girl Scouts; Co-Founder of Women of Email

CHAD S. WHITE has written more than 3,000 posts and articles about email marketing trends and best practices. He has served as lead email marketing researcher at three of the largest email service providers—Salesforce, ExactTarget, and Responsys—as well as at the Direct Marketing Association and Litmus.

A former journalist at Condé Nast and Dow Jones & Co., Chad has been featured in more than 100 publications, including *The New York Times*, *The Wall Street Journal*, *USA Today*, *U.S. News & World Report*, *Advertising Age*, *Adweek*, *MarketWatch*, and *SmartMoney*.

 EmailMarketingRules.com

 twitter.com/ChadSWhite

 linkedin.com/in/ChadSWhite

EMAIL MARKETING RULES

Checklists, Frameworks, and 150 Best Practices for Business Success

Chad S. White

Email Marketing Rules
Checklists, Frameworks, and 150 Best Practices for Business Success

Book cover by Jason Rodriguez

Charts, diagrams, and illustrations by Chad S. White

ISBN-13: 978-1546910633
ISBN-10: 1546910638

Third Edition: June 2017
Second Edition: September 2014
First Edition: March 2013

Printed in the United States of America

Contents

PART II
THE FRAMEWORKS

PART III
THE FUTURE

INTRO

Understanding Email Marketing's Power & Purpose

Email marketing's power is matched only by how incredibly misunderstood the channel is. It's only by understanding best practices that you can navigate the channel's complexities and find the best execution for your brand—one that serves the needs of your business and the needs of your subscribers.■

The Cure for Email Marketing's Complexity

The Best Executions Are Powered by an Understanding of Best Practices

> *"Email is funny because it has that stature of being a real pillar of effective marketing on the web, and then at the same time it is so often misunderstood."*
>
> —Sonia Simone, Chief Content Officer of Rainmaker Digital

Email marketing's return on investment is significantly higher than that of paid search, social media, and other digital channels—and way higher than that of direct marketing and other traditional channels. That's because email marketing has a number of compelling and unique characteristics.

WHY EMAIL MARKETING?

First, email is ubiquitous and available across a variety of platforms. Email, which has been called "the first social network," has far more users than Facebook. This gives email marketing unbeatable scale and reach.

Second, email is an open platform, controlled by many companies rather than just one. This gives it extra longevity and stability, but also keeps the cost of access low because of the competition.

Third, although consumers are incredibly omnichannel, they overwhelmingly prefer to receive commercial messages via email, because it's less intrusive as well as more convenient, searchable, and eco-friendly than other channels.

> **Marketers tend to force their way into every new communication channel, often confusing traffic with receptiveness.**

At a time when users increasingly block or skip ads and when closed platform social media sites increasingly require pay-to-play, having a marketing channel where commercial messages are welcome is tremendously powerful. It's worth stressing that email marketing is preferred by consumers both young and old.

Fourth, unlike noisy, untargeted broadcast mediums, email is a one-to-one communication channel. Its unparalleled targeting capabilities allow marketers to create messages that are highly relevant—even individually relevant.

Fifth, email is immediate, thanks to the age of mobile and the fact that checking email is a top activity on smartphones.

Sixth, although other channels excel at raising awareness, acquiring customers, and fostering conversations, email marketing is THE power channel for retention marketing. Consumers strongly associate email marketing with deals, product information, and service notifications, making it unrivaled at driving sales and boosting loyalty.

And **seventh**, email is the account of record for consumers. Email addresses serve as the most universal primary unique identifier online, essential to setting up accounts at most brands. The email inbox is where receipts, password resets, and notifications of all kinds are sent. The continued shift of messaging from postal mail to email will guarantee that people will be checking their inboxes regularly for decades to come.

THE DOWNSIDE

However, email marketing isn't without its negatives. In fact...

> **Many of email marketing's strengths are mirrored by equally powerful weaknesses.**

For instance, email's low cost of access makes it attractive to B2C brands, B2B companies, nonprofits, and every other kind of business—as well as for spammers. That makes the email inbox a crowded and unpleasant place for some people, although most consumers sign up to receive emails from only a handful of their favorite brands and aren't overwhelmed by the number of emails they receive.

The ability to personalize email content and use automation to send just the right content to the right subscriber at the right time creates super-effective messages. The downside here is that email's one-to-one targeting is raising people's expectation, which is making untargeted, broadcast messaging progressively less effective.

As a result, brands need to work harder than ever to be perceived as doing a decent job. Email's targeting capabilities also make email attractive to phishers, which erodes people's trust in the medium.

Anyone can sign up for an email account from a variety of providers and can easily access it across a range of devices, from desktops and laptops to mobile devices and wearables. However, since it is controlled by a patchwork of inbox providers, from inbox to inbox, there can be wild inconsistences in how an email is displayed, what content and functionality is supported, and what determines whether an email is blocked, junked, or makes it to the intended recipient successfully.

THE NEED FOR BEST PRACTICES

The good news is that you can overcome all of email's weaknesses if you use best practices to guide you.

After more than a decade of tracking the email marketing campaigns of many of the largest retailers and B2C brands in the U.S. and extensively researching their practices, I've never been more convinced that following best practices is critical to achieving spectacular results.

But what exactly do I mean when I say *best*

practices? Unfortunately, the term has been heavily abused over the past decade, to the point where some people have been convinced that best practices no longer exist.

Let's be clear: Best practices are not always determined by what the majority does, because adoption always lags. The exception does not disprove the rule. And while it sounds snappy, individualistic, and non-judgmental, the best practice is not "the practice that is best for you."

Best practices are those practices that generally produce the best results or minimize risk.

Even though email marketing is a dynamic, evolving channel—where consumer behavior, inbox provider protocols, inbox capabilities, email-reading devices, email marketing capabilities, and laws all change regularly—the industry has accumulated a lot of very stable conventional wisdom over the years. Ignoring them is inefficient at best and perilous at worst.

It's critical to recognize that...

The root of best practices is subscriber expectations and behaviors.

That's why there's rarely any significant competitive advantage in breaking best practices. Doing so just puts your program at odds with what subscribers expect.

That said, every brand is different, with different circumstances, different audiences, and different goals. So it should be fully expected that some companies can successfully deviate from industry accepted best practices through experimentation.

> **Best practices don't stop being best practices just because you don't follow them—just like beating the odds doesn't change the odds.**

Rather than being a surprise or disproving best practices, such instances only serve to illustrate why testing is itself a best practice.

If you're getting hung up on the implied absolutism or universalism of the word *best* in the term *best practice*, then feel free to call them industry accepted practices, accepted practices, recommended practices, or simply conventional wisdom as some people do. Whatever name you give them, these rules and guidelines will help you take your email marketing program to the next level.

THE BEST EXECUTION

Instead of putting a lot of effort into searching out those rare instances where you can break best practices, focus on bringing your business needs and your brand values and voice to your execution of best practices. Ask yourself:

☐ Do my email practices reflect my brand?

☐ Are my email practices in line with how I treat my customers in other channels?

☐ How do my email practices influence my customers' views about my brand?

☐ How do my subscribers respond to my email practices?

In other words, use best practices to guide you as you search for the best execution for your brand.

The on-brand execution of best practices tailored to your unique audience is what leads to the best execution.

Best practices generally allow for plenty of creativity in how they are implemented. Additionally, an ever-evolving array of techniques and tools are available to power your execution.

Therefore, you have numerous opportunities to express your unique brand and show off your marketing savvy and technological smarts. This is why best practices don't lead to mediocrity or sameness.

Think of best practices like a sheet of paper: You're confined only to the degree that you have to draw on the paper—and not on the table and floor and walls.

So, while following best practices separates average email marketers from poor ones, finding the best execution separates outstanding email marketers from average ones.

LOW-RISK STARTING POINT

Best practices are particularly valuable to those who are unfamiliar with email's unique, often confusing rules.

Even though email is a fairly mature channel, email marketing experience is not common and institutional support is subpar. Marketing degree programs rarely spend much—if any—time covering email marketing, which leads to a lot of on-the-job training. Some who are new to email marketing previously worked in the catalog and direct mail space, which has very different rules than email. And the small size of many email marketing teams may mean you don't have many coworkers to lean on, if you have any at all.

In this environment, avoiding assumptions based on personal preferences, experiences, behaviors, and tolerances is difficult. However, taking a "focus group of one" approach often leads to the wrong conclusions. That's because marketers and executives are very different from the average consumer, so your instincts may mislead you.

The chances are quite good that you have a lot less in common with your subscribers than you think. For instance, marketers are much more tech-savvy than the average person, are more likely to own the latest smartphone, are more involved in social media, are more likely to buy online, and are less concerned about privacy—to name just a few differences.

Given the reality of limited time and resources, best practices provide a valuable, low risk, default starting point.

Rather than using your gut, start by following conventional wisdom and then test to see how your audience responds to incremental changes. That said, although it's possible to test just about anything in email and nearly everything is worth testing on some level, very few things actually get tested.

WRANGLING THE COMPLEXITY

The bad news is that the growing complexity of email marketing can make it difficult to effectively execute on best practices.

On the technology side, one of the main reasons that email marketing doesn't reach its full potential is because of chronic underinvestment. It has been branded *cheap* and *simple*. That has misled some companies into thinking that maximizing email marketing's ROI is achieved by minimizing its budget, and that most of the money in the channel is in the low-hanging fruit.

I'm not sure that was ever true, but it's definitely not now. As email marketing has grown more complex, more of the ROI has migrated up the sophistication ladder. There's still plenty of low-hanging fruit, but competitive returns can only be reached through the savvy use of best practices, advanced targeting and automation, and cross-channel integration.

Investments in greater email marketing sophistication often lead to even higher returns, not diminishing returns.

On the human side, channel complexity has also hindered execution, as evidenced by the fact that the majority of the functionality offered by email service providers goes unused by most marketers.

In *The Checklist Manifesto*, Dr. Atul Gawande writes, "Avoidable failures are common and persistent, not to mention demoralizing and frustrating, across many fields—from medicine to finance, business to government. And the reason is increasingly evident: the volume and complexity of what we know has exceeded our individual ability to deliver its benefits correctly, safely, or reliably."

That's certainly the case with email marketing, which has become increasingly complex over the years as it has become more targeted, automated, personalized, interactive, and integrated across channels and functional areas.

THE SOLUTION

Dr. Gawande's prescription for better outcomes is the checklist. And it's mine as well.

In Part I of this book, I give you a checklist of best practices, breaking email marketing down into two sets of easy-to-understand rules that allow you to make focused improvements to your email program. The *Must-Follow Best Practices*—15 rules that are essential for all marketers to follow to the letter—separate legitimate marketers from spammers.

The *Recommended Best Practices*—covering everything from measuring success and email design to targeting and testing—are much more directional than prescriptive. How these rules are executed upon will vary from company to company, and some brands will discover through testing that they can bend or even break a few of these rules and achieve better results. These rules separate great marketers from the pack.

I've included *Words to Know* sections throughout Part I of this book. Although I try to keep the jargon to a minimum, an email marketing vocabulary is essential for you to know so you can effectively communicate with vendors, consultants, and other email marketers.

In Part II, I provide a more holistic perspective on key email marketing topics. The frameworks here give you more context for the rules and help you make strategic decisions about how to achieve your program goals, whether you're looking to...

☐ Optimize list growth

☐ Improve your deliverability

☐ Ratchet up the relevance of your emails

☐ Increase your email frequency wisely

☐ Maximize your subscriber lifecycle opportunities

☐ Develop cross-channel synergies

☐ Strengthen your email marketing workflow

☐ Better understand the performance of your emails and your email marketing program

And in Part III, I share my predictions about where email marketing is headed next.

In addition to the rules in Part I, over the course of the book you'll also find four overarching *Power Rules*, which bring a critical point of focus to the section they conclude.

However, one thing you won't find in this book is examples of real-world emails. Frankly, books are just a bad format to share such examples. Instead, throughout the book I refer to bonus collections of *Outstanding Email Marketing Examples* that you can explore online at EmailMarketingRules.com/Examples.

Having these online allows you to see them in color, zoom in on details, and share them more easily. You'll find lots more examples than I could possibly include in this book, plus I'll be updating the collections periodically to keep them current.

Since I've covered the U.S. retail industry for so long, you'll find that *Email Marketing Rules* slants toward American B2C marketers, who are among the heaviest users of email marketing. However, because of globalism, consolidation, changing consumer behavior, and other factors, the issues affecting email marketers have become fairly universal.

So, the vast majority of the rules and concepts also increasingly apply to B2B companies, nonprofits, and international businesses, both big and small.

GET OUT YOUR PEN

This book is designed to get you excited about the possibilities, thinking about your program's goals, planning improvements, and talking with your colleagues, new hires, bosses, and vendor partners.

When you're done reading this book, I encourage you to loan it out. But before you do that, mark up this book. You'll find plenty of white space throughout it. Use it. Jot down your ideas and questions, what you'd like to do and who you need to talk to in order to make it happen. Dog-ear the pages and underline and star the passages that are key for your email program. That way when you pass this book along, your associates will see your vision for how to improve your email program.

Ready? Let's go! But before we jump into the rules, let's first discuss the most critical framework for achieving email marketing success: The Hierarchy of Subscriber Needs.■

"Email's greatest strength lies in its ability to generate the highest ROI of any digital marketing channel. And therein lies also its greatest weakness: the tendency for many marketers to treat the channel lazily or nonchalantly because of its high ROI."

—Ryan Hofmann, Chief Marketing Officer at Global Access

The Hierarchy of Subscriber Needs

Creating Respectful, Functional, Valuable, and Remarkable Email Experiences

> *"Being useful and interesting and relevant needs to be the least of what your brand is known for, now and in the future."*
>
> —Jay Baer, President of Convince & Convert; author of *Hug Your Haters* and *Youtility*

Relevance has been the clarion call for email marketers for nearly a decade. However, this panacea for all email marketing ills is often discussed in vague, mystical terms or discussed within the narrow context of company-specific examples. Although relevance is indeed in the eye of the beholder, that doesn't mean it's indescribable or immeasurable.

Boiled down, relevance is about successfully fulfilling all four levels of the Hierarchy of Subscriber Needs (see Fig. 1 on next page)—that is, creating subscriber experiences that are…

☐ Respectful

☐ Functional

☐ Valuable

☐ Remarkable

Satisfying any one level is dependent on satisfying all of the previous levels. For instance, you can't create valuable experiences if your emails aren't functional and respectful. And you can't create remarkable experiences if your emails aren't valuable, functional, and respectful.

Whether you're meeting each of these needs can be gauged based on measuring common email activities: spam complaints, opens, unsubscribes, clicks, conversions, revenue, forwards, and social sharing.

Let's take a look at each subscriber need one at a time.

___

Hierarchy of Subscriber Needs

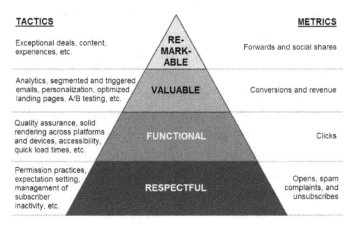

TACTICS		METRICS
Exceptional deals, content, experiences, etc.	RE-MARK-ABLE	Forwards and social shares
Analytics, segmented and triggered emails, personalization, optimized landing pages, A/B testing, etc.	VALUABLE	Conversions and revenue
Quality assurance, solid rendering across platforms and devices, accessibility, quick load times, etc.	FUNCTIONAL	Clicks
Permission practices, expectation setting, management of subscriber inactivity, etc.	RESPECTFUL	Opens, spam complaints, and unsubscribes

FIGURE 1

RESPECTFUL

At a minimum, subscribers need marketers to respect their permission grant. At the beginning of the email relationship, marketers should ensure that every person is aware that they are opting in to receive email. It also means setting the appropriate expectations around email frequency and content.

In the middle of the email relationship, emails should arrive at a frequency subscribers don't think are excessive and ideally they should arrive when subscribers are in the market to buy your products or services.

And at the end of the email relationship, it means an easy and quick unsubscribe process and managing inactive subscribers effectively. If a subscriber hasn't opened or clicked on one of your emails in a long time, marketers need to acknowledge that permission has been withdrawn and stop emailing that person.

Respect and trust are the foundations of all business relationships. And they serve as the foundation of email relationships as well.

While some think that a relevant message can compensate for a lack of permission, this is a losing strategy. Permission is foundational to creating relevance. This is borne out by the fact that the email element that has a biggest impact on whether an email is opened is the *from* name, which represents the person's previous interactions with your emails and your brand in general.

Disregarding permission puts your brand at an immediate disadvantage in the inbox, in addition to risking sender reputation damage and brand damage through negative word of mouth.

You can measure how respectful your emails are by looking at opens, spam complaints, and unsubscribes.

A lack of opens early in an email relationship likely indicates that you never really secured permission in the first place, and a lack of opens later likely indicates that permission has lapsed. High spam complaint and unsubscribe rates at the very beginning of an email relationship are also danger signs that your permission practices are too weak.

However, high spam complaint and unsubscribe rates later in an email relationship generally indicate that you're failing to meet another subscriber need.

FUNCTIONAL

The next need is for functional email experiences. That means, among other things, that:

- ☐ Emails display appropriately across the mobile, web, and desktop email clients that your subscribers use

- ☐ Text is legible and links are spaced far enough apart so they can be accurately clicked or, more importantly, tapped

- ☐ The links in your emails take them to the intended destinations

- ☐ The content is clear and free of errors

Essentially, all of this is about quality assurance. As in other forms of communications, errors distract your subscribers. But mistakes are especially detrimental in emails since you only have a few seconds to capture a subscriber's attention.

If they focus on an error in rendering, for instance, instead of your message, then engagement suffers. And if they're motivated enough to click through and then find themselves on an unexpected landing page or encounter a "404 page not found" error, then you've probably not only lost their attention in this instance, but they're also less likely to click through in the future.

You can measure how functional your emails are by looking primarily at clicks.

If your emails have broken links and images or have text that's too small to read on mobile devices, for example, your clicks will suffer.

VALUABLE

In order for marketers to have profitable relationships with subscribers, they have to create email experiences that subscribers find valuable, engaging, and compelling as individuals. Let's unpack that statement a little at a time.

First, *worthwhile*. Discounts, deals, and buying-related information are the No. 1 reason people signup for email. If you're a retailer, restaurant, or consumer brand, keep focused on fulfilling those needs. If you're a nonprofit, service, or B2B brand, stay focused on service information and brand-building.

Second, *engaging*. It's also important to engage subscribers who don't consider themselves in the market to make a purchase. Educational and instructional information can provide value to non-purchasers, as well as providing context that makes your products more compelling. Including non-promotional calls-to-action also helps keep your subscribers' attention between purchases.

Outside voices and cross-channel content can play a powerful role here. A disembodied corporate voice is far less compelling than the voices of customers, staffers, brand advocates, and outside experts—whether in the form of product reviews, testimonials, articles, videos, tweets, or pins.

And third, *compelling as individuals*. Beyond simply delivering what you promised subscribers when they signed up, you can discover what individual subscribers value by collecting demographic information, preferences, purchase history, behavioral data, and social data. And then you can use that information to power targeted email content.

You can measure how valuable your emails are by looking primarily at email conversions and revenue.

This is the point in the Hierarchy of Subscriber Needs where marketers often go wrong. Because of confusion, poor goal-setting, technical roadblocks, and other issues, marketers will use top-of-the-funnel metrics to gauge whether they're creating value instead of the bottom-of-the-funnel metrics they should be using.

REMARKABLE

And lastly, subscribers need the emails they receive to at least occasionally deliver remarkable experiences—that is, something that's worth telling someone else about. Like all humans, your subscribers are social beings. They want to evangelize for your brand, but you have to give them something worth sharing—be it an amazing deal, exclusive content, or a special experience.

Creating an email that subscribers will talk about isn't easy. Some tactics that aid with virality include:

☐ Targeting niche audiences with segmentation and triggered messages

☐ Making the most of topics such as events and charity efforts, which are innately more social and share-worthy

☐ Planning periodic emails with extra special content and using design to differentiate those emails from your run-of-the-mill emails

☐ Placing prominent "share with your network" calls-to-action in your most share-worthy emails

You can measure how remarkable your emails are by looking primarily at forwards and social shares.

In addition to raising awareness, aiding acquisition, boosting email engagement, and generating additional conversions, forwards and social shares are powerful indicators of the overall health of your email program. Used to measure the topmost portion of Hierarchy of Subscriber Needs pyramid, they're a sign that you're fulfilling your subscribers' needs at the highest level—that your emails are not just relevant, but deeply relevant.

An email program can be fairly successful while only fulfilling the first three subscriber needs, but a program can never be highly successful if it isn't creating remarkable experiences that convert subscribers into evangelists.

BUSINESS NEEDS

Of course, subscribers aren't the only ones with needs. Your business has needs, too, whether it's building awareness, nurturing leads, increasing customer loyalty, or some other goal.

If your email program spends all of its time completely focused on fulfilling subscribers needs, then the business reaps few benefits from the program. And if your email program spends all of its time completely focused on fulfilling business needs, then subscribers feel abused.

Ideally, you want to strike a balance between subscriber needs and business needs. Email marketing is about mutual benefits—not in every email, but over time. For the subscriber and the business, the email relationship should be a win-

Balancing Subscriber Needs & Business Needs

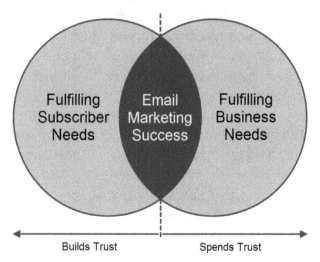

FIGURE 2

win situation. (See Fig. 2 above.)

But all successful email marketing relationships start with meeting your subscribers' needs, because...

If you're not fulfilling

your subscribers' needs, then

they won't help you fulfill

your business needs.

As you read this book, you'll find that most of the tactics and strategies explored relate back to fulfilling the Hierarchy of Subscriber Needs. Use that advice to build a foundation of trust with your subscribers. That's how to build a strong, effective email program.■

"The trust, the Emotional Bank Account, is the essence of Win/Win. ...Without trust, we lack the credibility for open, mutual learning and communication and real creativity."

—Stephen R. Covey, author of
7 Habits of Highly Successful People

PART I

The Rules

Email marketing is a big, complex channel with lots of moving parts. To help you avoid being overwhelmed by or lost in all that complexity, this part of the book breaks email marketing down into 150 individual best practices.

Divided into Must-Follow Best Practices and Recommended Best Practices, each rule zooms in on and addresses one element of email marketing at a time so you can focus on making targeted improvements to your program.■

WORDS TO KNOW

Controlling the Assault of Non-Solicited Pornography and Marketing Act of 2003 (CAN-SPAM): A law regulating commercial email messaging that forbids deceptive messaging, requires senders to include a working unsubscribe link and their mailing address in every email they send, and requires senders to honor opt-out requests, among other things

earned media: Media content produced by media outlets, bloggers, consumers, and other end users of a brand's products or services about that brand and distributed via any platform, such as publicity, social sharing, word of mouth, and ratings and reviews

email list: A list of the email addresses and other records associated with your subscribers

email service provider (ESP): A commercial provider of email marketing services that allows their clients to manage their email lists, send messages, track the response of message recipients, and process signups and unsubscribes, among other capabilities

engagement: Opens, clicks, and other positive indications that a subscriber is finding value in receiving emails from a brand

global filtering: When an inbox provider junks and blocks all email sent by a brand to any of its email users

granted media: Media content produced by a brand and distributed to an audience the brand developed via an open platform controlled by multiple third parties, such as email and SMS

inbox provider: Providers of web-based, desktop, and mobile email inboxes that send, store, and organize messages for users and manage and block spam (e.g., Gmail, Outlook, etc.); sometimes referred to as an internet service provider (ISP)

leased media: Media content produced by a brand and distributed to an audience the brand developed via a closed platform controlled by a third party, such as

Facebook, Twitter, and mobile app platforms

local-level filtering: When an inbox provider junks and blocks all email sent by a brand to one of its email users

opt-in email marketing: Sending email only to those who have given you permission to do so

opt-out email marketing: Sending email to those who have not given you permission to do so and requiring them to unsubscribe or mark your emails as spam if they don't want to receive future emails

owned media: Media content that's produced by a brand and distributed to an audience the brand developed via a closed platform controlled by the brand, such as a brand's website, brochures, in-store signage, and events

paid media: Media content produced by a brand and distributed to an audience developed by a third party via a closed platform controlled by that third party, such as TV ads, radio ads, newspaper ads, billboards, search ads, and display ads

permission: Actively or passively agreeing to receive promotional email

relevance: How valuable a subscriber thinks your emails are—which is largely determined by how many emails you send, when they arrive, their content, and how they look and function within whichever email client is being used

sender reputation: A reflection of your trustworthiness as an email sender that is affected by spam complaint rates and other factors that inbox providers use to determine whether to deliver, junk, or block your email

spam complaint: When an email recipient hits the *Report Spam* or *Junk* button, indicating to their inbox provider that the email was unwanted or irrelevant and that future emails from the sender are to be blocked

Must-Follow
Best Practices

The Rules that Separate Legitimate Marketers from Spammers

> *"Permission Marketing...offers the consumer an opportunity to volunteer to be marketed to. By talking only to volunteers, Permission Marketing guarantees that consumers pay more attention to the marketing messages."*
>
> —Seth Godin, author of *Permission Marketing* and many other books

For a long time, email has been caught between the opt-out marketing industry that's aligned with direct mail and the opt-in marketing industry that's aligned with mobile and social media.

Opt-out marketers have long argued for an expansive definition of permission and had a major victory in lobbying for the CAN-SPAM Act of 2003, which made it legal in the U.S. to send people promotional email without getting their permission first. They had hoped the law would perpetuate the free-wheeling, Wild West environment.

However, since the passage of the Act, a steady string of developments has undermined opt-out email marketing and rendered CAN-SPAM compliance a legal obligation that provides zero protection against having your emails junked or blocked by inbox providers—as well as zero protection against negative word of mouth and other brand damage.

GLOBALIZATION

First, the marketing laws of foreign countries—in particular, those of Canada, the U.K., and the European Union—stand in sharp contrast to those of the U.S. While CAN-SPAM focuses on the worst malicious and deceptive spammers, the laws elsewhere recognize that consumers also deserve protection from unwanted marketing emails.

> **Especially for global companies,**
> **the legal risks of not**
> **practicing permission-based**
> **email marketing are rising.**

Even if CAN-SPAM isn't strengthened at some point, many U.S. brands may find themselves needing to live up to the higher standards established by other countries. That's because all anti-spam laws are based on where a brand's subscribers live, not where the brand is based.

CONSUMER EXPECTATIONS

Second, many of today's other prominent digital marketing channels are opt-in, including social media, mobile apps, push notifications, and SMS. In these channels, consumers have total control.

Marketers can't make consumers follow them on Pinterest or push their app onto consumers' smartphones, and SMS requires an opt-in by law—with hefty penalties levied against lawbreakers. Permission is fundamental to these channels and can be given and taken away at will, with no recourse for the marketer.

As a result, consumers increasingly expect control over the commercial messages that reach them, including emails.

> **Many consumers now expect to not only have full control over permission, but also control over email content and frequency.**

The massive adoption of smartphones heightened these control expectations because consumers now carry their inboxes around with them everywhere they go. That's making the inbox an even more personal space.

EMPOWERED BY INBOX PROVIDERS

And third, inbox providers have nearly perfected spam filtering. It's incredibly rare that traditional malicious spam makes it to consumers' inboxes. So with that foe tamed, inbox providers now train their sights on grayer versions of spam sent by legitimate companies.

At the same time, because email usage

continues to grow, inbox providers continue to give their users more tools to manage their email— including tabs, auto-labelling, auto-foldering, priority marking, and more.

These inbox developments make it even less likely opt-out emails will get the attention of recipients.

THE COST OF EMAIL

The central reason that inbox providers and lawmakers abroad have moved so aggressively to protect inboxes is that the incremental cost to send an email is nearly zero. In contrast, the costs associated with traditional channels—such as TV ads, newspaper ads, and direct mail—ensure that marketers use those channels thoughtfully.

> **With email, recipients and inbox providers bear the vast majority of the cost of marketing messages.**

Email recipients bear the cost in terms of time and attention, while inbox providers bear the cost in terms of infrastructure. This difference is critical, because it exposes this channel to abuses on a scale that doesn't exist in other channels.

EMAIL MARKETING ISN'T OWNED MEDIA

Many marketers think about their email list as something they own. Some quietly sell their list to brokers, who quietly resell that list to others. Some bankrupt companies have publicly sold their list while liquidating their assets. And a few companies have been valued largely based on the size of their email list. Despite these occurrences...

Lists are owned only to the extent that someone can own a collection of nonbinding handshake agreements.

The truth is that inbox providers and their users own the email channel and that marketers are granted the right to use the email channel by meeting or exceeding subscribers' expectations and those of their inbox provider.

This is why email marketing has never sat comfortably in the owned bucket of the paid-owned-earned (POE) media model. It's a model that has also awkwardly forced social media into the owned bucket, since brands create the content and distribute it to an audience they've developed.

In both of those cases, however, new technologies are being forced into an outdated model that doesn't account for the type of platform being used to distribute the content. Taking that into consideration, social media is better categorized as *leased media* because it resides on a closed platform that's controlled by a single third party. And similarly, email marketing is better categorized as *granted media* because it is distributed via an open platform that's regulated and controlled by multiple third parties in the form of inbox providers. (See Fig. 3 on next page.)

The 5 Types of Media

Media Types ▶ / ▼ Characteristics		Paid	Owned	Granted	Leased	Earned
Content created by	Brand	✓	✓	✓	✓	
	Others					✓
Distributed to an audience developed by	Brand		✓	✓	✓	✓
	3rd Party	✓				✓
Via a	Closed platform controlled by brand		✓			✓
	Closed platform controlled by single 3rd party	✓			✓	✓
	Open platform controlled by multiple 3rd parties			✓		✓

FIGURE 3

This paid-owned-granted-leased-earned (POGLE) media model not only better accounts for email and social media, but for a range of digital channels. (See Fig. 4 on next page.)

EMAIL MARKETING IS GRANTED MEDIA

Unlike when brands hang signage in their stores, brands do not own the distribution platform for email. Inbox providers control distribution—and unlike the mail carrier who faithfully, passively, and transparently delivers everything you give them, inbox providers actively regulate the channel, globally junking and blocking email on behalf of all their users, or locally junking or blocking email on behalf of individual users.

Treating email like an ultra-cheap form of direct mail or a digital ad that you push into people's inboxes not only causes consumers to bad-mouth your brand on social media and to friends, but causes them to report your email as spam. When enough of an inbox provider's users do that, it starts junking or blocking your email. And after that happens, all the effort you spend crafting your messages is for naught, as most of the intended recipients will never see it.

PERMISSION IS FOUNDATIONAL

Permission takes effort to obtain, which is why spammers and some legitimate brands skip this step of the relationship-building process. Even though pushing unwanted email into inboxes is the equivalent of bursting into someone's house without being invited, some marketers believe their messages are so compelling that their trespassing will be forgiven.

Many marketers with strong permission practices and data on past purchases, click behavior, and preferences struggle to consistently create relevant messages and remain welcome in their subscribers' inboxes. So the idea that a company without permission could collect, purchase, harvest, or steal enough information to consistently create messages

---

POGLE Media Model
Paid-Owned-Granted-Leased-Earned

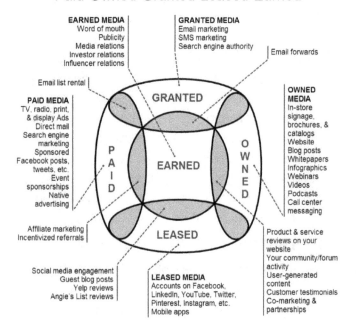

FIGURE 4

relevant enough to trump the need for permission is simply arrogant and delusional. Consumer expectations are just too high and inbox provider vigilance too unforgiving at this point.

Because it's not illegal, plenty of companies are more than happy to sell you lists of email addresses of "highly qualified" prospects or even of existing customers who haven't given you their email address. However, none of these companies can claim to sell you permission to email those prospects and customers, and permission is where all the value is. Without it, you're immediately at odds with that prospect or customer, damaging a relationship that you're hoping to build—while simultaneously risking your reputation with inbox providers.

> **While permission isn't a legal standard in the US, it is a de facto consumer standard globally.**

Instead of using unethical, unsustainable, and risky tactics to circumvent permission and the safeguards of inbox providers, you're better off investing that time in safe, proven methods for building long-term email marketing value.

It all starts with earning and respecting their permission, which is the focus of the first 15 rules.■

WORDS TO KNOW

active or express consent: Permission indicated when a person explicitly acts to indicate that they want you to add them to your email list (e.g., checking an unchecked box)

confirmed opt-in (COI) or double opt-in (DOI): A subscription process where a new email address is only added to your mailing address after the email address owner clicks a confirmation link in a subscription activation or opt-in confirmation request email that's sent to them after they opt in via a form or checkbox

email address append or e-append: Using a data broker to add email addresses to your customer profiles that don't have them

footer: The HTML text at the bottom of an email that includes the promotional fine print, legal language, unsubscribe link, mailing address, and other details

inactive subscriber: A subscriber who has not opened or clicked in any of your emails in a long time; the opposite of an active or engaged subscriber

list rental: Having a message sent on your behalf to an email list owned by someone else

malicious signups: When a person signs up to receive email from a brand using an address they know to be false, inaccurate, or a spam trap for the explicit purpose of harming that brand's sender reputation

opt-in confirmation page: Webpage or app messaging that follows a successful email signup

opt-in e-append: When a brand sends an email to people asking them for permission to email them in the future

opt-out e-append: When a brand sends an email to people informing them that they will continue to receive emails from the brand if they don't opt out

passive or implied consent: Permission indicated when a person does not act to keep you from adding them to your email list (e.g., not unchecking a pre-checked box)

re-confirmation or re-permission email: A message that asks a subscriber to reconfirm their subscription by clicking a link in the email in order to remain on your active mailing list

sender or *from* name: The name that appears in the *from* line in an email client; part of an email's envelope content

single opt-in (SOI): A subscription process where a new email address is added to your mailing list without requiring the owner of that email address to confirm definitively that they knowingly and willingly opted in

spam trap: These email addresses are used by inbox providers and blacklisting organizations to identify spammers

transactional email: A message sent to a current or former customer or user, regardless of whether they are a subscriber, in response to a transaction or administrative request made by that person or in response to a security, legal, or other company situation that may affect that person

unsubscribe or opt out: When a subscriber requests to be removed from your email list

unsubscribe or opt-out page: Webpage that is launched when subscribers click the unsubscribe link in your emails that allows subscribers to complete the unsubscribe process

unsubscribe process: How subscribers remove themselves from your email list

The Law

1

Follow the law, but recognize that doing so doesn't protect you from spam complaints, being blacklisted, or other negative outcomes.

In the U.S., the Controlling the Assault of Non-Solicited Pornography and Marketing (CAN-SPAM) Act of 2003 is the primary law regulating commercial email messaging, and it sets a very low bar for acceptable behavior. In fact, it sets the bar so low that legitimate email marketers should be much more concerned about getting into trouble with inbox providers than with the federal government.

CAN-SPAM requires email marketers to:

☐ Include a working unsubscribe link in every promotional email

☐ Honor opt-out requests as soon as possible

☐ Include their mailing address in every email they send

☐ Never use misleading or deceptive sender names, subject lines, or email copy

☐ Never attempt to conceal their identity or the fact that they're sending advertising

Besides violating CAN-SPAM, not following these requirements erode subscriber trust and lead to unsubscribes, spam complaints, and negative word of mouth. Recognize that misrepresenting who the sender is or falsely using *Re:* or *Fwd:* in a subject line, for instance, is not a marketing gimmick or tactic; it is a lie—and potentially a crime.

Depending on your target audience and countries of operation, your email program may be subject to other marketing laws. Other laws that might affect your program include, among others:

- ☐ Health Insurance Portability and Accountability Act (HIPAA) (US)
- ☐ California Online Privacy Protection Act (US)
- ☐ Canadian Anti-Spam Law (CASL)
- ☐ EU Opt-In Directive
- ☐ General Data Protection Regulation (EU)
- ☐ EU-US Privacy Shield
- ☐ Data Protection Act (UK)
- ☐ Federal Data Protection Act, and Telemedia Act (Germany)
- ☐ Article L. 34-5 of the French Postal and Electronic Communications Code
- ☐ Italian Data Protection Code
- ☐ SPAM Act (Australia)

Please consult an attorney to determine your legal risks and obligations.■

"The law is the low bar."

—Laura Atkins, Owner of Word to the Wise

Transactional Emails

2

Don't include too much promotional content in your transactional emails.

Transactional emails are so essential and expected that they are not permission-based—that is, they can be sent to people who haven't subscribed and they don't need to include unsubscribe links. To qualify as transactional, these emails need to meet at least one of the following criteria:

- ☐ Confirm, facilitate, or fulfill a purchase, registration, or other transaction

- ☐ Provide account balance information regarding a membership, subscription, account, loan, or other ongoing commercial relationship

- ☐ Provide warranty, recall, safety, or security information about a product or service purchased or used by the email address holder

- ☐ Provide information about a change in terms or policies initiated by the company

- ☐ Confirm user-initiated changes in account settings for security reasons

- ☐ Confirm the receipt of a user-initiated communication

- ☐ Provide information about an employment relationship or employee benefits

Most transactional emails that brands send are related to those first two criteria—that is, they are order confirmation, shipping confirmation, monthly account summary, and similar emails.

The primary purpose of these transactional emails legally needs to be to provide the customer with essential information about their transaction or account. However, in the U.S. and many other countries, transactional emails can provide more than that—within limits.

Marketers should take advantage of the high open rates that transactional emails enjoy by including promotional, educational, and other content in them. That's in addition to your standard promotional email navigation bar, if you typically include one.

For example, if a customer buys a computer, you could promote related accessories and software in the order confirmation email. Or if a supporter signs a petition, you could ask for a donation or promote an event in that email confirming the signing of the petition.

However, to stay in compliance with CAN-SPAM's definition of a transactional email, you should place additional content below the transactional content or in a right-hand column. Also, keep the amount of promotional content to no more than 20% of the overall email. That's the generally accepted limit, beyond which an email ceases to be transactional. (See Fig. 5 on next page.)

Be aware that some countries, including

Transactional Email Spectrum

Permission Not Required

Strictly Transactional Emails
Order/shipping/delivery/return confirmation
Download/e-product delivery
Monthly account summary
Overdrawn/near-limit alert
Subscription/membership/warranty
 expiration warning
Safety recall notice
Privacy policy/terms & conditions update
Password/address change confirmation
Account closed confirmation
Support/service inquiry confirmation

Transactional Emails
Any of the above with no more than 20%
 promotional content included

Non-Promotional Post-Purchase Emails
Installation instructions
Product care instructions
Service experience/satisfaction survey
Review/comment posted
Reactions/replies to review/comment

Promotional Post-Purchase Emails
Cross-sell/upsell based on purchase
Bounceback incentive for next purchase
Replenishment/short-supply notice
Purchase anniversary/end-of-product-life
 notification

Permission Required

All Other Automated and Promotional Emails

FIGURE 5

Germany, may require consent from customers before you can include promotional content in the transactional emails they receive. Without that consent, transactional emails must be kept strictly transactional.

Also, be aware that an email isn't necessarily transactional just because the content of an email is related to a transaction—even if that email isn't asking the recipient to spend more. Some post-purchase emails are not technically transactional, even though they aren't really promotional either.

Examples of non-promotional post-purchase emails include ones that contain installation instructions or care information for the product purchased. The same information in these emails may have been included in printed form with the product, but the intent is to make this information easier to store and retrieve. Product review request emails also fall into this category of emails.

While non-promotional post-purchase emails are unlikely to attract spam complaints or legal action if they don't include unsubscribe links, legally they should include them in most countries.

Many brands in the U.S. automatically opt new customers into receiving these emails, treating those opt-ins as separate from their promotional email opt-ins. That gives recipients the option of unsubscribing from these post-purchase emails.

Please consult an attorney to determine your legal risks and obligations.■

Permission

3

Don't buy email lists or barter for email addresses.

Very few consumers knowingly give a company permission to sell their email address to other companies. So if you purchase an email list, at best you'll reach inboxes overrun with marketing messages and spam. But more than likely you'll reach spam traps, abandoned email addresses, and unsuspecting and unreceptive people whose email addresses were scraped from the web and who are almost guaranteed to ignore or mark your emails as spam.

Sending email to a purchased email list is a quick and easy way to ruin your sender reputation and get you blocked by major inbox providers and blacklisting organizations.

Spamhaus and other blacklisting organizations create and hide pristine spam trap email addresses on websites where only email address scraping software used by spammers will find them. These email addresses routinely end up on email lists for sale. So if you use a purchased list, you will have likely signaled to blacklisting organizations that you're a spammer.

Moreover, all reputable email service providers (ESPs) have policies explicitly barring purchased lists from being uploaded to their platforms and will fire clients found using them. ESPs without these policies tend to attract lots of unscrupulous marketers, which then bring down the deliverability of every sender using those platforms.

Regrettably, some marketers refer to list rental as "buying a list." This perpetuates the myth that buying lists of email addresses is an acceptable practice.

I can't stress this enough: It is not.

List rental, on the other hand, is a fine practice when done correctly.■

"[Buying email addresses] is akin to playing Russian roulette with your email program."

—Ken Magill, Publisher of The Magill Report

Permission

4

When renting an email list, the list owner should never share the list with the renter.

If you rent a list from a company, you should supply the company with the message that you want sent. The list owner then sends that message on your behalf to their list—which you never see—using their usual name and email address, not yours. The unsubscribe link included in this email is an opt-out for the list owner only, not you. The list owner typically includes a tag in the subject line (e.g., *A message from our friends at* or *[Partner offer]*) and a message at the top of the email indicating that the message is from one of their partners.

This arrangement helps ensure that your message will be well received by the recipients, because the list owner would suffer unsubscribes and spam complaints if they sent a message from a partner that wasn't a good fit for their list.

List providers unwilling to follow this procedure should be viewed with great skepticism, as it's a sign that they either don't have permission to contact the people on their list or that the list is a poor match for your brand.

The message you send to a rented list should

ideally give you the chance to convert the recipients into customers, registered users, or into subscribers of your own. This allows you to strategically build your email list by renting the lists of partners, media, associations, and other groups that closely align with your business.■

Permission

5

Make sure consumers are aware that you are adding them to your email list.

If consumers are unaware that you've opted them into your email program, then they didn't give you permission. Hiding permission consent in your terms and conditions, privacy policy, or sweepstakes or contest rules is wholly insufficient. It's thoroughly established that consumers don't read privacy policies or terms and conditions.

Additionally, such consent doesn't protect you from spam complaints, nor does it constitute proof of signup when you're trying to get an inbox provider to stop blocking your emails or to get off a blacklist.

In countries where it's legal such as the U.S., using a prominently positioned and clearly worded pre-checked box of adequate size can make a consumer aware that they are opting in if they take no action. However, the strongest permission occurs when actively given—by checking a box or completing a signup form explicitly to receive email.∎

Permission

6

Never make an email opt-in mandatory for a customer interaction.

You can't force consumers to give you permission to send them promotional emails in exchange for the right to register a product, receive a receipt via email, enter a contest, or anything else. Permission granted in this fashion really isn't permission because they're only consenting to your demand to accomplish their goal.

Demanding permission in this fashion causes consumers to:

☐ Abandon the interaction with your brand

☐ Give you an old email address that they don't check anymore

☐ Give you a fake email address, which could potentially seriously affect your sender reputation

☐ Unsubscribe or mark your email as spam when they receive it

Instead, use the interaction as an opportunity to sell them on the value of becoming an email subscriber.■

Permission

7

Accept that permission grants are limited to the purpose stated when the subscriber opted in.

When asking a customer or prospect to opt-in, marketers need to be explicit as to what kind of email they will receive and not go beyond that.

For example, if a store rep asks a customer during checkout if they'd like to receive their receipt via email and they say yes, then the email address collected from that customer should only be used to send that receipt and nothing more.

Similarly, if a shopper signs up to receive a back-in-stock notification, you should only send that notification. Or if someone completes a form to download a whitepaper, unless you specify otherwise, their email address should only be used to deliver content in regards to that whitepaper.

It's tempting once you have someone's email address to want to send them additional messaging beyond what they signed up for. However, marketers risk spam complaints and more when they go counter to the expectations of subscribers.

Remember that getting someone's email address and getting their permission are not the same thing.■

Permission

8

Accept that permission grants are limited to the email address offered, even if you know one of the subscriber's other addresses.

So-called email change of address (ECOA) and other services that provide a consumer's other email addresses do not constitute permission.

Most consumers maintain multiple email addresses, using each one for different purposes. Consumers also abandon email addresses for various reasons. Using ECOA and other services to force your way into your subscribers' other inboxes because you're unhappy with the one you were granted entry to—even if you believe the address has been abandoned—is disrespectful and a violation of privacy and permission.■

Permission

9

Accept that securing an opt-in to another channel doesn't constitute permission to reach a consumer via email, too.

Knowing a customer's mailing address or phone number, or connecting with them on Facebook, LinkedIn, or another social network doesn't constitute having permission to add the customer to your email list.

Doing an email address append (e-append) or scraping an email address off a contact's profile page for mass marketing purposes is invasive, heavy-handed, and not how to build the foundation for a positive, profitable relationship.

If you must do an e-append, do an opt-in e-append, where you email people asking them for permission to email them in the future. That's in contrast to a more risky opt-out e-append, where you email people asking them to tell you if they don't want email from you in the future.

In some countries these practices are also illegal, which adds even more risk.

It's wiser to use your other channels to obtain email permissions for your customers and prospects.■

Permission

10

Don't share email addresses with other brands within your company.

Just because a consumer opts in to receive emails from one of your brands doesn't mean they're interested in getting emails from your other brands.

Consumers might not be aware of your other brands and, if they are, probably aren't aware that they are part of the same parent company. To protect yourself from souring the existing brand relationship, each of your sister brands must secure its own email permission.

The good news is that you can leverage one brand relationship to expose subscribers to your other brands and get additional opt-ins. Your opt-in confirmation page, welcome email series, preference center, and promotional emails can all be used to educate subscribers about your other brands and give them the chance to opt in to their email programs.■

Permission

11

When using a single opt-in process, treat new subscriptions as conditional on the subscriber engaging with your emails.

If you're not using a double opt-in process and a new subscriber hasn't opened or clicked any of your emails during their first 30 days on your list, you should stop mailing them.

This lack of activity may indicate that they...

☐ Didn't realize they opted in, which might be the result of poor permissioning practices

☐ Subscribed using a secondary or tertiary email account that they don't check often, if at all

☐ Have "subscriber's remorse" and immediately regretted subscribing

☐ Could be the result of bot activity

☐ Were signed up maliciously—that is, someone other than the email address holder signed up the address

All of those scenarios represent a risk—or at least a lack of opportunity—for the marketer.

For brands that email monthly or less often, a longer trial time period would be appropriate.

At the end of this period, consider sending

these "never-actives" a final email asking them to click a link in the email if they'd like to continue receiving messages from you. That way, on the off chance the email address does belong to a real live person and they go looking for your emails, they will have a clear way of reactivating their subscription.

Of course, if whole segments of new subscribers are not engaging with your emails—such as those with a Gmail address or those who signed up through your mobile website—then a broader deliverability or process problem likely exists rather than just an issue with the individual subscriber.■

Permission

12

Re-permission subscribers when you haven't honored their opt-in within 3 months of signup.

Whether due to human or technological errors, sometimes email marketing opt-ins aren't honored immediately. When this happens, if the delay has been longer than a few months, then it's highly recommended to re-permission these subscribers.

Re-permissioning is a form of double opt-in, where you send the would-be subscriber an email asking them to click a link in the email to confirm their signup. If they don't click the link, then they're not subscribed and you don't send them any more emails. With this kind of re-permission, you might want to explain that an error occurred and apologize for the delay. In addition to a *Yes, keep me subscribed* option, you might also consider giving recipients a *No, please unsubscribe me* option, as this has been found to increase response rates.

If you skip the re-permissioning, the risk is that the email address holder won't remember signing up, especially if they provided passive consent. That will likely translate into low engagement rates and high spam complaint rates. And the more time that passes, the higher the risk of each of those—with the risks becoming extremely high beyond a delay of 18 months.

The longer you go without emailing them, your risk of hard bounces also increases. Over time, some email accounts become closed or abandoned, which results in undeliverable email addresses that bounce.

To protect your deliverability, re-permission subscribers in small batches, perhaps starting with 100 at a time to get a sense of your average response. If the response is positive and the bounce rate is low, you can ramp up the re-permissioning.

However, if the response is negative, then you can avoid doing harm to your deliverability by keeping that re-permissioning process slow or perhaps abandoning the effort. While it's painful to walk away from the investment you made in attracting those people, sometimes that's the move that maximizes your return on investment.■

Permission

13

Make unsubscribing easy, taking no more than two clicks.

Your unsubscribe process constantly competes against the one-click, never-fail *Report Spam* button. Since unsubscribes don't hurt your sender reputation and spam complaints do, it's in your best interest to make opting out as friction-free as possible so subscribers don't resort to complaining. Here are some key ways to accomplish that:

First, the unsubscribe link needs to be easy to find upon scanning your promotional emails, so avoid small text and light gray fonts on white backgrounds. Use white space, bold text, and other typographical elements to make the link stand out.

Second, the unsubscribe link should never appear only in the form of graphical text or an image-based button because it will not display if images are blocked.

Third, it's best if the link text is the word *Unsubscribe* or a phrase that starts with that word, such as *Unsubscribe or Change Your Email Address* or *Unsubscribe or Update Your Email Preferences*, because consumers have been trained to look for that keyword. Avoid a generic *Click Here* call-to-action for your unsubscribe link.

Fourth, including an unsubscribe link at the top of certain emails or emails to certain groups of subscribers can often reduce complaints by encouraging unsubscribes instead. If you do this, you should also include one in your footer, because subscribers expect to find opt-out links there.

And lastly, the unsubscribe process should consist of no more than two clicks—one on the unsubscribe link in the email and one on the opt-out page. Requiring subscribers to login to access your unsubscribe page drives up spam complaints, and requiring anything besides the subscriber's email address to process an opt-out request is illegal.■

"Unsubscribes are healthy."
—Jacob Hansen, Deliverability Consultant at SendGrid

Permission

14

Honor opt-out requests immediately.

While the CAN-SPAM Act stipulates that you have up to 10 business days to process opt-outs, this regulation should not be interpreted as a green light to continue to email consumers who have unsubscribed.

That grace period was permitted solely to provide large, highly distributed companies with lots of independent agents the necessary time to suppress every instance of an address from their email lists. Even if your company fits this description, technology has improved drastically since CAN-SPAM was passed.

Any legitimate email service provider (ESP) will be able to process your opt-outs as they happen.

Regardless of what's legal, consumers that continue to receive emails from you after opting out are increasingly likely to believe that their attempt to unsubscribe has failed and then report your emails as spam in order to stop receiving them. In addition to thinking less of your email program, the former subscriber may question your trustworthiness as a brand.

Remember that just because a consumer wants

to stop receiving emails from you doesn't mean that they will stop buying from you or will stop interacting with you through other channels. Don't risk damaging a consumer's relationship with your brand by refusing to gracefully accept their desire to end their email relationship with your brand for the time being.■

Permission

15

Accept that permission expires when a subscriber hasn't engaged with your emails in a long time.

Subscribers lose interest in your emails for a variety of reasons, some of which have nothing to do with the content of your emails or even your brand. People find new hobbies, discover new brands they prefer more, go up- or down-market, change jobs, and move to new neighborhoods, cities, or countries. And even though they no longer want your emails, some subscribers will just never bother to unsubscribe.

Your emails also may not reach a subscriber for technical or logistical reasons, such as your emails being junked or routed into a folder that they never check or the subscriber abandoning their email address all-together. And, yes, sometimes subscribers die.

At a certain point, the reason doesn't matter. When a subscriber hasn't opened or clicked in a single email for a prolonged period of time, it's up to you to recognize that their silence means their permission has been withdrawn.

Individual brands can determine for themselves

how long a subscriber can be inactive before they stop sending emails to them based on the impact on their sender reputation and deliverability. However, a good default is to stop mailing or at least dramatically reduce the frequency of mailings to subscribers who have been inactive for 13 months, a period that takes into consideration once-a-year buying habits. And definitely do not send any mail to subscribers who have been inactive for 25 months or longer.

High-frequency senders like daily deal sites may find that they need to take action when a subscriber has been inactive for just a few months to avoid negative consequences.■

The Last Word on Must-Follow Best Practices

The Permission Rule

Most of the Must-Follow Best Practices focus on permission, because it is the foundation of the email marketing relationship. And in the minds of consumers, there's no clearer or more immediate marker of a spammer than violating permission.

Condensing those rules on permission gives us our first Power Rule, *The Permission Rule:*

> **Permission is consciously and willingly given, purpose-specific, email address–specific, channel-specific, brand-specific, and temporary.**

By taking the time to earn a consumer's permission and respecting the limits of that opt-in, you take a huge step toward fostering the trust necessary to build a profitable email relationship, as well as toward safeguarding your sender and brand reputation, protecting yourself from excessive spam complaints, and ensuring your deliverability remains high.

A strong focus on permission also puts you in a customer service frame of mind that's vital to achieving stellar email marketing performance—which is the subject of the remaining rules.■

"The ultimate goal of your email marketing program is to create one thing: trust."

—Andrea Mignolo, Head of Design and UX at Movable Ink

Recommended Best Practices

The Rules that Separate Great Marketers from Good Marketers

"Einstein knew what was inside the box before he thought outside of it. Creativity without knowledge can be an extremely dangerous thing."

—Walter Isaacson, author of *Jobs*

Permission is core to what makes email marketing so powerful, but having permission only gets you so far. It really just gets you in the door. It doesn't guarantee that you'll remain welcome.

That's because permission is only the starting point of a relationship. From that point forward, email marketing is all about maintaining that relationship by meeting or exceeding subscribers' expectations. And they have a *lot* of expectations.

EXPECTATIONS AND RELEVANCE

Marketers set expectations during the signup process by how they attract subscribers, the information they require from subscribers, the content they say they'll send, and how frequently they say they'll send it. Word of mouth about your brand or emails also sets expectations.

Of course, individual brands don't operate in a vacuum. The experiences people have with other brands' email programs impacts expectations, too. Leading email marketing programs are constantly raising the bar, making it increasingly difficult for laggards to compete.

Marketers' ability to clear that expectation bar has been boiled down into a single word: relevance.

> **While permission grants marketers access to inboxes, sending relevant messaging maintains that permission.**

Relevance means that you're meeting your subscriber's need for respectful, functional, valuable, and occasionally remarkable email experiences. When you don't meet those needs, your subscribers will decide your emails aren't relevant and your email frequency is too high. Those are consistently the top two reasons given by subscribers for leaving email lists, either via the unsubscribe link or the never-fail *Report Spam* button.

Frustratingly, subscribers now use the *Report Spam* button liberally, mostly because of the success inbox providers have had in combatting spam. (And the *Report Phishing* button is now used to combat truly malicious and dangerous spam that the Report Spam button was originally designed to address.)

NEW DEFINITION OF SPAM

Inbox providers and spam watchdog groups have become so effective at blocking traditional, malicious spam that....

> **Consumers now consider spam to be any unwanted, irrelevant, or non-actionable email—even if it's from brands they gave permission to.**

The definition of spam now goes well beyond unexpected emails with malicious content from unknown senders. (See Fig. 6 below.) And with consumers' definition of spam changed, inbox providers have adapted their spam filtering

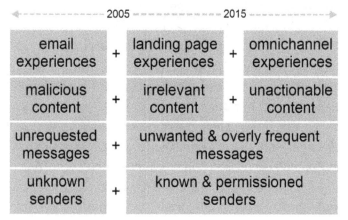

The Evolution of Consumers' Definition of Spam

◄------------------ 2005 ------------------ 2015 ------------------►		
email experiences +	landing page experiences +	omnichannel experiences
malicious content +	irrelevant content +	unactionable content
unrequested messages +	unwanted & overly frequent messages	
unknown senders +	known & permissioned senders	

FIGURE 6

algorithms accordingly.

The biggest shift is that inbox providers now track positive email signals, not just negative ones like spam complaints.

ENGAGEMENT-BASED FILTERING

Negative feedback loops were the entire basis for email filtering for a long time. Email users would hit the *Report Spam* button and inbox providers would block senders whose spam complaint rate got too high.

Some brands used to keep their complaint rates low by filling their email marketing lists with unresponsive subscribers who wouldn't engage with emails, but who also wouldn't unsubscribe or mark their emails as spam.

However, around 2010, inbox providers expanded their filtering algorithm to also include positive signals such as opens, making endlessly emailing unresponsive inboxes harmful to a brand's sender reputation.

> **It's impossible to game the system now that inbox providers require users to engage with—not just tolerate—a brand's emails.**

But now that inbox providers factor in engagement, a focus on quality must moderate a focus on quantity when it comes to building an effective email marketing list.

END-TO-END EXPERIENCES

Complicating matters further, subscribers now have email expectations that go well beyond the inbox. The rise of mobile created disjointed email experiences for some subscribers. It's not just that some brands sent emails that didn't display or function well on smartphones; many also delivered poor mobile web and mobile app experiences. The rise of wearables and the Internet of Things will again challenge brands to create compelling emails experiences that cross channels.

If that end-to-end, email-to-landing page experience isn't good, subscribers start tuning out, opting out, and reporting email as spam. Some consumers also report emails as spam after having a bad customer experience—using it like a bad review on Yelp—further proving that a subscriber's satisfaction goes well beyond the email channel.

Put all those factors together and unsubscribes and spam complaints can be the result of...

☐ Emails that are sent too frequently

☐ Emails that contain irrelevant content

☐ Emails that are difficult to read or don't function well on the subscriber's device of choice

☐ Landing pages, websites, or mobile apps that are difficult to read or don't function well on the subscriber's device of choice

☐ Negative customer service experiences

And those are just the primary reasons. It perhaps begs the question:

ARE SUBSCRIBERS TOO DEMANDING?

No, they're not. The reason that they expect so much is that...

Subscribers' time is far more valuable than the pittance it costs to email them.

As a result, marketers must fill that cost-value gap with relevant email experiences. Marketers must *deserve* their subscribers' attention.

All marketers should feel pressure to boost the relevance of their email programs and ensure that they provide positive end-to-end experiences to their subscribers. Leading email marketers invest in more data analytics for targeting and personalization, more automation for messaging, and more design and coding resources to increase the functionality and user-friendliness of their emails. These leaders continue to cause the expectations of all email users to rise.

Relevance is the key to succeeding in the current email marketing environment and creating relevance is a major focus of the remaining rules, which cover everything from measuring program success and building a productive list to email design and testing.

These Recommended Best Practices are not an absolute answer to what you should do, but rather provide strong directional guidance. You have to find the best execution for your organization within these guidelines.■

Email Metrics & Program Success

> *"Data-driven marketing is the engine behind improved marketing results, and it creates measurable internal accountability as marketers become more effective in planning, executing, and proving the value of their work."*
>
> —Lisa Arthur, author of *Big Data Marketing*

Most CEOs could care less about what your open and click rates are. While such metrics are important secondary indicators of program health, CEOs want to know how the email program is helping the business succeed.

For most brands, success is quantifiable in terms of the revenue and profits generated by the email program, email average order size, subscriber lifetime value, and other financial-focused metrics.■

WORDS TO KNOW

click: When a subscriber selects a link or linked image in an email with a mouse, trackpad, tap of a touchscreen, etc. and visits the associated webpage

email client or reader: An application or web interface that displays emails and allows users to reply, forward, and interact with the content of the message

webmail: An email client accessible via a web browser

email or campaign conversion: When a subscriber completes the action requested by an email's call-to-action

email metrics: Measurements of the effectiveness of your email campaigns and overall marketing program

image blocking: When inbox providers or subscribers don't allow the images in an email to load

open: When the images in an email are loaded or rendered, which typically happens when a subscriber views an email with images enabled

sales or business conversion: When a customer or prospect makes a purchase or takes another action of monetary significance

subscriber lifetime value: The cumulative profit generated by a subscriber during their time on your list

Email Metrics & Program Success

16

Translate email success
into business success.

Email metrics like opens, clicks, unsubscribes, and spam complaints are important to track because they indicate campaign engagement and email channel health. However, none of those necessarily directly translate into business success.

Supplement those email-centric metrics with business-focused metrics such as sales conversions, average order size, revenue per subscriber, return on investment, and email marketing's impact on customer lifetime value. Those metrics directly impact email campaign success, email channel success, and business success. (See Fig. 7 on next page.)

For that reason, use these metrics when communicating success to your leaders. Too often, marketers try to speak email to business leaders when they should be speaking business to them. This is particularly critical when arguing for new software, resources to improve or launch new campaigns, or other growth initiatives.∎

"Marketers have to stop reporting on activities and start reporting on business outcomes."

—Allen Gannett, CEO of TrackMaven

Email Metrics Matrix

	Email-Centric	Business-Centric

Customer-Level	**Subscriber Optimization**
	subscriber lifetime value
	subscriber RFM (recency,
	  frequency, monetary)
	length of email inactivity
		Business Success
		customer lifetime value
		customer RFM (recency,
		  frequency, monetary)
		length of customer
		  inactivity

Channel-Level	**Email Channel Health**
	hard & soft bounce rates
	spam complaint rate
	delivered rate
	inbox placement rate
	inactivity rate
	open & click reach
	engagement reach
	acquisition source metrics
	metrics per ISP
	list size & list growth rate
	list churn & list churn rate
		Email Channel Success
		email marketing revenue
		revenue per email
		revenue per subscriber
		sales conversions &
		  conversion rate
		email marketing profit
		email marketing return on
		  investment
		incremental lift across all
		  channels from email
		lead generation

Campaign-Level	**Email Campaign Optimization**
	unique & total opens
	open rate
	unique & total clicks
	click rate
	click-to-open rate
	mobile/desktop opens &
	  clicks
	mobile/desktop open &
	  click rates
	engagement rate (opens
	  or clicks)
	spam complaint rate
	unsubscribes &
	  unsubscribe rate
	shares & share rate
		Email Campaign Success
		email campaign revenue
		email conversions &
		  conversion rate
		post-click metrics (browsing,
		  carting, etc.)

FIGURE 7

Email Metrics & Program Success

17

Focus on maximizing the value of a subscriber, not on maximizing the results of a campaign.

Every company faces pressure to maximize short-term results; however, the ultimate goal of every business should be to maximize long-term results. In email marketing, that means looking at the lifetime value of a subscriber rather than per-campaign results, which can be deceptive since some campaigns work indirectly by boosting the effectiveness of future campaigns.

Although you can use a variety of methods, the simplest way to calculate subscriber lifetime value is to multiply the average monthly profit per subscriber by the average retention time of a subscriber in months.

This holistic, subscriber-centric approach looks at the cumulative effect of your email marketing efforts on your subscribers. And although this view focuses on profits, it also recognizes that campaigns and content that keep subscribers engaged and primed to convert in the future are also valuable.

This approach also acknowledges that tactics, content, gimmicks, and tricks that diminish trust, lower engagement, or increase unsubscribes and spam complaints must be minimized because they diminish lifetime value.

In addition to lifetime value—or as a crude alternative to it—you might consider looking at your subscribers' behavior over a period of time by using open reach, click reach, and conversion reach metrics. For instance, measuring your click reach over the past quarter would mean measuring the percentage of your subscribers who clicked at least once during that time.

The key is to avoid a campaign-by-campaign mentality when looking at data, because that can cause you to misunderstand how subscribers are reacting to your overall messaging and unintentionally make campaign-specific decisions that reduce the overall effectiveness of your email program.■

Email Metrics & Program Success

18

Measure your negative performance metrics, not just your positive ones.

When evaluating strategies and tactics, make sure you're seeing the whole picture by measuring negative metrics such as unsubscribes and spam complaints—and perhaps even negative social media chatter, word of mouth, and other indications of brand impression.

Ignoring negative indicators is tempting, especially when positive indicators are high. However, if you don't understand the impact of disengagement and opt-outs, for instance, you won't be able to minimize their threat to the success of your future campaigns.■

Email Metrics & Program Success

19

View email performance by subscriber segments, paying close attention to how your most valuable subscribers react.

Looking at the performance of a campaign or series of campaigns on your entire subscriber base can conceal important trends. In particular, it can conceal how your campaigns are affecting your most valuable subscribers.

Email marketing follows the 80-20 rule: A minority of your subscribers generate the majority of your email marketing revenue. So pay extra attention to how your campaigns affect these subscribers, especially in terms of complaints and unsubscribes.

If you find some of your campaigns work best on certain groups of subscribers, then in the future, segment those campaigns so they're sent only to the groups that reacted positively.■

Email Metrics & Program Success

20

Recognize that many of the actions prompted by emails are not easily trackable or measurable.

Although email is more quantifiable than most other channels, it is not nearly as measureable as it's often portrayed. Subscribers often respond to emails in ways that are untrackable or very difficult to track. Depending on your audience and business model, more than 50% of your email response might not be readily apparent.

For instance, some subscribers will type in the URL of your site into their browser or search for your brand on a social media site rather than clicking though one of your emails. Others will visit your store or event offline after seeing it promoted in an email. Some use one email address to subscribe to promotional emails and another account when making purchases. Still others will forward an email to their spouse or to friends, who will take action. And then there's word of mouth and social sharing.

Using promo codes that are unique to a particular subscriber and promoting printable and mobile coupons—particularly if those are also trackable back to individual subscribers—are a couple of ways to help measure the pass-along and offline influence of email.

Another, even better, way is to do a withhold study, where you do not send promotional emails to a group of subscribers for a while (often a month) and then compare their activity across all channels to subscribers who received emails. This approach provides insights into the incremental sales attributable solely to email while filtering out sales that would have happened anyway without email's influence.

While you clearly forego revenue from the group you withheld emails from, the results of these studies can provide powerful evidence of email's impact on your customers, evidence that you can use to make a business case for more investments and to get stronger buy-in from other groups within your business.■

Email Metrics & Program Success

21

Don't attach too much meaning to open rates and other surface metrics.

The open rate is really a misnomer, because it doesn't accurately reflect the percent of recipients that viewed the content of your email. In fact, some factors inflate opens, while others obscure them.

For instance, an open is registered only if a recipient views an email with images enabled so that an invisible tracking pixel renders. So if a recipient reads an email with images blocked, no open is recorded. Because image blocking is fairly common, roughly 30% of email reads aren't tracked as opens.

Also, some email clients download or cache images automatically, generating false opens.

Moreover, just because you're seeing an open doesn't mean that the recipient gave the email much or any consideration. They could have just been flipping through their emails and the images in your email loaded for a split second before they continued on to the next email.

More importantly, opens are of marginal use as a success metric because generating opens is rarely the primary goal of a campaign and lots of opens don't necessarily translate into lots of sales. In fact,

Surface Metrics vs. Deep Metrics

Surface Metrics	Deep Metrics
Email list size	Email list productivity
Email opens	Email conversions
Web traffic	Sales conversions
Campaign metrics	Subscriber metrics

FIGURE 8

maximizing your open rate on individual campaigns can actually lead to fewer clicks and lower conversions, because the tactics that increase opens—such as short, vague subject lines—often suppress the response to the email's call-to-action.

While tracking opens can help you understand some basic things about the health of your program, it's ultimately not very revealing. For truly meaningful activity, look further down the email funnel at deep metrics like email conversions. (See Fig. 8 above.)

If your products are high-consideration and purchased infrequently like computers and cars, then your brand might focus on email conversions and other forms of engagement that lead to sales.■

"If you get stuck measuring the wrong thing, you could end up wasting your time on the wrong initiatives."

—Sarah Tavelnative, Partner at Greylock Partners

Email Metrics & Program Success

22

Benchmark yourself primarily against yourself.

Everyone wants to know how their email program stacks up against others, but external benchmarks are of little use for a number of reasons.

First, most aggregations of data are not going to be relevant to your industry or company. Even if the benchmark is for your industry, accounting for differences between companies of different sizes that operate within different sub-verticals is impossible.

Second, the open rate and click rate data that is typically shared may not be very useful. Because brands manage their lists differently, these numbers don't provide an apples-to-apples comparison.

And third, beating an external benchmark can give you a false sense of security and make you complacent when you shouldn't be.

All of that said, if you are massively trailing external benchmarks, changes might be needed. Otherwise, focus on systematically beating your own performance.■

"Our goal is to beat yesterday."

—Andy Crestodina, author of *Content Chemistry*

Deliverability & Sender Reputation

> *"If your reputation sucks, none of it matters.*
> *People with lousy products, crummy business practices,*
> *and shady backgrounds get found out.*
> *And word spreads with frightening speed."*
>
> —Sonia Simone, Chief Marketing Officer of
> Rainmaker Digital

Your sender reputation and the percentage of your emails that make it to your subscribers' inboxes are heavily influenced by your permission practices, but your signup processes, complaint rate, and other factors also play a role. ■

WORDS TO KNOW

blacklist: A list of senders of spam, typically maintained by an independent organization, used by inbox providers to determine whether and where to deliver email

blocked: When an inbox provider prevents your emails from being delivered to their users

bounced: When an inbox provider rejects an email because it was sent to an unknown email address (hard bounce) or because of a temporary condition like the recipient's mailbox being full (soft bounce)

CAPTCHA: Anti-bot security mechanism for forms that include reCAPTCHA, No Captcha reCAPTCHA, and Invisible reCAPTCHA

content filtering: When an inbox provider evaluates an email's subject line and other content as part of its process to decide whether and where to deliver the mail

deliverability: All issues involved with getting commercial emails delivered to their intended recipients' inboxes

delivered: When email makes it to the intended recipient's inbox or junk folder, as opposed to being blocked

double entry confirmation: Requiring a would-be subscriber to enter their email address a second time in a confirmation field on a subscription form and requiring that the two entries match in order to reduce entry errors

email authentication: A variety of methods that help inbox providers accurately identify email sent by a brand, including Domain Keys Identified Mail (DKIM), Sender Policy Framework (SPF), and Domain-based Message Authentication, Reporting & Conformance (DMARC)

feedback loop (FBL): A mechanism through which inbox providers notify email senders of spam complaints by their subscribers using a standard Abuse Report Format (ARF), allowing senders to unsubscribe those subscribers

freemail: An email account that is available for free from Yahoo, Gmail, Outlook.com, or another inbox provider

inbox placement rate: The percentage of emails sent by a brand or from an IP address that reaches their intended recipients' inboxes, as opposed to being blocked or junked, based on delivery to a panel or seed list

junked or bulked: When inbox providers route emails to a recipient's junk or spam folder

list hygiene: Ensuring that your email list is free of invalid and undeliverable email addresses, role-based email addresses, spam traps, unconfirmed email addresses, and chronically inactive subscribers

open subscription form: An email signup form accessible

without purchase, account creation, registration, etc.

opportunistic TLS: When senders enable this, your ESP will always attempt to send your email encrypted; but if an inbox provider can't handle encryption, your email will be sent unencrypted

private or dedicated IP address: An IP address from which only one company sends email, making that company solely responsible for the sender reputation of that address

proof of consent: Details on how, when, and where a subscriber opted in to receive emails from your brand

role-based email address: An email address that begins with *info@*, *webmaster@*, *sales@*, *press@*, *support@*, *test@*, or a similar function-based descriptor denoting that messages sent to this address are likely seen by or forwarded to more than one person

shared IP address: An IP address from which multiple companies send email, with all of them contributing at least partially to the sender reputation of that IP address

spoof: When spammers, phishers, and others falsify the sender name and address of an email, making it appear to come from a reputable person or brand in an attempt to deceive the recipient

statement of permission: A reminder of how the subscriber opted in to receive your emails and an explanation of why they received this particular email

subscriber acquisition source: The form or mechanism through which a subscriber opts in to receive emails from a brand, or the ad, sign, or other messaging that drove them to opt in

throttling or rate limiting: When an inbox provider slows the rate or volume at which they accept a sender's emails, or when a sender or email service provider manages the rate at which they send email to an inbox provider to avoid throttling or bounces

unknown user: An email address that is invalid, either because the address never existed or because the address has been long abandoned

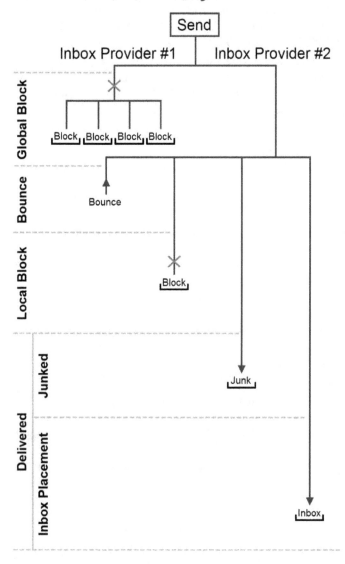

FIGURE 9

Deliverability & Sender Reputation

23

Use an email service provider to send your commercial email.

The technical issues around sending commercial email are now so complicated that using anything less than a professional-grade email service provider (ESP) risks your deliverability.

That's because—in addition to providing analytics, targeting, testing, and other functionality—ESPs handle many issues that affect your ability to reach the inbox, including:

☐ Removing email addresses that hard bounce

☐ Monitoring feedback loops and removing complainers

☐ Setting up servers and authentication properly

☐ Sending emails at a rate that's acceptable to each inbox provider

☐ Helping you determine whether a shared or dedicated IP address is best

Using a homegrown platform for anything other than sending simple transactional email is unwise for all but the most sophisticated companies

Thankfully, no matter how small or large your email needs are or what industry you're in, many ESPs are available to choose from.■

Deliverability & Sender Reputation

24

Accept that email service providers have relatively little control over the deliverability of your emails, especially if you're sending from a dedicated IP address.

If you're using a shared IP address, then the sender reputation of all the other senders using that IP address may impact your deliverability. In these cases, your email service provider ensures that everyone maintains healthy sender reputations— which they generally do by mandating high permission standards such as using a confirmed opt-in process.

However, if you're using a dedicated IP address, your deliverability is largely in your own hands. That's because the most critical factor affecting whether your emails reach your subscribers' inboxes is your sender reputation.

So while your ESP's infrastructure affects your deliverability, a much bigger component is whether your email sends generate too many bounces from bad email addresses, too many spam complaints, and too little engagement in terms of opens and clicks, causing inbox providers to throttle, junk, or block your emails.

Your permission practices, how well you set expectations, your email frequency, how relevant your emails are, and how you handle subscribers who are no longer engaging with your emails all drive those metrics.

Moreover, domain reputation is increasingly supplementing IP reputation, because senders can't escape the reputation of their domain by changing their IP address or engaging in "snowshoeing," where a sender spreads their send volume across a large number of IP addresses in an attempt to evade inbox providers' spam filters.

So while it's tempting to want to blame your ESP for your deliverability issues, it's rarely fair to do so. Moreover, it's just wishful thinking to expect your deliverability to improve long-term if you change ESPs but don't change your behavior.■

"Marketers aren't making good decisions about what to send to whom. We've abdicated that decision to ISPs."

—Alex Timlin, Head of Client Success at Emarsys

Deliverability & Sender Reputation

25

Recognize that 100% deliverability is not a realistic expectation nor an achievable goal.

Flawless deliverability is a myth, and any email service provider, vendor, agency, or consultant promising you that should be viewed with suspicion.

Generally speaking, inbox placement rates of 98% and higher on average are excellent, and rates in the mid 90% range are good.

Companies should be concerned with inbox placement rates that average in the low 90% range, and very alarmed by anything lower than 90%.

Factors partially or completely out of your control that may lower deliverability rates include:

☐ Sending email to a huge audience

☐ Sending email at high frequencies

☐ Having many subscribers outside of the U.S. and Europe

☐ Being a brand that's frequently spoofed or the subject of spam

If your program doesn't have any of those challenges, then you should expect to be able to achieve excellent deliverability rates. If you're not, then you'll need to change your behavior.■

Deliverability & Sender Reputation

26

Use email authentication and send from a domain you control.

Email authentication involves a variety of methods that help inbox providers accurately identify email sent by a brand. Authenticating your emails aids your deliverability, protects your sender reputation, and makes it easier for inbox providers to identify when spammers and phishers spoof your brand.

It's highly recommended that you use all three major authentication methods:

☐ Domain Keys Identified Mail (DKIM)

☐ Sender Policy Framework (SPF)

☐ Domain-based Message Authentication, Reporting & Conformance (DMARC)

Your email service provider or a consultant can help you authenticate your email.

Because of developments around DMARC, do not use a Yahoo, AOL, Gmail, Hotmail, or other freemail address as your *from* address because many inbox providers will block your email. Instead, send emails from a domain you control, which makes for a stronger brand impression anyway.■

Deliverability & Sender Reputation

27

Enable opportunistic encryption
for your emails.

Encryption currently only has an indirect effect on deliverability, but it may become a direct factor in the future if momentum continues.

Gmail leads the way on encryption. Their interface uses a little green or red padlock icon to indicate if an email was sent using transport layer security (TLS) or not.

For financial, insurance, and other similar companies, a lack of encryption may undermine confidence in those emails for subscribers.

More widely, with email hyper-personalization across all brands on the rise, more and more subscribers may find encryption comforting and influence how they view the sender.

Encryption may also get a push from governments around the world in the wake of foreign hacking—primarily by the U.S. and Russia.

Because of those factors, it's recommended that you enable opportunistic TLS, if your email service provider offers it. By doing so, your ESP will always attempt to send your email encrypted; but if an inbox provider can't handle encryption, your email will be sent unencrypted.■

Deliverability & Sender Reputation

28

Send your promotional emails from a different IP address and subdomain than you use for your transactional and other critical emails.

Keeping your promotional emails separate is necessary because they tend to generate far more complaints and much lower engagement than other emails you send. That means they're more prone to deliverability problems, and you don't want those problems affecting your ability to deliver vital emails like order confirmation emails and password reset emails, or your corporate email.

If at all possible, send your promotional emails from a different IP address. Even better, use a different subdomain as well.

For instance, if you're sending your corporate email from yourbrand.com and your transactional emails from email.yourbrand.com, then use a different subdomain like shopping.yourbrand.com, mail.yourbrand.com, or online.yourbrand.com to send your promotional emails.

If you send a large array of non-transactional triggered emails, you might want to use yet another subdomain for those emails.■

Deliverability & Sender Reputation

29

Keep your unknown user rate under 2%, preferably well under.

Unknown users are email addresses that are invalid for one of four reasons:

☐ The domain doesn't exist

☐ The domain doesn't accept email

☐ The address has never existed

☐ The address has been long abandoned

Getting rid of unknown users post-send is generally easy, as most email service providers automatically remove them from your active list when they hard bounce at an inbox provider.

The bigger concern is keeping these addresses off your list. The most common ways that unknown users get on your list include:

☐ Typos when entering an email address

☐ Malicious signups

☐ Emailing subscribers you haven't sent to in years

☐ Buying email lists or harvesting addresses

It's this last reason that makes unknown users dangerous. Inbox providers assume that senders with high hard bounce rates are spammers, and treat them appropriately by blocking their emails.

While you probably won't see any effect on your deliverability until your unknown user rate is consistently above 2%, it's best to minimize this figure as much as possible.

Sometimes, rather than a hard bounce, email addresses soft bounce. Unlike the permanent failure of a hard bounce, soft bounces are temporary failures to deliver email because:

☐ The email message is too large

☐ The recipient's mailbox is full

☐ The recipient's inbox provider's email servers are down

Sometimes soft bounces eventually turn into hard bounces. For example, a full mailbox is potentially a sign of an abandoned inbox and that the email address will eventually be shutdown.

For this reason, most ESPs have a default limit on how many times an email address can soft bounce within a certain time period. If exceeded, they treat the address as though it hard bounced and remove it from your active email list.■

Deliverability & Sender Reputation

30

Avoid error-prone manual methods of email address collection, when possible.

Human error is a huge challenge with data collection of all types. So when it comes to collecting email addresses, use a process that only requires the participation of one human: the subscriber.

That means avoiding methods that involve a store or customer service representative transcribing an email address:

☐ From a paper signup form

☐ Given to them verbally

In both cases, transcription error rates are very high. Not only do you risk disappointing the person who thought they'd signed up, but you also risk high bounce rates and perhaps even adding a typo spam trap to your list.

When the would-be subscriber is still present, you can show them the transcription on a pin pad, tablet, or other screen and have them visually verify it's correct. But if the person isn't present, then the safest recourse is to confirm the address using a double opt-in process.■

Deliverability & Sender Reputation

31

Use double opt-in and other safeguards to protect yourself from error-prone, low-quality, and bot-vulnerable subscriber acquisition sources.

Using a double opt-in (DOI) process can protect your list quality from slipping when using subscriber acquisition sources that:

☐ Are high-value but prone to transcription errors, such as collecting email addresses verbally in store or through a call center

☐ Are high-value but prone to entry errors, such as collecting email addresses via a mobile app and other environment with virtual keyboards and autocorrect functionality

☐ Include open subscription forms

☐ Have proven to produce low-quality or high-complaint subscribers for you in the past

☐ Are outside of your organization, such as list rentals and co-registration

A DOI process involves sending an opt-in confirmation request email or subscription activation request email to a new would-be subscriber that requires them to click a link in it to confirm that

Single Opt-In (SOI) vs. Double Opt-In (DOI)

Single Opt-In (SOI)	Double Opt-In (DOI)
Faster List Growth	**Slower List Growth**
- One-step opt-in process - Higher completion rates for opt-in process - Lower failure rates for opt-in process	- Two-step opt-in process - Lower completion rates for opt-in process - Higher failure rates for opt-in process
Higher Total Engagement	**Lower Total Engagement**
- More opens, clicks, and conversions	- Fewer opens, clicks, and conversions
Lower Engagement Rates	**Higher Engagement Rates**
- Lower open, click, and conversion rates - Higher inactivity rates - Higher unsubscribe rates	- Higher open, click, and conversion rates - Lower inactivity rates - Lower unsubscribe rates
Higher Risks to Deliverability	**Lower Risks to Deliverability**
- Higher need to monitor deliverability - Higher risk of needing to intervene to fix deliverability - Higher spam complaint rates - Weaker protection from malicious signups - Weaker production from typo spam traps	- Lower need to monitor deliverability - Lower risk of needing to intervene to fix deliverability - Lower spam complaint rates - Stronger protection from malicious signups - Stronger production from typo spam traps
Weaker Proof of Consent	**Stronger Proof of Consent**
- Do not have opt-in confirmation from email address owner	- Have opt-in confirmation from email address owner

FIGURE 10

they did indeed want to sign up. If they don't confirm, then they receive no additional emails.

Having subscribers confirm their permission ensures that you're adding valid and active email addresses to your list and subscribers who have a genuine interest in receiving your emails.

The downside of DOI is that it adds additional friction to your opt-in process. Anywhere from 20% to 50% of new email addresses won't be confirmed when using a DOI process. So while it protects your list from low-quality subscribers, it does so at the cost of some high-value subscribers. (See Fig. 10 on previous page.)

For this reason, DOI isn't recommended in all instances and for all brands. For instance, if a current customer who has received transactional emails from you in the past goes into your preference center and opts in to receive promotional emails or a newsletter, having them confirm that opt-in using DOI is pointless. You already know their email address is correct because you've mailed it before and you know that the email address holder is opting in because they accessed their preferences while logged in.

Moreover, process improvements can compensate for the email address accuracy and signup intent risks of using a single opt-in (SOI) process for some subscriber acquisition sources. For instance, consider:

☐ Having subscribers enter their email addresses in an extra field as part of a double entry confirmation process

☐ Adding honeypot techniques or any of the many forms of CAPTCHA protections to open subscription forms that are susceptible to bot activity and malicious signups

☐ Adding an email validation service to catch improperly formatted email addresses or those that contain common misspellings of domain names, such as *someone@outloko.com*

☐ Adding an email verification service that checks to see if an email address belongs to a real person using lists developed by the vendor

☐ Using engagement-based confirmation, where you stop emailing new subscribers who don't engage with any emails soon after opting in

Even with these additional safeguards in place, SOI isn't a viable option for everyone. For instance, SOI isn't for you if:

☐ Your email service provider requires all of its customers to use double opt-in

☐ You don't have good visibility into your deliverability

☐ You are not prepared to deal with potentially being blacklisted, or blocked or junked at one or more inbox providers

☐ Your industry requires stronger permission because of regulations concerning marketing to minors, healthcare or financial information, etc.

☐ Your company is a target of harassment

Please consult an attorney to determine your legal risks and obligations.■

Deliverability & Sender Reputation

32

Send only one opt-in confirmation request email as part of your double opt-in process.

Sending multiple reminder emails to try to get non-confirmers to verify their opt-in undermines many of the benefits of using a double opt-in (DOI) process in the first place.

For instance, sending reminders means that you're repeatedly hitting any typo spam traps based on misspelled domains. That dramatically increases your risk of being blacklisted.

And people who are signed up maliciously or simply had second thoughts about signing up may resort to marking your emails as spam to get you to stop mailing after they see more than one email asking for opt-in confirmation.

The latter contributed to the blacklisting of hundreds of brands by Spamhaus in August of 2016. Bots signed up roughly 100 email addresses—many belonging to government officials—to more than 10,000 email lists each. Many of the brands targeted used DOI processes, but some of them sent multiple reminder emails and ended up with their emails blocked by several inbox providers as a result.■

Deliverability & Sender Reputation

33

Keep records of proof of consent for each of your subscribers.

If legal action is brought against you under an anti-spam law or if a blacklist organization lists you, having detailed proof of consent will help you resolve any issues.

When tracking proof of consent include:

☐ URL, address, or location of subscriber acquisition source and whether signups at this source are active or passive

☐ Data and time of signup

☐ IP address of subscriber at time of signup

☐ Date and time of opt-in confirmation, if using a double opt-in process

☐ IP address of subscriber at time of confirmation

Your email service provider should track proof of consent for you for the subscriber acquisition sources that tie into it, and provide a way to export that data. However, you'll want to check with your ESP to see exactly what information they collect.

Also, for an opt-ins that you collect offline or through other mechanisms, you'll want to keep a separate record of those proofs of consent.■

Deliverability & Sender Reputation

34

Include a statement of permission in the footer of every email.

Subscribers get lots of emails and don't always immediately understand why they're getting every message from brands. Help them by including a statement of permission right before your unsubscribe link or preference center link, as this can avert some opt-outs and spam complaints.

A simple statement of permission might say, *You are receiving this email because you signed up for promotional emails from Brand X*. However, you can strengthen your permission statement by including more details, such as:

☐ How they subscribed (i.e., *via our preference center*, *during checkout*, *during registration*)

☐ Where they subscribed (i.e., *at Conference X*, *at our store at 123 Street Rd.*)

☐ Whether the email is the result of a transaction (i.e., *because you purchased X*)

☐ Whether this is a one-time email, part of an email series, or part of a regular mailing

Essentially, including a statement of permission reflects the proof of consent back to subscribers. Consider moving this statement to the top of your higher-complaint emails.∎

Deliverability & Sender Reputation

35

Don't add role-based email addresses to your email list.

Role-based email addresses are those that begin with function-based descriptors such as *info@*, *webmaster@*, *sales@*, *press@*, *support@*, and *test@*. These addresses pose a serious risk to your deliverability for a couple of reasons.

First, emails sent to these addresses are likely seen by or forwarded to multiple people, all of whom might not be as interested in receiving your messages as the one person who opted in. Because of that, messages sent to these addresses are more likely to generate spam complaints.

And second, these addresses tend to be published publicly on websites, which means they are scraped, harvested, and collected by spammers, who send the addresses a lot of spam and sell the addresses to others. Inbox providers are aware of this, so having role-based addresses on your email list may be seen as a sign that you are harvesting email addresses or buying lists. Either gets you labeled a spammer and gets your emails blocked.

Reject these addresses at the time of signup, asking people to instead use their personal email address to subscribe.■

Deliverability & Sender Reputation

36

Block email signups from irrelevant or non-preferred locations or domains.

Setting some reasonable restrictions on who can sign up for emails from you can potentially save you from deliverability headaches in the future.

Some blocking criteria might include signups:

☐ Using free webmail (freemail) accounts like Gmail, Outlook.com, and Yahoo

☐ Using temporary or expiring email addresses

☐ From geolocations outside your region, country, or state of operation

☐ Using top-level domains that aren't related to your business

For example, some B2B brands don't allow prospects to enter a freemail address because entering a business email address helps qualify that lead as indeed working at the company that the person indicated.

If you care about being able to reach your user or customer in the future, you probably don't want them using an email account that's designed to expire shortly after its creation. Some of the domains associated with these accounts include:

- ☐ mailinator.com
- ☐ maildrop.cc
- ☐ fakeinbox.com
- ☐ abyssmail.com
- ☐ dispostable.com
- ☐ getnada.com
- ☐ 20mail.it
- ☐ pokemail.net
- ☐ spam4.me
- ☐ guerrillamail.info
- ☐ guerrillamail.biz
- ☐ guerrillamail.com
- ☐ guerrillamail.de
- ☐ guerrillamail.net
- ☐ guerrillamail.org
- ☐ grr.la

Some retailers block signups from countries they don't ship to in order to avoid frustrating these customers, keep their list focused on customer opportunities, and avoid possible legal compliance obligations with other nations.

And as a safety measure, some companies block signups using country and other top-level domains that might lead to trouble such as:

- ☐ .gov
- ☐ .mil
- ☐ .int
- ☐ .airforce
- ☐ .army
- ☐ .navy
- ☐ .adult
- ☐ .porn
- ☐ .sex
- ☐ .xxx
- ☐ .casino
- ☐ .poker
- ☐ .attorney
- ☐ .lawyer
- ☐ .legal
- ☐ .democrat
- ☐ .gop
- ☐ .republican

You should make blocking decisions based on your own business needs and intended audience.■

Deliverability & Sender Reputation

37

Keep your spam complaint rate under 0.1%, preferably well under.

Consult with your email service provider (ESP) for their recommendations and understand your contractual obligations to them, but in general keeping your complaint rate under 1 for every 1,000 emails you send keeps you in the good graces of both inbox providers and your ESP. Your ESP will report your complaint rate to you based on the feedback loops of inbox providers.

Exceeding that 0.1% limit puts you at risk of having your emails junked or blocked by inbox providers and of being sanctioned or terminated as a client by your ESP.

Although that's the recommended limit, be aware that most brands are able to maintain a complaint rate of less than 0.05%, so it would be wise to aim to be in the company of the majority. If the standard does change, it's more likely to get tighter rather than looser.■

Deliverability & Sender Reputation

38

When worrying about content filtering, focus more on the code of your emails than the subject lines, text, and images.

Although it used to be a major concern, nowadays your subject lines and the words and images in your emails have relatively little weight when inbox providers determine whether to deliver your emails. Using exclamation marks, all caps, and words such as *free* and *offer* in your subject lines will not affect your deliverability unless you have other serious factors that cause inbox providers to view your emails as spam.

Foreign languages are one of the few areas where the words you use can cause you filtering trouble. If an email user hasn't received other emails written in a particular language before, an email in that language will likely get flagged. So make sure that your language preferences and targeting are good.

That said, content filtering is now much more focused on the coding of your emails. For instance, a very poorly coded HTML email with many unclosed tags and other imperfections may raise red flags.

Excessive code comments can also, because it looks like you're trying to conceal content.

While filters do not react negatively to the use of responsive email design or most interactive email elements, they do react harshly to HTML forms, JavaScript, Flash, and *<object>* and *<embed>* tags because of their ability to carry malicious payloads. Inbox providers will strip out this code and may block or junk your email because of it.

Inbox providers also pay attention to the sites you're linking to and take note if you use shortened URLs or IP addresses as URLs, which are routinely used by spammers to conceal the destination of a link. Only link to reputable sites using full, unmasked URLs, although redirect links created by your ESP for tracking purposes are fine.

Corporate email filters might give more weight to subject lines and email content, so business-to-business email marketers face some additional uncertainties that business-to-consumer email marketers don't have to worry about as much. Content scoring tools exist that can help you identify potential problems.

The good news here is that more and more installed, on-premise email systems are being replaced by cloud-based ones provided by Google, Microsoft, and other vendors that run consumer email platforms as well. As a result of this consolidation, deliverability is becoming a bit more predictable and more uniform across both B2C and B2B audiences.■

Deliverability & Sender Reputation

39

Do not include attachments
on your commercial emails.

Consumers are very hesitant to open attachments because of the risk of viruses and other malicious payloads. For that reason, inbox providers and corporate email servers are more likely to block your emails if you include attachments. They also provide a poor subscriber experience because they can dramatically increase the time it takes for subscribers to download your email, which can be frustrating.

Instead, host any PDF coupons, documents, or other files on the web and link to them from the email. That approach lets subscribers download these materials and then easily navigate to other parts of your website.■

Deliverability & Sender Reputation

40

Avoid overreacting to the introduction of new inbox organization tools and services.

The inbox is a dynamic place. Not only do inbox providers release new functionality on a regular basis, but third parties also create add-ons and services that affect inboxes. Many of these are aimed at helping people better organize and sort through the emails they receive.

Historically, announcements of these kinds of tools generate the greatest buzz, the most handwringing, and the biggest distractions. The introduction of Priority Inbox and later Tabs by Gmail, the addition of Sweep functionality by Outlook.com, and the launch of Unroll.Me are all great examples of events that received more attention than they deserved.

Marketers' fear is always that their emails will get less attention or, worse, be exiled to a place that email users never check.

However, these developments generally benefit email marketers by making inboxes a more pleasant and efficient place for consumers to visit and spend time. What has happened consistently is that marketers who send at least modestly relevant emails are rewarded with increases in engagement by these tools, while marketers sending emails that are poorly received by subscribers see their engagement fall further.

For those marketers who are concerned that they'll be negatively impacted by these developments, the best protection is to focus on sending relevant emails.

Trying to fight or game these tools is a losing strategy. Not only is the trend toward users having more control of their inboxes gaining momentum, but inbox providers do not appreciate it when marketers and spammers try to trick their algorithms. In particular, Google has proven to be quite punitive toward brands that try to get rankings and placements they don't deserve.■

_____

"Good marketing leads to good inbox placement."
—Kevin Senne, Senior Director of Global Deliverability at Oracle Marketing Cloud

Deliverability & Sender Reputation

41

Maintain a minimum email frequency.

While over-mailing risks annoyance, unsubscribes, and spam complaints, under-mailing also carries risks. If your subscribers receive emails from you too infrequently:

☐ They might forget that they subscribed and either ignore your emails or mark them as spam.

☐ Your low inbox presence may result in months passing between email interactions.

☐ Individual campaigns could have a sizable impact on your sender reputation, resulting in erratic deliverability.

☐ It becomes more difficult to identify inactive subscribers who are no longer responding to your emails or who have abandoned their email address.

Using a shared IP address can mitigate some of those risks, but not all. It's recommended that brands send at least one marketing email a month, as an absolute minimum.■

Deliverability & Sender Reputation

42

Recognize that high-volume senders are subject to more scrutiny by inbox providers.

While it may not seem fair, inbox providers have higher standards for higher volume senders, because those senders affect more of their users. As a result, these senders are more likely to have their email junked or blocked.

Inbox providers expect high-volume senders to also be high-sophistication senders and to more diligently follow all the rules of deliverability—ensuring that they set up their infrastructure properly and have appropriate permission policies and strong list hygiene.

That's not to say that low-volume senders don't have to follow the rules; they do. But inbox providers may overlook some of their lack of sophistication because of their lower volumes.

If you're using a shared IP address, recognize that inbox providers at least partially view you collectively as a high-volume sender because your email volume is being sent along with many other senders' over the same IP address.∎

List Building & Profiling

> *"Customer loyalty is mostly about choosing the right customers."*
> —John Jantsch, author of *Duct Tape Marketing*

Locating the best sources of quality subscribers and creating a subscription process that's as friction-free as possible are key to building a productive, low-risk email list. Determine what information to ask for, when to ask for it, and how to ask for it to maximize form completions, either during acquisition or later in the email relationship.■

WORDS TO KNOW

list building or acquisition: The process of adding email addresses to your mailing list

mailstream: The emails resulting from a single opt-in or preference selection

preference center: Webpage that displays a subscriber's email address and other details, such as profile information (i.e., zip code, etc.) and communication preferences (i.e., topics of interest, etc.), and allows them to make changes as well as unsubscribe

progressive profiling: Collecting additional demographic data and information about interests from subscribers by periodically prompting them to answer questions, take quizzes, or interact with a guided selling program

social sign-in: Using the login information from a social network to sign in to a third-party website

List Building & Profiling

43

Recognize that not all subscribers are equally valuable or desirable.

The expectations of your subscribers—and therefore, their value—can be very different depending on where and why they opt in.

You can acquire email addresses through many sources, including via your website, your store checkout, your blog, a signup request on product packaging or a receipt, an SMS text-to-subscribe sign, your Facebook page, a sweepstakes or contest entry form, co-registration on someone else's website, and on and on. The subscriber who signs up on your homepage is a very different subscriber than the one that signed up because they wanted to enter your sweepstakes.

Tracking the performance of your subscribers by their acquisition source will allow you to see how each is performing and make decisions about which sources to continue, improve, or abandon.■

List Building & Profiling

44

Focus on adding engaged subscribers to your list.

Growing your list expands the reach of your messages only if you're adding engaged subscribers. Adding low-quality subscribers to your list who are more likely to ignore or junk your emails than open and act on them is pointless and counterproductive.

Lists that generate too many spam complaints and are bloated with unengaged subscribers are more likely to be blocked or junked by inbox providers. In addition to costing time and effort to correct, deliverability problems mean that your emails aren't reaching any of your subscribers—not even your most engaged ones.

Unqualified list growth is a poor goal and an even worse key performance indicator. Instead, focus on engaged list growth, where list size is grown while maintaining or expanding the percentage of engaged subscribers. That is a much safer and more effective goal.■

List Building & Profiling

45

Recognize that the best subscriber acquisition sources are closest to your shopping and customer service operations.

People who are on your website, using your mobile app, buying your products, shopping at your stores, and talking to your service representatives are more familiar with and interested in your brand than those who haven't done those things. That naturally makes such people more valuable and less risky subscribers, and that makes your website, online checkout, mobile app, store checkout, product packaging, and call centers your best subscriber acquisition sources.

Subscriber quality declines and the risk of spam complaints rises the further away you get from these operations. Signups that come from sources outside of your business—such as co-registrations and list rentals—are among the least valuable and most prone to generating spam complaints, but even your social channels might produce subpar subscribers.

To maximize your returns, focus your acquisition efforts on those sources that generate the most valuable subscribers.■

List Building & Profiling

46

Don't force people to register as a customer in order to receive promotional emails from you.

The word *register* conjures up visions of long, over-reaching forms and troublesome site passwords in the minds of consumers—and the reward for registering is highly inconsistent from company to company.

So don't only have your email signup as part of your customer registration form. Also have it as a separate form that you highlight on your homepage and throughout your website.

Even though signing up for email is a lower bar than customer registration, if you treat these subscribers well and demonstrate your value over time, you can get the same information from them as someone who registered.■

List Building & Profiling

47

Make your email signup forms and links prominent to boost their performance.

Opt-in forms and links convert best when they're prominently placed high on your website where visitors don't have to scroll to find them. Forcing visitors to scroll to find your email opt-in can reduce signups by 50% or more.

To a much smaller degree, opt-ins placed in the right-hand corners tend to outperform those placed in the left-hand corners, because consumers have been trained to expect email opt-in forms in those spots.

Placing your email signup in the header or footer of your website so it appears on every page of your website will also increase signups.

Lightboxes, popovers, and other in-your-face signup requests can also be effective, but be aware that these might annoy some visitors, especially if they are forced to view them repeatedly. Therefore, it's important to test when and how often they are displayed to optimize the overall impact.

If you have offline operations, use those to build your email list as well. Messaging on shopping carts, in-store signage, product packaging, menus, coasters, and other places can be very effective.■

List Building & Profiling

48

Tell consumers why they should sign up to receive your emails.

No one wants to join a list, and few people want to get more email. However, people do want to receive discounts, product updates, helpful advice, and even company news.

Be sure to sell people on the benefits of subscribing to your email program—whether you have the space to list comprehensive benefits with images and links to sample emails or you only have space for 30 characters. What's in it for them?

Keep in mind the level of convincing needed to convert would-be subscribers will vary depending on their acquisition source and persona group. For example, customers signing up for email during checkout should take less convincing than people that you're reaching out to via a list rental.

Consider adding some social proof to your signup form, noting how many subscribers you have and why they love to receive your emails. This can lower signup anxiety.

It's also worth reassuring would-be subscribers that your brand won't ever share their email address with anyone else. Some brands also include this reassurance on the opt-in confirmation page.■

List Building & Profiling

49

Avoid over-incentivizing signups because that attracts low-quality subscribers.

Coupons, freebies, and other incentives can significantly boost email signups. However, some consumers will subscribe to your emails just for the incentive and then turn around and unsubscribe or report your email as spam.

One approach to mitigating this risk is to keep sign-up incentives to a moderate value. An even better approach is to ensure the incentive is only attractive to strong prospects and loyal customers.

A final approach is simply to avoid signup incentives altogether to make certain that people are subscribing solely because they want your emails. That said, not promoting a signup incentive doesn't mean you can't provide a surprise reward for subscribing in a welcome email.

Relatedly, don't incentivize sales associates or other employees to collect email addresses or set collection goals or quotas. These tactics have been known to lead some employees to make up email addresses, resulting in a spike in unknown users and even spam traps hits.∎

List Building & Profiling

50

Deliver email signup incentives to the email address provided.

If offered a discount, coupon or freebie on the spot in exchange for their email address, some consumers will give you false email addresses to get the reward.

To protect your list quality, deliver any signup incentives to the email address provided. That encourages people to give you their real address and to spell or enter it correctly.■

List Building & Profiling

51

Set expectations regarding how many emails you'll be sending subscribers and what content will be in them.

The top two reasons given by subscribers for why they unsubscribe are consistently that they received too many emails and that the emails weren't relevant. Use your signup messaging, signup confirmation page, and welcome emails to set expectations appropriately.

Consider providing images of or links to previous emails as examples of the kind of content you will send. Regarding email frequency, set general expectations, but avoid being overly specific so that you have some wiggle room to increase frequency during key selling seasons.

If you offer multiple mailstreams during your opt-in process, be reasonably clear about what each one of them entails.■

"Email is all about delivering on promises."
—Gary Vaynerchuk, CEO of VaynerMedia

List Building & Profiling

52

Keep your email signup forms short and simple, and collect additional information after signups.

For most brands, the only piece of information that is absolutely necessary for an email signup is the person's email address. Every bit of information beyond that generally adds friction to the process and decreases signups.

Opportunities to collect additional information after an email signup include your opt-in confirmation page, preference center, welcome emails, registration forms, online checkouts, sweepstakes entries, and progressive profiling efforts, such as email surveys. As a relationship grows, subscribers will be willing to share more.

If you do require more information at signup for business or compliance reasons, consider breaking the signup process into two or more steps, where each step consists of a short form.

Also consider using a social sign-in for email opt-ins. This convenient option for consumers has the added benefit of providing brands with useful profile information, such as birth date.

The one major caveat: Although longer forms generate fewer signups and leads, those that do signup are better qualified leads. That's not just because you can include fields on your form that allow you to identify subscribers and prospects who will be a better fit for your brand, but also because people who take the time to complete a longer form have higher intent, proving that they're very interested in your brand.

Some B2B brands and high-touch B2C brand may find that the tradeoff in lower form completions and higher quality subscribers and leads to be well worthwhile, especially if there's significant human intervention in the sales or service process. But most brands won't find this tradeoff worth it. Do some experiments and decide which approach is best for your brand.■

List Building & Profiling

53

Recognize that requiring email subscribers to share additional contact information lowers signups significantly.

Consumers are fairly willing to share their email addresses with brands. That's because consumers overwhelming prefer to receive commercial communications via email.

The flipside of that is consumers don't like to receive brand communications via other channels. As a result, consumers are very hesitant to share their mailing address, phone number, and cellphone number because they know doing so exposes them to additional marketing communications in less-preferred channels.

So think twice before asking would-be subscribers to share additional contact information—even as an optional field—as this may significantly increase form abandonment, decreasing signups.■

List Building & Profiling

54

Only ask subscribers for information you will use.

Whether on your subscription form, on your opt-in confirmation page, in your welcome email, or further along in the email relationship, asking for information sets the expectation that you'll use it for the subscriber's benefit.

Don't ask for information that you think you might use eventually. You can always get that information later; in the meantime, you will avoid setting false expectations or dampening the response to a form.

For instance, don't ask subscribers which product categories they are most interested in if you don't plan to use that information to create targeted messages.

Additionally, collecting and retaining too much and unnecessary information potentially opens you up to legal liabilities, particularly in the case of data breaches.

Please consult an attorney to determine your legal risks and obligations.■

List Building & Profiling

55

Explain to subscribers how sharing additional information with you will benefit them.

If you require additional information, tell subscribers how you will use it to their benefit.

For instance, if you require their zip code so you can send them news about local events or merchandise carried by stores near them, make that clear. If you require their birth date (perhaps for regulatory reasons) and will use it to send them a special birthday offer, tell them that and make sure you're prepared to follow through.■

List Building & Profiling

56

When profiling subscribers, ask them questions that lead you to a clear response.

Try to be as direct as possible when asking about interests and collecting other information during signups, in your preference center, or elsewhere. Avoid making assumptions about your subscribers and instead focus on gather clear intel.

For instance, if you want to know if a subscriber is interested in men's or women's apparel, ask them that. Don't ask their gender and assume that men are only interested in buying clothes for themselves.

Similarly, if you have brick-and-mortar stores, don't ask for a subscriber's zip code and assume that their preferred store is the one that's closest to their home. It might be your store that's closest to their workplace or elsewhere, so use their zip code as a starting point, but give them the freedom to select a different preferred location.

Making it easy for your subscribers to clearly state their interests allows you to send more targeted and relevant messages backed by data, rather than educated guesses.■

List Building & Profiling

57

Keep an inventory of all of your subscriber acquisition sources and track the performance of each one.

Signup mechanisms can break. And the performance of a subscriber acquisition source can change dramatically over time because of new technologies, process changes, or shifts in consumer behavior.

But you won't notice any of those changes if you're not keeping an inventory of all your acquisition sources and tracking their performance. For each subscriber acquisition source, note:

☐ The name or description of the source (i.e., homepage lightbox)

☐ A log of changes or A/B tests, along with screenshots, call center scripts, and other materials documenting those iterations

☐ Performance metrics, including:

- o Signups

- o Net list growth (signups minus hard bounces, unsubscribes, and spam complaints during first 30/90 days)

- o Hard bounces

- o Unsubscribes (all time, first 30/90 days)

- o Spam complaints (all time, first 30/90 days)
- o Engagement (opens and clicks)
- o Sales conversions and revenue
- o Subscriber lifetime value

Consider tracking those performance metrics on a weekly, monthly, quarterly, and annual basis. That will allow you to follow trends, fix breakdowns in a source's signup process, and identify which sources you should further optimize and which you should perhaps abandon.

Common acquisition sources include:

Website

- ☐ Homepage signup form
- ☐ Lightbox, overlay, popup, slide-in, exit intent, and similar signup forms
- ☐ Checkout opt-in
- ☐ Lead generation form
- ☐ Report/asset download form
- ☐ Webinar registration form
- ☐ Post-survey/petition opt-in
- ☐ Sweepstakes/contest entry form

Mobile

- ☐ Mobile app signup form
- ☐ Text to subscribe to email

Social

- ☐ Facebook tab email signup form
- ☐ Twitter Cards

☐ Social ads targeting lookalikes with email opt-in messaging

Customer Support

☐ Call center script signup prompt

☐ Customer support emails

☐ Chat

Store

☐ Store signage

☐ Checkout via POS, pin pad, tablet, etc.

☐ Kiosk

Other Channels

☐ Product packaging

☐ QR codes in magazines, playbills, etc.

☐ TV commercials

☐ Radio commercials

In addition to tracking each of these sources, you'll likely also want to track individual signup campaigns. Doing so allows you to measure the effectiveness of different signup messaging, processes, and other variables.■

Bonus Resource:

Outstanding Email Marketing Examples
of List Growth Tactics

EmailMarketingRules.com/Examples

List Building & Profiling

58

Routinely audit your subscriber acquisition sources and preference center to make sure they are up to date and working properly.

In addition to keeping an inventory of all your acquisition sources, you should regularly check these subscription pathways for errors by using them to sign up as if you were a customer. This is especially advised after you:

☐ Relaunch, redesign, or otherwise significantly change your website, mobile app, blog, etc.

☐ Change email service providers

☐ Change data warehouses or make any other major infrastructure change

The opportunity cost associated with failures of signup sources can be significant. For instance, in 2013, retailers Lands' End and Northern Tool each had issues that delayed the honoring of some email signups through their homepages' opt-in forms by at least 6 months. And in 2011, home improvement retailer Lowe's discovered a problem with their homepage's subscription process that delayed honoring some opt-ins by more than two years!

Since most brands collect email signups through a variety of sources, the failure of any one source probably isn't going to drop list growth enough to raise red flags. Only by keeping track of individual signup sources can you see any process failures that might occur.

Additionally, you should also routinely review your signup language and preference center content. Make sure you're not offering choices or incentives you no longer offer, such as a discontinued newsletter or content choice. And if you're asking about equipment, items, or brands your subscribers own, make sure those selections are up to date as well.

For instance, in 2008, Best Buy's preference center asked subscribers which video game consoles they owned, but hadn't been updated to include any of the current platforms. That's a huge missed opportunity to collect information that would have allowed them to target their subscribers with more relevant video game offers.■

"Broken acquisition sources are more common than you'd imagine. Approach all of your acquisition sources as an outsider, signing up with new email addresses, and monitor what happens."

—April Mullen, Senior Marketing Strategist at Selligent

Welcome Emails & Onboarding

"[A welcome email] sets the stage—the tone—for the rest of the email you will send. More importantly, a welcome email can increase your business and help you better understand your new subscribers."

—DJ Waldow and Jason Falls, coauthors of
The Rebel's Guide to Email Marketing

Confirming a successful signup is the bare minimum signup confirmation pages and welcome emails can do. Because opting in is a strong signal of buyer intent, these onboarding components reach subscribers when they are most likely to take another high-value action. Use these touchpoints to deepen the relationship and drive conversions.■

WORDS TO KNOW

onboarding: The process of familiarizing new subscribers with your email program and your brand using your signup confirmation page and welcome emails

welcome email: A message automatically sent to a new subscriber just after they've opted in that welcomes them to your email program and seeks further engagement

welcome email series: Multiple emails automatically sent to a new subscriber over time that seek to maximize engagement

Welcome Emails & Onboarding

59

Use the signup confirmation page as a "pre-welcome message" to continue to engage new subscribers.

When a person signs up to receive your emails, they are reaching out to you and expressing a desire to hear more. So don't stop talking after they subscribe.

First, use your signup confirmation page to clearly confirm that the person successfully signed up to receive promotional emails from you, showing them the email address they signed up with so they can verify they entered it correctly.

Second, capitalize on the moment and engage the new subscriber further. Treat it like a pre-welcome message.

For instance, it could be used to ask subscribers to add your email address to their address book, to collect optional preferences and other information, to drive them to key webpages, to educate them about sister brands, or to expose them to your social media channels.

If you plan to send a welcome email immediately, you can tell the subscriber to look for that. Moreover, you can use the signup confirmation page to remind subscribers to check their junk or spam folders if they don't see the welcome email in their inbox.

Although a signup confirmation page could be used in all those ways, focus on one or two of them, because asking subscribers to do too many things at once often dilutes your message and lowers response.■

Welcome Emails & Onboarding

60

Send a welcome email immediately after signup.

Consumers have been trained to look to their inbox after subscribing, registering, and checkout, so the longer you wait before sending a welcome email, the more likely the subscriber will move on to other things. Delays that stretch into days or weeks also increase spam complaints because sometimes people forget that they signed up.

Sending a welcome email immediately maximizes its effectiveness by continuing the momentum of a signup and engaging the subscriber further.■

Welcome Emails & Onboarding

61

Send a series of welcome emails to inform and engage new subscribers.

Although sending one welcome email prevents subscribers from abruptly dropping into your promotional mailstream, you can ease that transition further and quickly engage subscribers more deeply by sending a series of welcome emails.

For instance, if you're a B2B brand, you might want to send a new subscriber a three-email welcome series consisting of:

☐ An email highlighting your most popular blog posts, videos, podcasts, or ebooks; followed by

☐ An email promoting an upcoming webinar, event, or conference; followed by

☐ An email explaining the benefits of your products or service with an offer for a demonstration or free trial

A three-email welcome series is the most common to send, but the series can range from two all the way up to six or more messages. It all depends on your brand and what new subscribers need to know.■

Welcome Emails & Onboarding

62

Message new subscribers differently depending on their acquisition source and customer history.

Tailor your onboarding messaging to the individual subscriber based on what you know about them and what you know about other subscribers who opted in via the same acquisition source.

For example, people who subscribe through your homepage or while entering a contest are more likely to be prospects, in contrast to the customers opting in during checkout. So consider delivering a richer offer to those prospects to spur their first purchase, while giving your existing customers, who already see your value, a less rich offer.

Similarly, you probably shouldn't use your welcome email to push someone who subscribed via your Facebook page to "like" you. Instead, promote something they're more likely to be unfamiliar with, such as your mobile app or Twitter presence.

Additionally, analyze the behavior of your subscribers by acquisition source and look for patterns of behavior you can amplify or address in your onboarding messaging.■

Welcome Emails & Onboarding

63

Include an unsubscribe link in your welcome emails.

Some people argue welcome emails don't need to include an unsubscribe link because they are transactional emails, which CAN-SPAM exempts from requiring opt-out links. However, brands should always include an opt-out link in their welcome emails for two reasons:

First, well-crafted welcome emails are promotional emails. These emails should be promoting your products and services, offering deals and discounts, and otherwise trying to get subscribers to convert.

And second, even if you don't take advantage of the promotional power of welcome emails and only send a transactional email that confirms the signup and nothing more, denying subscribers the opportunity to unsubscribe only drives them to use the *Report Spam* button instead.

Similar to using a confirmed opt-in process to protect your list from low-quality acquisition sources, you can use a more prominent unsubscribe link in your welcome email to give regretful subscribers a clear way to opt out, other than marking your email as spam. A prominent opt-out link also builds trust by signaling to subscribers that you'll make it easy for them to unsubscribe in the future as well.

Making an opt-out link prominent typically involves positioning one in the upper right-corner of the email design opposite your logo or incorporating it into your welcome message, in addition to the usual one positioned at the bottom in the footer of the email. Font size and styling—in particular, color—can also ensure that subscribers who go looking your unsubscribe link can easily find it.■

Welcome Emails & Onboarding

64

Fulfill subscriptions quickly after sending your welcome email(s).

Just like a delay in sending your first welcome email increases spam complaints, so too do delays in fulfilling subscriptions. Minimize this gap as best makes sense.

For instance, if a subscriber signed up for a weekly or monthly email program and your next regular email isn't due for a while, send the most recent email immediately to start demonstrating the value of your program.■

Welcome Emails & Onboarding

65

Pay special attention to subscribers during their first weeks on your list, as this is when they are most engaged.

This "signup honeymoon" period of heightened engagement right after a subscriber has opted in is one of the reasons that sending a welcome email or a series of welcome emails immediately and minimizing subscription fulfillment delays are so important.

However, you may find it worth taking other actions, such as sending emails triggered by low initial engagement or a lack of sales conversions that ask new subscribers more about themselves and their interests so you can send more targeted offers going forward.■

Subject Lines & Envelope Content

"Far from the waterfalls of social media feeds, email and SMS inboxes are more akin to 'to-do' lists that consumers check off, one message at a time. Your email and SMS messages tend to have far greater reach than social media, because every message the user receives creates an impression from its 'from' and subject lines—even if they never open it."

—Jeffrey K. Rohrs, Chief Marketing Officer of Yext; author of *AUDIENCE*

Email interactions generally involve three stages, with reading the envelope content being the first stage. The envelope content consists of the:

- ☐ Sender or *from* name
- ☐ *From* email address
- ☐ *Reply-to* email address
- ☐ Subject line
- ☐ Snippet or preview text

Not every envelope content element will appear in every email client.■

WORDS TO KNOW

body content or copy: The text, images, and other content inside your email that becomes visible once opened

call-to-action (CTA): What a message asks a subscriber to do, but more specifically the buttons and links subscribers click to take action

envelope content: The portion of an email that's visible to subscribers before they open it, which generally includes the sender name, sent date, subject line, and preview text

***from* email address:** The email address from which your emails are sent to your subscribers; in some email clients, this appears next to or instead of your sender name

preheader text: Visible or hidden HTML text positioned at the very top of an email's body content that is used to control what appears as preview text

reply-to email address: Replies to your emails go to this address instead of your *from* email address

snippet or preview text: A portion of the first text from inside the email that some email clients display after the subject line in the inbox, when highlighting a new email's arrival, or in other situations; part of an email's envelope content

subject line: The text that appears in the subject line in an email client; part of an email's envelope content

Subject Lines & Envelope Content

66

Use a recognizable and consistent sender name for your emails.

Although much is written about the power of subject lines, the email sender's identity actually has a greater impact on whether a recipient opens an email. After all, email marketing is a permission- and relationship-driven channel.

The sender name, which appears as the *from* name in the inbox, is the first thing that many email users look at when receiving an email. And when recipients don't instantly recognize a sender, they ignore, delete, or mark those emails as spam.

For this reason, using a sender name that subscribers will immediately recognize is critical. For most marketers, that will be your brand name.

Avoid using less recognizable and less stable alternatives, such as:

☐ Generic terms such as *newsletter*, *info*, and *customer service*

☐ The name of your parent company

☐ The name of your CEO, president, or other officers or agents

After you decide on the appropriate sender name,

always use it. Subscribers will become trained to look for it and will instantly recognize you. Resist the temptation to change it for "really special" one-off emails, to be funny, or any other reason.

Your sender name is the equivalent of your logo, the sign on your storefront, and your signature. You wouldn't casually change those. So be consistent with your sender name and use your subject line and preview text to express your brand personality and call out brand ambassadors.

The one caveat to this is that B2B marketers might find that using the name of a client's service representative, for instance, is more powerful than the name of their company. However, use this approach with caution, since you're elevating a person above your brand.

As a compromise, some brands have found success with using their brand name plus some other rotating element as their sender name. That additional element could be the name of a person (i.e., *Person's Name from Brand*, or *Brand, Person's Name*) or the name of a kind of email that the brand sends (i.e., *Brand Notification* or *Brand Alert*). In these cases, you're at least still leveraging your brand equity, even if you're diluting the focus a little.

Whatever your approach, keep your sender name to 20 characters or less to ensure that it doesn't get truncated in any major email clients.■

Subject Lines & Envelope Content

67

Use a well-branded *from* email address and *reply-to* email address.

Your *from* email address sometimes displays either next to or instead of your sender name. However, in some email clients, it is only revealed when subscribers click for more details about the sender, add the sender to their address book, or reply to the email.

In all cases, you want your *from* address to give the recipient confidence that you did indeed send the email. Accomplish this by using a *from* address that includes your brand name both before and after the @ sign, if possible.

Examples of well-branded *from* address structures include:

☐ brand@email.brand.com

☐ brand@shop.brand.com

☐ brandnews@e.brand.com

☐ brand@brandemail.com

If you use a *reply-to* email address that's different from your *from* address, make sure that is well-branded as well.∎

Subject Lines & Envelope Content

68

Measure the success of a subject line by how well it drives clicks and conversions.

Perhaps the biggest myth in all of email marketing is that subject lines should be measured on how well they generate opens. This thinking assumes that subject lines exist in a vacuum, isolated from the performance of the email content and the web page that they land on after they click through.

In reality, a subject line impacts performance all the way down the email interaction funnel because it is key in selecting the subscribers who enter that funnel. As with all other digital marketing channels, you maximize performance by targeting the right people to enter the top of your funnel.

Subject lines target the right openers by setting expectations about what they'll find if they open the email. Align your subject line with your email copy and your email copy with your landing page's call-to-action to maximize performance. Poorly aligned subject lines may attract a lot of openers, but they're worthless if they aren't good candidates to convert. (See Fig. 11 on next page.)

Because email marketing is an ongoing relationship, a poor subject line doesn't just

Good Subject Lines Generate High-Converting Openers

Email #1: Subject line B is the winner.

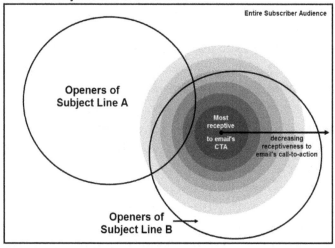

Email #2: Subject line A is the winner.

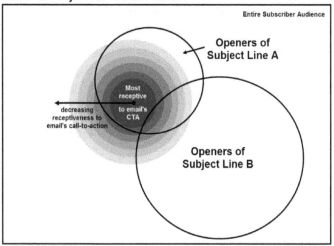

FIGURE 11

dampen the results of the one email. It can damage the performance of future campaigns by causing disappointed openers to be reluctant to open future emails, to unsubscribe, or to report the email as spam in frustration.

So a good subject line not only encourages the right subscribers to open the email, it dissuades subscribers from opening who would likely be disappointed by or uninterested in the email's content.

Putting those two considerations together, a subject line that produces fewer opens but more conversions is preferable to one that produces more opens but fewer conversions. At the same time, be sure to look at unsubscribe and spam complaint rates, because you always want to keep these rates low.

If you're at all skeptical of a subject line's ability to impact performance all the way through to conversion, A/B test some subject lines, keeping both the email content and the landing pages the same. You'll see for yourself that subject lines affect clicks, post-click activity, and conversions.∎

Subject Lines & Envelope Content

69

Keep your subject lines short, but still coherent and descriptive.

People scan their inboxes quickly to decide which emails to open. Overly long subject lines are a turnoff to many consumers and generally don't lead to more clicks or conversions among those who do open.

At the other end of the spectrum, very short subject lines often generate higher-than-average open rates, but lower-than-average click rates. These subject lines tend to be more intriguing and mysterious but, as a result, attract curious subscribers rather than the subscribers most likely to respond to the calls-to-action in the email. Additionally, using too many vague, short subject lines might cause fewer subscribers to open your emails over time because the email content has repeatedly disappointed them.

Barrack Obama's infamous "Hey" subject line for a March 31, 2012, fundraising email is sometimes held up as evidence that intriguing subject lines can be highly effective. While that email did raise the most money for them during the campaign, don't lose sight of the context: That email was sent by a very popular presidential candidate on the eve of a major fundraising deadline and that the call-to-action of virtually every email he sent was the same: *Donate*. The sender, timing, predictability of the call-to-action, and external factors like news coverage were likely more powerful contributors to the email's success than the subject line alone.

Although growing smartphone readership and the rise of smart watches and other wearables will continue to put downward pressure on subject line length, the sweet spot appears to be between 20 to 40 characters, which generally produces above average conversions and clicks, as well as opens. That range includes enough characters to clearly convey two or more aspects of the email's content— perhaps some details about the offer plus a time factor to create urgency or some emotional appeal— while staying true to your brand's voice.

If you decide to use a subject line that's more than 40 characters long, consider frontloading it with your keywords and main call-to-action to limit the impact of it being truncated.

Be aware that word choice can affect perceived subject line length because several long words can be easier to read than a bunch of short words.

Of all the email elements covered in this book, subject lines are the most frequently tested—and rightfully so. The perfect subject line lies at the intersection of your brand voice, message goal, and audience preferences—that is, how your brand projects itself, what you want to communicate with

Elements of a Perfect Subject Line

FIGURE 12

the email, and which kind of messaging your subscribers respond to best. (See Fig. 12 above.) Finding that point requires a deep understanding of all three elements, which is a process that's as much art as it is science.■

> *"The best subject lines tell what's inside, and the worst subject lines sell what's inside."*
>
> —MailChimp

Subject Lines & Envelope Content

70

Don't use misleading subject lines.

Many anti-spam laws, including CAN-SPAM, stipulate that marketers should not use deceptive or misleading sender names or subject lines to misrepresent who the email is from or its content. In terms of enforcement, we're talking about deceptions that rise to the level of fraud and false advertising.

However, lesser levels of deception are unfortunately not uncommon among legitimate email marketers, often justified as cleverness or creativity. While not likely to draw criminal charges, these deceptions lead to email fatigue, unsubscribes, spam complaints, and, more broadly, brand damage.

To avoid those consequences, refrain from misleading subscribers about:

☐ Who the email is from

☐ Actions taken by the subscriber

☐ The content of the email or a previous email

For example, for a May 10, 2013 email, the American Red Cross nonprofit group used the subject line *Fwd: Mom will love this*. The message was indeed a forward, but it was a forward of an

American Red Cross email from seven days earlier, which is surely not what subscribers expected.

Falsely using *Fwd:* implies that the content of the email is from someone other than the sender. *Re:* is similarly misused in subject lines to falsely signal that the subscriber had emailed the brand about the content of the email previously when they didn't.

Beyond *Fwd:* and *Re:*, there are other ways that subject lines can mislead. For a 2015 April Fool's email, home goods retailer West Elm used the subject line *Thanks for your order!* for a broadcast email sent to its full list. The email included a *receipt from the future* and a discount offer, but some subscribers saw the subject line and thought their credit card had been stolen or account had been hacked. Some of those subscribers took to social media to express their unhappiness with the joke.

For a Sept. 7, 2016 email, apparel retailer Chubbies used the cryptic, one-word subject line *Oops*. Words like *oops* and *correction* are subject line keywords used for apology and correction emails, which generally see higher-than-average open rates because people want to know what about the previous messaging is now different. However, this Chubbies email wasn't a correction email at all. It was just a regular (albeit quite funny) promotional email.

And for a Sept. 27, 2016 email that was designed to look like an internal email that was accidently sent to subscribers, apparel retailer Threadless used the subject line *Urgent: Hoody prices are incorrect, way too low.* The text-only email even used *Jason Macatangay*, the name of their VP of Finance, as the sender name to enhance the deception.

None of those examples were at high-risk of drawing legal action, but they do break subscriber trust to one degree or another. Think beyond the open to how your subscribers will react to the entire email experience.■

"Your most important job as an email designer is to get them to open the next one."

—Alex Williams, Vice President, Creative Director, Trendline Interactive

Subject Lines & Envelope Content

71

Use preview text like a "second subject line" to support and extend your subject line.

Preview, or snippet, text plays a unique role in email design because while it's technically body copy, it's also sometimes envelope copy. That's because some email clients display a small portion of the first body copy after the subject line in the inbox, when highlighting a new email's arrival, or in other situations.

Make the most of preview text by including either visible or hidden preheader text, which is HTML text positioned at the very top of an email's body content. Ensure that it supports and extends the subject line of your email. In other words, treat it like a second subject line.

Avoid having your preheader text repeat the subject line and try to keep administrative preheader text from showing up as preview text. For instance, preheaders might also include links to view the web-hosted version of the email, to visit your social media pages, to update preferences, or to unsubscribe.

If you include any of those options in your preheader, make sure they're not among the first 70 or so HTML text characters in your email as to avoid

Envelope Content

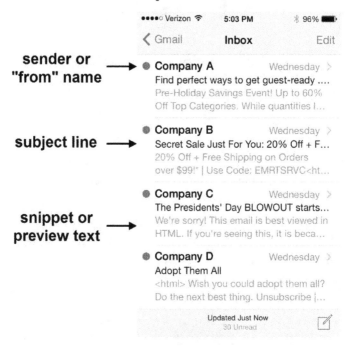

sender or "from" name →

subject line →

snippet or preview text →

FIGURE 13

squandering the opportunity provided by preview text. (See Fig. 13 above for two good examples of preview text followed by two bad ones.)

Similarly, don't ask your subscribers to add your email address to their address book in the preheader of every email you send. Make that request on your signup confirmation page and in your welcome email series. If subscribers haven't done it after being asked a few times, they're unlikely to ever do it and you're just wasting valuable screen real estate by endlessly asking.

Consider including a more direct call-to-action in your preheader text by linking all or a portion of it to the primary landing page for the email so subscribers can easily click through and take action after they open the message.

It's worth noting that preview text may be on the cusp of a reimagining in the wake of Gmail introducing Highlights. That feature uses the preview text space in the inbox to display text and images from the email and from webpages linked to in the email. Given this change, we should probably start calling it *snippet content*, since it's no longer just text and it's not always a preview of the email.∎

Subject Lines & Envelope Content

72

Recognize that an unopened email delivers a brand impression and call-to-action through its envelope content.

Although every marketer wants every single one of their emails opened, very few subscribers are that engaged. Even so, emails still generate value when they go unopened by subscribers who at least occasionally engage with your emails.

First, a subscriber who deletes an email unopened is still exposed to your brand name in the *from* line, which helps keep your brand top of mind and might prompt interactions in other online or offline channels.

Second, if the subject line is clear about what action you want subscribers to take, it has an even better chance of prompting interactions in other channels or generating word of mouth. For instance, a subject line about summer apparel might serve as a general reminder for the subscriber to stop by their local store to refresh their summer wardrobe. And including a promo code in a subject line might spur a subscriber to make a purchase without even needing to open the email.

And third, the subject line can affect subscriber interest in opening future emails. For example, if the subject line promotes a good deal but the recipient is just not ready to shop at the moment, the savings message still reaffirms the subscriber's belief in the value of your emails and would keep them interested in future ones.

For those reasons, avoid relying too much on vague and mysterious subject lines to generate opens. Over time, this approach erodes trust by making subscribers feel manipulated into opening your emails to find out what the email is truly about and misled when subject lines don't align with the content of your emails.

Instead, try to be descriptive, using keywords connected to the primary message and maybe an important secondary message. A subject line should help subscribers decide whether opening the email will be a good use of their time. Respecting your subscribers' time makes them less likely to tune you out and more likely to stay subscribed.■

Email Design & Body Content

"There's really only one central principle of good content: it should be appropriate for your business, for your users, and for its context. Appropriate in its method of delivery, in its style and structure, and above all in its substance."

—Erin Kissane, author of
The Elements of Content Strategy

When a subscriber opens your email, they've reached the second stage of email interaction: reading the body content of your email.

For a small percentage of brands, this is the end game; however, for the vast majority, this is just one step closer to the goal of generating a conversion. Effective email design and compelling body copy help propel subscribers on to the next and final stage of email interaction.■

WORDS TO KNOW

above the fold: The portion of an email that displays before a subscriber scrolls

adaptive design: Email design approach that uses media queries to establish one or more breakpoints at set screen widths at which the email content is reformatted, rearranged, or hidden so it's optimized for the subscriber's screen size

alt **text:** Text coded into an *<img>* tag that is displayed when the image is blocked and when recipients mouse over the image, although support is not consistent across email clients

animated GIF: An image file that displays multiple images sequentially over time, sometimes in a loop

below the fold: The portion of an email that displays only after a subscriber scrolls

bulletproof button: A non-graphical button created from styled and linked HTML text inside a table cell with a background color that suffers minimal or no degradation when email images are blocked

cinemagraph: A picture composed of both static images and one or more animated GIFs, which give motion, often subtle, to a small portion of the overall picture

defensive design: Design techniques that allow an email to communicate its message effectively when images are blocked

desktop-centric design: Email design approach that uses basic coding techniques to create a single email rendering that's optimized for viewing on large-screened desktops, which can easily handle multi-column designs, small text, and tightly clustered links and buttons

email template: Reusable, preformatted email file that includes all essential email elements, plus content blocks that can be switched out to create individual emails

forward to a friend (FTAF): Providing a link in your email that takes subscribers to a form that allows them to forward all or a portion of your email to one or more people that they know

fully responsive email design: Email design approach that uses adaptive design's breakpoints to reformat, rearrange, and hide email content at set screen widths and uses fluid design's 100% width scaling to optimize the size of images, fonts, buttons, and other elements between those breakpoints

Anatomy of a Mobile Email

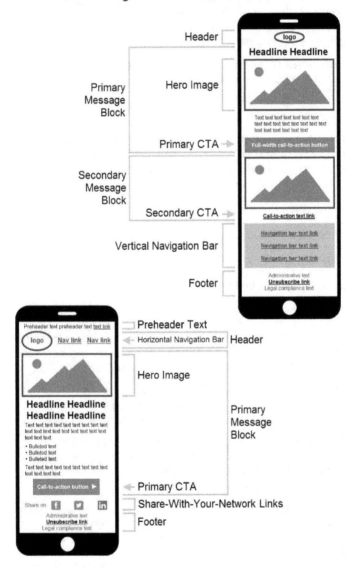

FIGURE 14

graceful degradation: Using fallbacks to provide adequate email experiences when advanced coding, animated GIFs, images, HTML, and other elements aren't supported

graphical text: Text that is part of an image

header: The upper portion of an email that includes your brand's logo

HTML version or part: The HTML part of a multipart MIME email that supports images, a range of HTML text formatting, and other functionality

HTML weight: The file size of the HTML coding of an email

images-off mosaic: Using background colors on the cells of elaborate tables to create pixel art pictures that only display when images are blocked in your email

liquid or fluid email design: Email design approach that uses 100% width images and table cells to have the email content expand to completely fill the subscriber's screen, up to a max width that's set using media queries

live content: Images and other email content that vary based on when the email is opened, what kind of device it's opened on, and other factors

live, system, or HTML text: Text from a limited number of fonts that are universally or widely supported across email clients

loaded or total weight: The file size of the HTML coding of an email plus the total file size of all the images used in the email

progressive enhancement: A technique that provides improved rendering or advanced functionality in certain email environments

media queries: CSS that allows the rendering of an email's content to vary depending on conditions such as screen size

multipart MIME (Multipurpose Internet Mail Extensions) protocol: An email format standard that

Anatomy of a Desktop Email

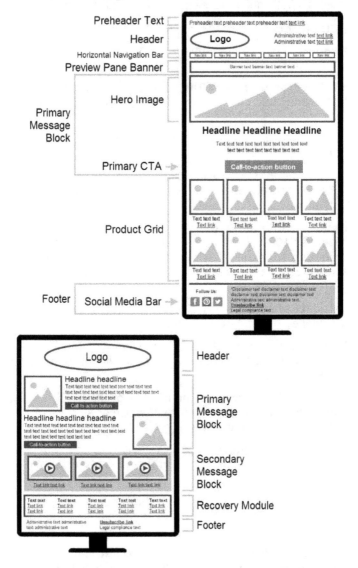

FIGURE 15

allows you to bundle an HTML version, plain-text version, and other versions of your email together in one package; the receiving device's capabilities or the subscriber's preferences then determine which version is displayed

navigation bar: A row of links to important pages on your website

newsjacking: Leveraging the popularity of a news story, event, or cultural phenomena to promote yourself or your company

plain text version or part: The text-only part of a multipart MIME email that supports only text and some basic symbols

reading or preview pane: A window in some email clients that allows subscribers to view a smaller portion of an email than if the email were opened in its own window

preview pane banner: A banner placed right above or right below the header (or navigation bar, if used) in the body of an email so that the banner always appears above the fold

primary message or content block, or hero: The main message of an email, usually positioned at the top and larger than other messages in the email

product grid: A multi-column and usually multi-row layout where each grid cell contains a product image and other information, such as product name, brand, and price

recovery module: A secondary content block usually positioned right before the footer that contains many links to different product categories, brands, or other areas of your website with the intent to appeal to subscribers who were uninterested in the other calls-to-action in the email

rendering: How an email displays and functions in a particular email client; this can vary wildly from email client to email client

responsive email design: A variety of email design approaches that use media queries and other progressive enhancement techniques to control the formatting, layout, and display of email content depending on the subscriber's screen size

responsive-aware email design: Email design approach that uses responsive design for the header, navigation bar, recovery module, and footer of an email, and uses mobile-aware design for the rest of the email

scalable, mobile-first, or mobile-aware design: Email design approach that uses basic coding techniques to create a single email rendering that's suitable for a range of screen sizes, but is deferential to smartphones

secondary message or content block: The other message(s) in an email, usually following and smaller than the primary message

share with your network (SWYN): Functionality that allows subscribers to add content from your email to their social media timeline

social media bar: A row of social media icons that link to your brand's pages on those social media sites

spongy or hybrid email design: Email design approach that generates the effects of adaptive or fully responsive design without relying on media queries

static or still image: An image that doesn't change over time, unlike an animated GIF

styled *alt* text: Alt text that has had its font type, size, weight, or color changed through the application of inline CSS styling

swipe file: A record of your top-performing emails, subject lines, calls-to-action, content blocks, landing pages, and other email elements that you return to for learnings and inspiration

video gif: A compressed, streaming animated GIF capable of video-quality frame rates

Email Design & Body Content

73

Design your emails to render well and function properly across a wide range of platforms and devices.

Very few subscribers will open your emails more than once, so make sure your emails display well on desktops, tablets, and smartphones—and potentially even smart watches and devices that are part of the Internet of Things.

In fact, a considerable percentage of email users would rather unsubscribe than try to navigate emails that render poorly on their preferred email client or device.

This issue has become more critical as an increasing percentage of subscribers read email on their smartphones. Small screens can make it hard to easily read and engage with marketing emails not designed with mobile devices in mind.

For this reason, it's highly recommended that you use a mobile-friendly design approach for your emails—rather than a desktop-centric design that has multi-column layouts, small text, and small and tightly grouped links and buttons.

You can no longer expect subscribers who have lackluster experiences on mobile devices to save the emails and reopen them later on laptops or

desktops. The vast majority will just delete them—
or worse, they'll unsubscribe or even mark your
emails as spam.

Mobile-friendly design approaches range from
straightforward mobile-aware design to sophisticated
responsive design (see Fig. 16 on next page):

Mobile-aware design, or scalable design,
involves basic techniques to create a single email that
functions well across a range of screen sizes, but is
deferential to smartphones. Those techniques include:

☐ Employing a single-column layout (two-column
product grids are okay)

☐ Using large text, with at least 14px text for
body copy and 18px for headlines

☐ Using large images, as well as and large, easily
tapped buttons that are at least 44x44px

☐ Spacing out links and buttons—including those
in navigation, social, and administrative bars—
so subscribers can tap them accurately

☐ Using high contrast values and colors for ease
of reading outdoors and in other less-than-ideal
environments

Responsive design has become a general term
for a basket of techniques that use CSS media
queries and other progressive enhancements to
produce renderings or versions of an email that are
optimized for particular screen resolutions or email
clients. These approaches include:

☐ *Liquid or fluid design*, which uses 100% width
images and table cells to have the email content
expand to completely fill the subscriber's

Environment Biases of Email Design Approaches

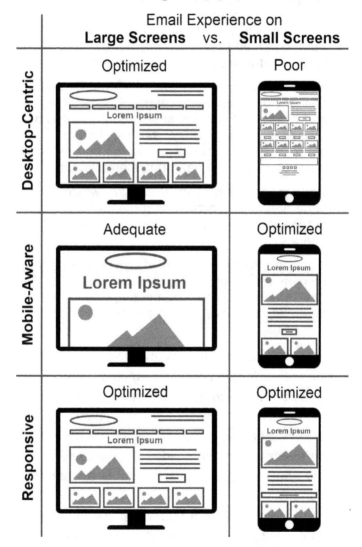

FIGURE 16

screen, up to a max width that's set using media queries

☐ **_Adaptive design_**, which uses media queries to establish one or more breakpoints at set screen widths at which the email content is reformatted, rearranged, and revealed or hidden so it's optimized for the subscriber's screen size

☐ **_Fully responsive design_**, which uses adaptive design's breakpoints to reformat, rearrange, and hide email content at set screen widths and uses fluid design's 100% width scaling to optimize the size of images, fonts, buttons, and other elements between those breakpoints

☐ **_Spongy or hybrid email design_**, which generates the effects of adaptive or fully responsive design without relying on media queries

☐ **_Responsive-aware design_**, which uses responsive design just for the header, navigation bar, recovery module, and footer of an email, and uses mobile-aware design for the rest of the email

Each of these techniques involve extra email design and coding, with hybrid email design involving the most complex and heaviest coding, and responsive-aware email design minimizing the extra work by allowing you to build most of the responsiveness into the header and footer sections of your email template, which tend not to change very often.

Beyond ensuring that your email displays and functions well across a range of screen sizes, media queries can also create device-targeted content. For instance, they can be used to display calls-to-action to download your mobile app and to display tap-to-call CTAs that take advantage of the ability of smartphones to make phone calls.

Consult with your ESP or an email design specialist to determine the design approach that's best for your brand and circumstances. Consider the subscriber experience, but also keep in mind the workload that your design approach choice will create. Depending on the content and frequency of your emails, the more efficient design approaches like mobile-aware and responsive-aware may make more sense than the more sophisticated ones like adaptive and hybrid.

That said, be sure to focus on the returns from your email production efforts rather than just the costs of those efforts.■

"Responsive design is really about strategy, not design."
—Loren McDonald, Marketing Evangelist at
IBM Watson Marketing

Email Design & Body Content

74

Recognize that your emails won't render or function exactly the same in every email environment—and that a consistent experience isn't a good design goal.

Support for fonts, emojis, animated GIFs, and other coding elements varies across email environments, so any email you create likely won't look or function exactly the same everywhere. The rise of wearables and other Internet of Things devices—some of which don't support images, links, or HTML—exacerbate this disparity.

While consistency-loving brand management folks may cringe, trying to create email experiences that are 100% identical for each of your subscribers is a poor email design goal. Instead, be open to having a range of acceptable experiences that raise the bar overall for functionality and accessibility.

Rather than playing down to the lowest common denominator in terms of email coding support, look for opportunities to give some of your subscribers better experiences by using progressive enhancement, a technique that provides improved rendering or advanced functionality in certain email environments. Be mindful to provide graceful degradation, or fallbacks, when coding isn't supported to ensure an adequate baseline experience.

Some types of progressive enhancements, such as media queries, work across a number of email clients. Others, such as Microsoft conditional comments, allow you to target a single email client or family of email clients. Regardless of your coding techniques, it's important to expect—and indeed plan—for your subscribers to have different experiences in different email clients and on different devices.

In the end, if you are providing a consistent experience to all of your subscribers, then it's probably not a great experience.∎

———————————————

"Pixel perfection only exists in a static environment like Photoshop. We need to recognize and accept that different canvases will show slightly different results, and then use that in a positive way."

—Mike Ragan, Senior Developer at Action Rocket

Email Design & Body Content

75

Design your emails so they convey their message even when images are blocked.

Many email clients block images by default and some subscribers don't turn images on, so relying too heavily on images to communicate your message can be a losing strategy. Defend against image-blocking ruining your message by using three common defensive design techniques:

☐ Adding *alt* text to your image coding—or better yet, styled *alt* text

☐ Using HTML or system text as much as feasibly possible instead of embedding all of your text into your images

☐ Using background colors on table cells either to create content blocks, simple structures, or complex mosaic pixel art

Alt text generally appears when the image is blocked and when recipients mouse over enabled images, although support isn't consistent across email clients. If an image contains graphical text, use the *alt* text to replicate all or some of that text so recipients can read it when images are not enabled. As an added bonus, *alt* text also helps subscribers who use a screen reader.

You can create emphasis and better mimic the images-on version of your email by applying inline CSS to change the font type, size, weight, and color of your *alt* text. However, support for styled *alt* text is again inconsistent.

Use HTML text at the very top of your emails before the header to create preheader text, which most often communicates the primary call-to-action of the email or builds on the content of the subject line. HTML text can also be used for your navigation bar links; throughout your primary and secondary messaging blocks, particularly for headlines, coupon codes, and calls-to-action; and in a product grid. And, of course, HTML text should be used for all footer text and administrative links, such as your mailing address and unsubscribe link.

Traditionally, HTML text has been limited to just a small number of popular web safe font families—including Arial, Courier New, Georgia, Times New Roman, and Verdana—because these fonts are universally supported. And in most cases, those fonts can also be styled in different sizes and colors.

However, web fonts are also a possibility now, although they are not universally supported. So you'll need to use web safe fonts as fallbacks.

Background colors can be used in table cells to stand in for blocked images or to otherwise recreate the structure, patterns, and flow of content blocks, images, and text in your emails.

If you're feeling ambitious, create pixel art or mosaics using this technique. Some brands have used mosaics to create a low-resolution version of their logo, replicate the primary product or lifestyle image in the email, or to create a picture of something completely different that is related to the primary message of the email.

A high-effort tactic, mosaics should be used sparingly. They are best for executions with a long shelf-life, such as for your logo or for a high-impact triggered email.

HTML text and background colors can be used in combination to create bulletproof buttons that retain their effectiveness even when images are blocked, unlike image-based buttons. You can create bulletproof buttons using a few different methods, but most involve using a table cell with a background color to create the button and styled and linked HTML text in the table cell to create the clickable call-to-action.

These defensive design tactics are especially critical in the first emails that a consumer receives from you, such as your welcome email and transactional emails, when recipients are most likely to have the images in your emails turned off. They're also important for reengagement and re-permission emails, which are sent in response to a subscriber not engaging with your emails and are therefore more likely to land in the spam folder where images are typically blocked.

While you shouldn't ignore image blocking as a design consideration, you shouldn't let it deter you from using images either. The vast majority of B2C brands send emails that are at least 50% image-based. And lifestyle, aspirational, and high-end brands send emails that are almost entirely image-based, since pictures are key to conveying the appeal of these brands' products.

B2B brands tend to use much more HTML text in their emails and a lot fewer images. In fact, it's not uncommon for some B2B emails to be entirely HTML text with no images. Some B2B brands can't easily depict their products or services visually, so images are less vital to how they communicate.

Wherever your brand falls on that visual spectrum, use defensive design thoughtfully, but don't let it cause you to sacrifice how you project your brand image.■

Bonus Resource:

Outstanding Email Marketing Examples
of Defensive Design

EmailMarketingRules.com/Examples

Email Design & Body Content

76

Design your emails with an appropriate balance of text and images.

The issue of how much text and how much visual imagery to include in your emails goes well beyond the concerns around defensive design, accessibility, and deliverability.

Decisions around text-image balance impact your message. Certain kinds of brands do better and certain messages do better when the email is text-heavy, while others do better when emails are image-heavy. (See Fig. 17 on next page.)

For example, it's difficult to promote clothing using words alone. You have to show the clothing—and you may even want to use animation to show how the clothing moves when worn. Similarly, it's difficult to promote travel without showing pictures of the available activities, venues, and points of interest. For those reason, B2C brands almost universally have high image-to-text ratios in their emails.

On the other hand, if you're promoting legal advice, software, and other kinds of B2B products and services, text plays a much bigger role since visuals have difficulty communicating the benefits in these cases. Text also comes across as more

Factors that Influence Text-Image Balance in Email Design

B2B brands	B2C brands
Value brands	Lifestyle brands
Transactional and apology emails	Promotional and newsletter emails
Person's name as sender name	Brand's name as sender name
More Text	More Images

FIGURE 17

personal and sincere, so it's frequently used for messages that are sent on the behalf of sales representatives and for apology emails.

It's worth stressing that even the most text-heavy of emails shouldn't be plain text. You still want to be sending an HMTL email so you can at least include a tracking pixel to measure opens and perhaps to include your logo, even if it's only at the bottom of the message as part of your email signature.■

Email Design & Body Content

77

Send a plain text version of your email using multipart MIME.

The vast majority of email clients can handle most HTML coding, and most subscribers prefer HTML emails. But some email clients can't display HTML and some subscribers don't like HTML emails. To make sure your message is accessible to every subscriber, you need to send a plain text version along with the HTML version of your email.

You do this using multipart MIME (Multipurpose Internet Mail Extensions), which allows you to bundle both an HTML and plain text version of your email together in one package. The email client then decides which version to display, based either on its capabilities or the subscriber's preference.

In addition to being more subscriber-friendly, including at least a plain text version is good for your deliverability, especially if the HTML version of your email is image-heavy with little HTML text.

Some email service providers automatically generate a plain text version of your email based on the HTML text in the HTML version. Even if that's the case, you'll want to edit that auto-generated version to clean up the formatting and add text, as necessary.

Although plain text limits your design elements,

Anatomy of a Plain-Text Email

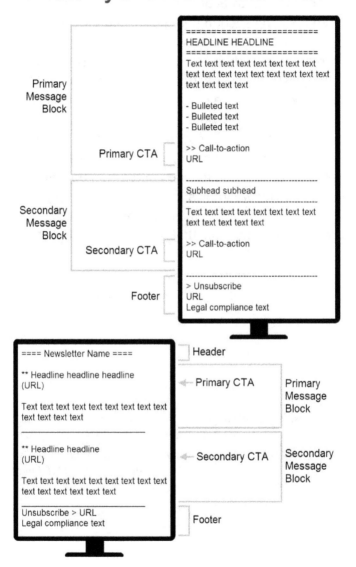

FIGURE 18

you should still create a clear content hierarchy and clear calls-to-action. Consider setting off headlines and section heads by using all-caps or enclosing them in asterisks (*), separating sections with lines of hyphens (-) or equal signs (=), and highlighting calls-to-action by preceding or following it with one or two greater than signs (>). (See Fig. 18 on previous page.)

It's worth noting that the Apple Watch supports a new watch-html version, which lets marketers optimize a message for the limited-functionality device. Other wearables may end up adopting this new version, and new devices may lead to the creation of additional MIME parts in the future.■

"It is...extremely important that your plain text email is just as well-designed as its HTML counterpart."

—Jason Rodriguez, author of *Professional Email Design* and *Modern HTML Email*

Email Design & Body Content

78

Design your emails with a clear content hierarchy so they can be easily scanned.

Subscribers don't read emails; they scan them. So make your content skimmable by:

☐ Using strong headlines that are substantially larger than the text that falls under them

☐ Making the primary message block, or hero, larger than any secondary content blocks and having it immediately or closely follow the header

☐ Using large (44x44px minimum) colored buttons for primary calls-to-action, and ghost buttons and text links for secondary CTAs

☐ Using bulleted items rather than full sentences

☐ Avoiding blocks of text that are more than five lines long when using full sentences

In most cases, your email is just a gateway to your website or some other final destination, so you only need to convey enough content to compel subscribers to click through.■

"When you emphasize everything, you emphasize nothing."
—Herschell Gordon Lewis, author of *Effective E-mail Marketing*

Email Design & Body Content

79

Make your calls-to-action action-oriented and clear in language and positioning.

If you want subscribers to do something, tell them! Use direct language in your calls-to-action, instead of a generic and less compelling *Click Here*.

Use action words like *get*, *shop*, *read*, *view*, *start*, *find*, and *join*. Follow those words with descriptors that clarify the action, such as *Shop New Arrivals*, *Get the Report*, or *View Your Statement*.

Place your CTAs so that they punctuate the copy that's associated with it. For example, if you want subscribers to share a discount code in an email with their friends and family on Twitter, Facebook, and other social networks, place a share-with-your-network (SWYN) link with a *Share This Deal* CTA right next to the discount code just as you'd place a *Shop Now* button next to product information.

Primary CTAs should generally be in the form of a button that stands out from the surrounding content.■

"I like big buttons and I cannot lie."

—Justine Jordan, Vice President of Marketing at Litmus

Email Design & Body Content

80

Offer subscribers many paths to click through from an email.

Generally, when we talk about calls-to-action, we're referring to buttons and text links. However, subscribers think of CTAs more broadly.

They see the logo in your header, the headlines, and any image in your email (whether it is a product shot or not), as a CTA that they'll try to click. Make the most of their interest by making as many of these elements clickable as possible—even if most of these links take the subscriber to the same landing page.

There's no rule about the right number of unique links to include in an email, as emails with a single destination and emails with lots of destinations can be equally effective. But the right number of total links is generally not one.

All of that said, don't cluster non-identical links too closely together because subscribers reading your email on tablets and, especially, smartphones might have difficulty accurately selecting a link with their finger.■

Email Design & Body Content

81

Don't limit your email calls-to-action to online only.

Email can drive subscribers to act offline just as effectively as it can drive them to act online, so don't shy away from promoting store events and other happenings. In fact, the increase in mobile email reading makes offline calls-to-action more effective, because you can increasingly reach subscribers when they are out and about.

Subscribers are more likely to be out of the home on weekends, during the warmer months, and especially on big shopping days like Thanksgiving Eve, Thanksgiving Day, Black Friday, and the day after Christmas. Those are all occasions to be more mindful of mobile readers and to consider including store-only deals, mobile coupons, and store-specific information such as hours in your emails to make acting offline easier.■

Email Design & Body Content

82

Design your email content so it can be viewed in screen-sized chunks.

Don't design your emails as you would posters or store signage. Unless a particular email is small, subscribers don't see an entire email at once. They see the email in screen-sized chunks as they scroll.

How much of an email is displayed at one time varies by device and email client, and is considerably smaller when a subscriber is using a preview or reading pane, which shows less of the email at a time than if it were opened in its own window. However, a good rule of thumb is to design your emails assuming that subscribers will only see about 500 pixels of height at a time.

Make your text easy to read by designing your emails so that logical groups of text are visible on a single screen so they can be read at once. Create clear breaks between content blocks by using containers, lines or rules, and white space.

Large images that take several screens to scroll through can create intrigue, encourage subscribers to scroll, and highlight the details of the image. However, be strategic about where you place copy and calls-to-action. Near the top and near the bottom tend to be effective.■

Email Design & Body Content

83

Pay extra attention to the top portion of your email that appears "above the fold" and ensure it's well-branded.

The email content that appears above the fold on that first screen-sized chunk is the most critical because some subscribers will not scroll down to see the content that's below the fold. Again, assume that your subscribers will only see 500-pixel-tall chunks of your email at a time on average.

Depending on the email client used to read the email and the design of the email, the following elements will likely appear above the fold:

☐ Sender name

☐ Recipient's name or email address

☐ Date email was received

☐ Subject line (in some email clients)

☐ Preheader text, if used and if displayed at the top of the email in the rendering of the particular device or screen size

☐ Header, which includes your logo

☐ Navigation bar, if used and if displayed at the top of the email in the rendering of the particular device or screen size

☐ Preview pane banner, if used

☐ Primary content block

The key is to use your above-the-fold space wisely, avoiding placing low-value content there. Just because the top portion of your email is the most read, don't try to cram too much content up top. Content still needs room to breathe so it's accessible, and messaging still needs enough runway to become persuasive.

Having your logo visible above the fold is essential as it provides additional confirmation of who the sender is. However, keep the size of your logo modest to avoid pushing additional content below the fold. Most marketers position their logo on the left side of the header, so it's seen immediately as subscribers scan downward from the left side of the screen. Centered logos are less common but also an option.

Some marketers like to position their primary call-to-action above the fold, but this isn't an absolute rule by far. Depending on the complexity of the product or service or what is being asked of the subscriber, some CTAs are far more effective if they're prefaced by persuasive content that convinces them to the need to convert.

More pivotal is positioning headlines and other key text toward the top of your primary content block. While images can be powerful, sometimes leading with those pushes headlines below the fold, making your message less clear and less compelling.

Responsive design allows marketers to make more nuanced decisions about what appears above the fold in different reading environments, which is helpful because the fold can be much higher in mobile environments. Two common adaptations entail using responsive design to:

☐ Hide preheader text in mobile renderings

☐ Have a horizontal navigation bar after the header in desktop renderings and a vertical navigation bar before the footer in mobile renderings

In both cases, you will probably want to do some testing to see what your audience responds to best.■

"Higher conversion rates have nothing to do with whether the button is above the fold, and everything to do with whether the button is below the right amount of good copy."

—D Bnonn Tennant, copywriter

Email Design & Body Content

84

Design your emails so they are harmonious with— but don't necessarily mirror— your website's design.

You should use consistent branding and general style across all your channels, including email, but recognize that every channel is different.

For example, emails enjoy less design freedom than websites because of inferior and inconsistent coding support across the various email clients. Emails have less screen real estate to work with than websites because emails often share the screen with inbox navigation and sometimes ads. And subscribers often act differently than website visitors because they are more engaged with your brand and because emails aren't usually intended to deliver a complete experience without clicking through to a website.

For those reasons, don't shrink your website design and use it in your emails. Instead, design your emails so they incorporate key branding elements from your website while being optimized for the email channel. Use the same color scheme, but be flexible on the layout and design elements, such as fonts. For instance, opt for a widely supported HTML font rather than the exact font you use on your website.

Navigation bars are another area where you're better off using a derivative of what's on your website. Because emails are generally narrower than websites, you typically have room for fewer links in a horizontal navigation bar. Generally, mobile-friendly email designs have horizontal navigation bars with two to four links, while desktop-optimized designs have six to eight.

Given those limitations, include only the navigation links that will be of most interest to your email subscribers. Also, consider changing up your navigation bar links from one email to the next in order to support the primary message of each one.

A vertical navigation bar at the bottom of the email and an interactive hamburger menu at the top are alternatives that avoid space constraints. Brands often use those to replicate their full website navigation.

Of course, the combination of a few key links in a top horizontal navigation bar along with a bottom vertical navigation bar with less popular links gets you the best of both worlds.■

Email Design & Body Content

85

Provide context for products featured in your emails.

Don't assume that subscribers know what your products are for, how to use them, or the differences between similar products. Provide context for your products to help inspire subscribers to purchase.

For instance, an apparel retailer might show the same blouse used in two outfits, one dressed up and one dressed down, to show its versatility. An electronics retailer might link to an article or blog post that explains the different kinds of HDTV display technologies. A B2B software vendor might explain how their software integrates with other software or works within an overarching workflow. And a home improvement retailer might promote a video that demonstrates all the uses of a power washer.

In other words, think of ways to strengthen the appeal of your promotional content by weaving in elements of content marketing. All brands should think of themselves as publishers.■

Email Design & Body Content

86

Offer subscribers non-promotional content and calls-to-action.

Although the goal of your email program is likely to generate sales, that doesn't mean that every message has to scream, *Buy Now!*

Subscribers are not always in the market, so incessantly asking them to buy can be off-putting and cause them to tune you out or unsubscribe. Keep your subscribers engaged between purchases by including educational, instructional, editorial, social, inspirational, and other non-promotional content in your emails.

This content could include:

☐ Promotions of blog posts, articles, infographics, ebooks, podcast, videos, and other content— whether they were created by your company, a partner, or someone else

☐ Surveys and polls, which have the added benefit of giving you progressive profiling data

☐ Updates on social media activity, such has event photos shared on Instagram, most insightful tweets from a Twitter chat, etc.

☐ Information about your charity, conservation efforts, volunteer work, etc.

☐ Season's greetings and other messages of thanks

The soft sell can be surprisingly effective. Not only can it engage, inspire, and motivate subscribers to buy when they didn't consider themselves ready to buy, it can move them down the sales funnel, making them more receptive to future hard-sell messaging.■

"Best way to sell something—Don't sell anything. Earn the awareness, respect, and trust of those who might buy."

—Rand Fishkin, Founder of Moz

Email Design & Body Content

87

Use faster channels to help determine the content of your emails.

Improve the results of your email marketing campaigns by incorporating learnings from faster channels like site search, pay-per-click (PPC) search campaigns, and Twitter.

For instance, look at the terms that visitors are putting into your website's search box and use the most popular terms in your subject lines or body copy. You can also fine-tune the landing page of a PPC search campaign before using it for an email campaign or use insights from PPC search ad headlines and body copy for subject lines and preheader text. And tweets that generate high engagement should be used to inform subject lines and headline copy.

The converse is also possible. You can use the results of your email campaigns to inform slower channels. For instance, you can test product images in emails and use the winners in your upcoming catalog.■

Email Design & Body Content

88

Give your customers and other people a voice in your emails.

Consumers trust what others do and say more than they trust what companies say, so give your customers, outside experts, media outlets, bloggers, celebrities, and others a presence in your emails.

Consider promoting user-generated content—pictures, videos, testimonials, reviews, tweets, and other content provided by customers. Promote top-selling, top-rated, most-liked, most-tweeted, and most-pinned items. Poll your customers and include the results in an email.

Outside experts boost your credibility, too. Consider including advice, curated product assortments, and other content from outside experts, as well as pointing out media coverage of your products.

And don't forget your employees. The voice of your staffers can also ring more true and authentic than anonymous, disembodied corporate content.■

Email Design & Body Content

89

Keep the weight of your emails reasonable to avoid long load times and deliverability issues.

When the file size of an email message is too large, inbox providers might display only a portion of the message or block it completely. Very large emails also load more slowly for subscribers, causing some to hit the *Delete* button in frustration.

To avoid trouble, aim to keep the HTML weight of your emails to around 60 KB or less—and be very wary of exceeding 100 KB.

That HTML weight excludes the file size of web-hosted images associated with an email, which could be an additional several hundred kilobytes—or even upwards of 2 MB for graphic-heavy messages. For a quick load time, it's best to keep the loaded or total weight—email coding plus images—to less than 1 MB, especially if you have subscribers in countries with slow internet speeds.■

"Load time is a much bigger deal than image blocking nowadays."

—Kristina Huffman, Sr. Manager of Creative Services at Salesforce Marketing Cloud

Email Design & Body Content

90

Use motion selectively
in emails to engage subscribers.

Because most email content is static, movement really stands out in an email.

Animated GIFs are the most common way to add motion to an email because most email clients support them. CSS animation is also an option. It loads more quickly than animated GIFs, but is not as widely supported.

Animation can be used to:

☐ Demonstrate how a product works

☐ Show color or style variations of a product

☐ Draw attention to a call-to-action or secondary message

☐ Add some fun and whimsy to a design

Be mindful of the size and frame counts of your animated GIFs to prevent the file size from getting too large. Luckily, cinemagraphs and other small animations can be just as effective as large ones. And many very effective animated GIFs get away with containing only three to five frames.

While animated GIFs can be great at drawing attention, too many animations in a single email can make the message seem overly busy and distract the recipient. Try to avoid having more than one animation active in a viewing pane at once.

Another risk is that an animated GIF can distract subscribers from the goal of your email. Avoid this by using animated GIFs primarily in association with your main call-to-action.

If using an animated GIF for a fade in, keep in mind that attention spans are short in the inbox, so start your fade-in quickly.

Some email clients block animated GIFs and only show the first frame of the animation. You should plan for that possibility by using an image that can stand on its own as your first frame. Often, that means placing what you'd typically consider the last frame of your animation first.

You can also use HTML5 video, video GIFs, live content, and other mechanisms to add video-quality motion to your email designs. These tools are best reserved for content where you're showing complex motion. Support for these various video methods is highly inconsistent across email clients, so make sure that you incorporate fallbacks, such as animated GIFs and static images, for those email clients that don't support your selected form of video.

Video in email can be quite tricky to implement, so it's best to consult with your ESP or an email design specialist to determine the best approach for your brand.■

Email Design & Body Content

91

Don't include sound effects or auto-play videos with sound enabled by default in your emails.

People expect the internet to be a largely silent experience unless they press a *Play* button. That's even truer of their expectations around email, especially as more emails are read on mobile devices in stores and restaurants, in meetings, during presentations, and at other times when sounds might be embarrassing and otherwise unwelcome.

Avoid the temptation to use sound as a tactic to stand out from the crowd. Standing out with this tactic will likely earn you a spike in negative attention in the form of unsubscribes and spam complaints.■

Email Design & Body Content

92

Don't avoid creating long emails.

Although higher email frequencies and more consumers reading emails on smartphones are driving many marketers to send shorter emails, subscribers will engage with long emails. Beyond compelling content, marketers can use several techniques to encourage subscribers to scroll and, in doing so, expose the recipient to more of the content in your emails.

First, use a single-column rather than a two-column format to make it easier for subscribers to scroll. Including product grids generally doesn't impede scrolling, as long as the grid isn't more than two columns on mobile devices and four columns on desktops.

Second, look for opportunities to use an S-curve layout, where a content grouping with an image on the left and text on the right is followed on the next row down by a content grouping with text on the left and an image on the right, and so on. Subscribers often find this arrangement easier to read than having all images on the left and all text on the right, or vice versa.

Third, use images with strong vertical or sloping lines, as subscribers' eyes naturally follow them, especially if the image is only partially revealed. For instance, if subscribers see the top of a Christmas tree or part of a necklace chain, many will be intrigued enough to scroll to see the entire tree or necklace.

And fourth, consistently place some high-value content deep in your emails. If you stick with a consistent layout, you'll train your subscribers to look for certain types of content throughout your email. For instance, if you always place a coupon at the bottom of your email—and perhaps refer to it in your subject line, preheader, or header—subscribers will learn that they have to scroll down to find that coupon.

When you send long emails, be thoughtful about the content you place at the very bottom before the footer, as that content tends to attract more attention than the content in the middle of an email.

You can determine if your email content is scroll-worthy by looking at a heat map of where the clicks are in an email. If there are little to no clicks on the content toward the bottom of your emails, then they are too long or you need better content.∎

"Scrolling is easier than clicking."
—Joshua Porter, Co-Founder of Rocket Insights

Email Design & Body Content

93

Don't expect subscribers to scroll back to the top of your emails.

Expecting subscribers to scroll to the bottom of very long emails is reasonable; however, expecting them to scroll back to the top is not. For that reason, consider using content with a high link density at the bottom of your emails to give subscribers alternatives to the message blocks higher up.

One tactic is to include a recovery module, which is a content block that contains many links to different product categories, product sub-categories, price points, or brands, for instance. Sometimes recovery modules relate to the theme of the email, but other times they just promote sale or clearance items in various product categories.

Another tactic is to repeat your navigation bar before your footer or elsewhere in the email.■

Email Design & Body Content

94

Include links to your social media pages and your mobile app in your emails.

Email subscribers are among your best customers and you can make them even better customers if you can also engage them through social media, your blog, and your mobile app. Providing links to these channels in your emails is a constant reminder of other ways to interact with your brand and see what other customers are saying.

Most marketers include these links right before their footer in a social media bar, but some include them in their header to the right of their logo. Above the fold space is precious, so if you include these links in your header, make sure they perform well enough to earn that position.

If you include both share-with-your-network (SWYN) links and social community links in your emails, differentiating them by prefacing your SWYN links with *Share:* and your social community links with *Follow Us:* or something similar.■

Email Design & Body Content

95

**Place all important content
"before the credits" in your emails
to increase its chances of being
seen by subscribers.**

Borrowed from newspaper terminology, "above the fold" refers to the content that appears first when an email is opened. Borrowing from film terminology, "before the credits" refers to the content that appears above the email footer and other standard text and links that are in every email a brand sends.

Just like most moviegoers leave when the credits start to roll, the vast majority of subscribers stop scrolling when they see the following bottom-of-the-email content:

☐ Navigation bars, especial vertically stacked ones

☐ Social media bars and social sharing links

☐ Offer exclusions and other legalese

☐ Administrative links like unsubscribe and preference center links

☐ Your company's mailing address and other information required for compliance with CAN-SPAM and other anti-spam laws

Anything positioned after this content is likely to go unseen by subscribers.∎

Email Design & Body Content

96

Use a consistent email design, but don't be afraid to deviate from it occasionally.

Having a consistent email design is brand-building, makes you more recognizable in the inbox, and creates familiarity among your subscribers. However, it can also give the false impression that all your messages are equally important. Monotony can lull subscribers into paying less attention to you.

Significantly changing your email design on a one-off basis every once in a while can deliver a wake-up call to get your subscribers' complete attention again.

Occasions where it might make sense to deviate from your usual email design and use a breakout design instead include:

☐ A major product launch

☐ Entry into a new product category

☐ Collaboration with another brand

☐ A charity effort

☐ A big social media or mobile campaign

☐ A reengagement campaign aimed at subscribers who haven't opened or clicked in a long time

☐ A win-back campaign aimed at subscribers who haven't converted in a long time

In situations like those, consider one of these options for deviating from your usual email template in a significant or even dramatic way:

☐ Depart from your usual color palette

☐ Drop your navigation bar and similar links to draw attention to your primary message

☐ Send a plain-text email to express urgency

☐ Use a video as the main call-to-action

☐ Break the grid, where a portion of an image extends past the usual boundaries of the email

Although some consider these tactics breaking the rules, I consider it a rule to mix things up periodically to keep things interesting and create emphasis. One-off breakout designs help you accomplish that.■

Bonus Resource:

Outstanding Email Marketing Examples
of Breakout Designs

EmailMarketingRules.com/Examples

Email Design & Body Content

97

Keep a swipe file of your most successful email campaigns and components to inspire future campaigns.

A swipe file is a record of your emails, subject lines, calls-to-action, content blocks, landing pages, and other email elements that performed really well. You can return to this file for learnings and inspiration.

For instance, a swipe file helps you keep track of subject line arrangements, keywords, and offers that your subscribers responded to best. It works the same for email designs, allowing you to model new designs off previously successful ones. You can even reuse past winners, although it's best to reimagine, re-skin, or further optimize them.

Monitoring what your competitors and others do with their email programs can inspire new ideas that you can then test and make your own. You can do that by signing up for their emails yourself or by using a service that aggregates and categorizes commercial emails, making monitoring easier.■

Seasonality

"Holidays are an opportunity to market to your subscribers when they may be most receptive to offers."

—Scott Hardigree, Founder of Email Industries

Most brands don't have consistent demand for their products or services over the course of the year. Moreover, most brands have one or more events or deadlines around which they'd like to drive a spike in engagement. Therefore, most brands shouldn't have a consistent email cadence.

In addition to increasing their email frequency during their peak seasons, brands should adapt the appearance and content their emails and adjust their subscriber acquisition messaging.

Some brands live and die by their performance during their peak seasons. If that's the case for you, ensure that you're doing everything you can to have your email program support the business during these periods.■

WORDS TO KNOW

gift services footer: A secondary content block typically positioned just before the footer that pulls together links to gift guides, order-by deadlines, return policies, and other important seasonal buying information

holiday header: A temporary, holiday-themed header design supporting the seasonal messaging of your emails

seasonality: Related to an upcoming or current season, holiday, or buying occasion

secondary navigation bar: Typically positioned right below your standard navigation bar, this one provides deeper navigation into one of your standard navigation bar links, links to seasonal merchandise and content, or links that support the primary message or theme of the email

Seasonality

98

Send subscribers more email when they are predisposed to take action.

Subscribers tolerate—and even welcome—more email when it arrives at a time that's helpful to them.

For instance, retailers wisely send more promotional emails during the holiday season, knowing their subscribers are actively looking for gift ideas and buying heavily. Similarly, many charities and nonprofits send more email toward the end of the year, knowing that many people make most of their charitable donations just before the end of the calendar year for tax purposes.

Put another way: Look at your customers' natural buying patterns. The times of the year that they buy more, send more email to reinforce and strengthen that pattern. And send fewer emails when they're less active to avoid annoying them.

As you increase email frequency during peak season periods, keep a close eye on how your subscribers respond. If engagement dips and spam complaints and unsubscribes rise too much, that's a sign to back down.■

Seasonality

99

Message your subscribers differently during the holiday season.

Consumers use email differently during November and December than they do the other 10 months of the year. During the holiday season, people are extremely busy, travel more, might have to deal with bad weather, and have longer-than-usual lists of things to do. In short, they're more stressed.

They turn to promotional emails to make their lives easier by helping them find great gifts at great prices—and that's about it. Marketers can adjust their email content by simplifying, reducing, or eliminating video and social media calls-to-action, contests, advice and lifestyle content, and other content that requires too much of a time commitment from subscribers. The holiday season is the time to simplify messaging.

It's also a time to increase customer service messaging, such as clarifying return policies, promoting order-by deadlines, and highlighting store hours.■

Seasonality

100

Recognize that once-a-year gift-buying makes subscribers' interests less predictable during the holiday season.

Consumers are mostly buying for others during the holiday season, so downplay or disregard content preferences and previous browse and purchase behavior when making decisions about what content to send individual subscribers.

Instead, promote a wider selection of products and product categories and direct subscribers to a gift guide that helps them find gifts by interest, gender, age, price, or other variables. Also, consider promoting fewer product category sales in favor of more sitewide sales.

Similarly, be wary of using the behavior of subscribers in December to send them targeted messages in January.■

Seasonality

101

Signal the arrival of the holiday season and other seasonal events by altering your email designs.

Stores hang garlands, decorate Christmas trees, and put up lots of red and green signage to indicate the arrival of the holiday season. Email designs should similarly signal to subscribers that it's time to start thinking about gift buying.

You can accomplish this in a few different ways. First, add seasonal imagery to your email designs, particularly to your header, because it appears above the fold.

Second, add a link to your navigation bar that directs subscribers to seasonal merchandise or your gift guide. You might also consider adding a holiday-themed secondary navigation bar dedicated entirely to promoting your seasonal merchandise and content.

And third, add a gift services footer, which pulls together links to gift guides, order-by deadlines, return policies, and other important seasonal buying information into a single content block.∎

Seasonality

102

Make your opt-in forms, welcome emails, and other email marketing components seasonally relevant.

In addition to changing your email design and content in response to seasonality, you should adjust other aspects of your email program, too, including your opt-in forms, welcome emails, transactional emails, preference center, and unsubscribe page.

For instance, the email signup call-to-action on your homepage could be changed in November to read, *Don't miss our exclusive Black Friday and Cyber Monday email deals*. That makes for a much more compelling call-to-action because the value statement is much more pointed and urgent with those two key shopping days approaching.

Similarly, you could also add a Valentine's Day gift services footer to your order confirmation and shipping confirmation emails in January and early February. This will spur additional purchases from customers who were buying things for themselves.■

Targeting & Automation

"We are quickly moving from mass media to personalized media, which means audience segments are refined and refined until they reach one. It's what I'm calling Marketing's Law of One."

—Scott McCorkle, former CEO of Salesforce Marketing Cloud

The effectiveness of "one size fits all" broadcast emails is steadily declining. Consumers expect more. They expect marketers to listen to them—both to what they say and how they act—and respond with messages that are tailored to their individual interests.

This takes more effort than broadcast emails, but your subscribers will handsomely reward your efforts. Whether through personalization, segmentation, or automation, targeted emails often generate multifold better results than broadcast emails. (See Fig. 19 on next page.) They also have the added benefit of lower unsubscribe and spam complaint rates.

While marketing automation is valuable across all industries for addressing key moments in a customer's lifecycle, it is the No. 1 tactic among B2B brands for lead generation and lead nurturing.■

WORDS TO KNOW

automated or triggered email: A message sent to an individual subscriber in response to an action taken by that person (e.g., cart abandoned), to a lack of action (e.g., reengagement), to the arrival of an event (e.g., birthday), or to the requirements or instructions of an internet-of-things (IoT) device (e.g., battery low)

back-in-stock notification email: A message sent to an individual subscriber when a product comes back into stock in response to that person either browsing that product

Degrees of Message Targeting

Redefining the "The Right Message to the Right Person at the Right Time" Paradigm

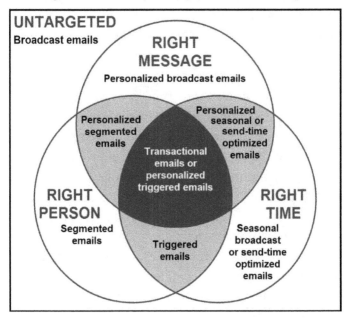

FIGURE 19

when it was out of stock or opting in to be notified when that out-of-stock product becomes available again

broadcast email: An email sent to all subscribers

browse abandonment or browse retargeting email: A message sent to an individual subscriber in response to that person browsing certain pages of your website but not making a purchase

checkout abandonment email: A message sent to an individual subscriber in response to that person starting, but not completing, the checkout process

dynamic content: A portion of an email that contains different content for different groups of subscribers or individuals based on their geography, demographics, behavior, or other factors

email automation: Triggered emails, personalization, dynamic content, and other tools that send emails or add content to emails on a one-to-one or one-to-some basis without manual intervention according to rules established by a brand

email fatigue: When a subscriber opens a brand's emails less frequently because previous emails disappointed them

expressed preferences: The topics, activities, and other things that subscribers tell you they are interested in

implied preferences: The topics, activities, and other things that subscribers indicate they are interested in based on their interactions with your brand

opt up: When a subscriber chooses to receive a brand's emails more frequently, either by receiving current communications more often or opting in to receive additional communications

personalization: Including information that's unique or particular to the recipient in the subject line or body copy of an email

reengagement or reactivation email: A message sent to an individual subscriber in response to that person having not engaged with your emails in a long time in an effort to get them to engage again

replenishment, short-supply, or re-order email: A message sent to an individual subscriber in response to a product that person purchased being near or at its recommended or typical lifespan, maximum number of usages or servings, etc.

segmentation: Sending a particular message to only those subscribers who are likely to respond favorably based on geographic, demographic, psychographic, or behavioral factors; using a suppression list to avoid sending a particular message to certain subscribers; or sending a message at a time based on their time zone or geographic region

shopping cart abandonment email: A message sent to an individual subscriber in response to that person leaving one or more unpurchased items in their shopping cart

suppression list: A list of subscribers to whom you don't want a particular message to be sent

targeting: Achieving at least one facet of sending the right message to the right subscriber at the right time

win-back or lapsed-customer email: A message sent to an individual subscriber in response to that person having not made a purchase in a long time in an effort to get them to make a purchase again

Targeting & Automation

103

Recognize that what subscribers do is more important than what they say.

Expressed preferences—what subscribers tell you they are interested in during signup, through progressive profiling, and at other times—can become outdated rather quickly. People are not always the best judges of their own interests and sometimes their circumstances, intentions, and plans change suddenly.

Expressed preferences are a good starting point. However, as time passes, they are trumped by implied preferences, which subscribers communicate through their behavior. For example, if a subscriber says they are interested in hockey but begins buying baseball gear, then start mixing some baseball promotions into their emails.

A major caveat to this (as already discussed) is subscribers' behavior during the holiday season, which can be less predictable due to gift buying.∎

"The most important thing in communication is hearing what isn't said."

—Peter Drucker

Targeting & Automation

104

Send subscribers some segmented messages based on their expressed and implied preferences.

In addition to sending broadcast messages about broad topics to all your active subscribers, use your subscribers' expressed and implied preferences to regularly send messages about a narrow topic only to those subscribers who are likely to respond. This reduces email fatigue and boosts engagement.

For instance, if you're opening a new store, segment your list by zip code and send a store-opening announcement to only your subscribers that live nearby. Segmenting by geography can also ensure that, for instance, all subscribers receive a promotion of winter gear at a time when their local temperatures start to cool.

In addition to geography and demographics, segment by subscriber interest. For example, if you're promoting rock climbing gear, send the message to only those subscribers who have purchased or browsed that product category recently.■

"There's no magic number for how many segments to target—but the 'unmagic' number is 1."

—Experian

Targeting & Automation

105

Use dynamic content and personalization to add tailored content to emails.

Dynamic content and personalization can make even broadcast emails feel like one-to-one communications. These tools allow you to inject individual data and tailored content into emails, making them more personally relevant to recipients.

A decade ago, personalization was largely synonymous with addressing an email recipient by name. Now, first-name personalization has become so overused that, used on its own, it's as likely to hurt your email's performance as help it.

Today, marketers have moved beyond such superficial gestures and dramatically broadened their personalization efforts, especially with the advent of Big Data. Customers know that you're tracking their interactions with your brand—and they expect you to use that tracking to help serve them better.

Consider personalizing your subscribers' emails based on the following information:

- ☐ **Who they are**, including their name, where they work, what their birthday is, their age, and other personal data points

- ☐ **Who they care about**, including information about their family members, friends, and work associates

- ☐ **What they did**, including browsing, purchases, physical activity, electricity usage, media consumption, and other behaviors

- ☐ **What they did not do**, including not completing their profile, not selecting options, and other actions not taken

- ☐ **What others did in reaction**, including social media influence, the impact of the subscriber's reviews, and other actions taken

- ☐ **What they have**, including account and reward point balances, accessories for a purchased product, care or service instructions for a purchased product, and similar information

- ☐ **Where they are**, including their city, town, or neighborhood of residence, local store information, local weather forecasts, geolocation-based messaging, and other location-based data

In all of these instances, it's now about demonstrating that you know a subscriber on a deeper level and can translate that knowledge into tailored content and deals.

An extra benefit of effective personalization is that it also gives email recipients confidence that the email they're reading is actually from you, and not from a phisher, who wouldn't have the knowledge you have.∎

Targeting & Automation

106

When personalizing content, have a good default set up for when you don't have data for a particular subscriber.

If you're personalizing an email, you can end up with some pretty embarrassing results when you try to pull a data point and encounter a null set. Protect yourself from blank spaces, showing code, and other issues by establishing a default value for an attribute.

For example, if you're using first-name personalization in a subject line, set a default value of *Valued Customer* or something less corporate, such as *Deal-Seeker*, to avoid an awkward *Dear <$First_Name$>* or *Dear ,* in case you don't have a subscriber's name on record.

Additionally, depending on the size of the personalized content block, the default could be a call-to-action to supply the missing data point. For instance, your emails could highlight *Special Deals at Your Local Store*. Subscribers who have indicated a favorite store would see the deals, while those that haven't would see a call-to-action to *Tell us your favorite store to see these deals.* ∎

Targeting & Automation

107

Avoid misleading uses of personalization that suggest an email's content is deeply personalized when it is not.

Expectations are powerful. If you include a subscriber's name in a subject line, many subscribers will expect the content in the email to be tailored to them. If it isn't, some recipients will be disappointed.

For that reason, reserve first-name personalization in subject lines for segmented emails, emails that contain dynamic content or personal information, or emails sent directly in response to an action taken by a subscriber.

Similarly, in the body of an email, if you use language similar to *Recommendations for You* or *Just for You* and the content is generic, then you've trained your subscribers to pay less attention the next time you use that language.■

"The companies that succeed in this new Internet of Me era will become the next generation of household names."

—Accenture

Targeting & Automation

108

Optimize the delivery time of your emails to increase their effectiveness.

Although inbox providers and third-party tool providers continue to roll out features that threaten the "last in, on top" inbox paradigm, there's still an advantage to timing the arrival of your email so that it's at the top of the recipient's inbox or promotional email folder.

For B2C brands, the beginning of the work day (around 8 am local time), toward the end of the workday (around 4pm), and after dinner when the kids are in bed (around 8 pm) are times when engaging subscribers is generally easiest. For B2B brands, mornings tend to be better. Consider segmenting your list by time zone to target these periods more precisely.

However, as more and more emails are read on smartphones, these peak engagement periods are flattening out. Consider testing different send tactics for your mobile readers and desktop readers, or even tailoring send times to the behavior of individual subscribers.

Keep in mind that the call-to-action of your email may also affect the ideal send time. For instance, you might find that social CTAs more interest in the morning and promotional CTAs generate more interest in the evening.

In addition to time of day, you might also see a benefit in optimizing the day of the week to send your emails. Targeting different days of the month, especially those around common paydays like the 15th and last day of the month, can also be fruitful.

However, in all of these cases, balance subscriber behavior and preferences with your business operations and concerns. For instance, the timing of a promotion or event or the hours of your stores will drive the timing of the email promoting it. Also, call center hours and staffing should also be considered.

Send time optimization isn't just about maximizing opens and conversions. It's also about maximizing the chances that subscribers will have a great customer or user experience.■

Targeting & Automation

109

Create a customer journey map and use triggered emails to address the moments that matter.

Triggered emails tend to perform the best of any type of email, regularly generating multifold more revenue per email than broadcast emails. (See Fig. 20 on next page.) They are super-effective because they are delivered at a time when subscribers are most receptive to their content.

The key is to identify moments that matter— the events that have a high impact on customer satisfaction, engagement, and purchase intent— and then use those events to trigger messaging that maximizes the positive impact.

However, to do that you need to understand how your customer generally interact with your brand via your primary channels. In many ways it boils down to a few questions:

☐ What actions do they take on their path to converting?

☐ What information can you give them to smooth that path?

☐ What would increase their satisfaction with their purchase?

Broadcast Emails vs. Triggered Emails

Broadcast Emails	Triggered Emails
Are **company**-centric in their timing and messaging	Are **subscriber**-centric in their timing and messaging
Raise awareness and spark intent	**Capitalize on intent and serve customer needs**
Create **common** experience	Create **personal** experience
Are often part of a **short-term tactic**	Are part of a **long-term strategy**
Typically represent **80% or more** of the email volume a brand sends	Typically represent **5% or less** of the email volume a brand sends
Produce **modest** returns on investment	Produce **very high** returns on investment
Are responsible for most of a brand's **email fatigue and disengagement**	Are responsible for most of a brand's **most engaging subscriber moments**
Generate **most** of a brand's unsubscribes	Generate **almost none** of a brand's unsubscribes
Generate **most** of a brand's spam complaints	Generate **almost none** of a brand's spam complaints
Spark moral outrage on social media and via word of mouth when deemed **too frequent**	Spark moral outrage on social media and via word of mouth when deemed **creepy and stalkerish**
Are the subject of **considerable** testing (although still inadequate)	Are the subject of **little** testing, falling victim to "set it and forget it" thinking
Are **maintenance-free**	Need **regular maintenance and optimization**
Occupy **much (too much?)** of an email marketing team's time	Occupy **little (too little?)** of an email marketing team's time

FIGURE 20

☐ What causes them to buy again or remain loyal?

☐ What could you do to recognize them as an individual and show your appreciation?

Once you've answered these questions, determine what kinds of triggers best accomplish your goals. Triggered emails come in four varieties:

1. ***Action-triggered emails***, which are triggered emails sent in response to a subscriber taking a particular action

2. ***Inaction-triggered emails***, which are triggered emails sent in response to a subscriber not having taken a particular action in a certain amount of time

3. ***Date-triggered emails***, which are triggered emails sent in response to the arrival of a particular date

4. ***Machine-triggered emails***, which are triggered emails sent in response to the requirements or instructions of an internet-of-things (IoT) device

Common triggers and the resulting automated messages include:

ACTION-TRIGGERED EMAILS
☐ **Registering at a website**

   o Registration confirmation email

☐ **Signing up to receive email, joined loyalty program**

   o Subscription confirmation request email

   o Welcome email

☐ **Making a purchase**

- o Order confirmation email
- o Activation or installation instructions email
- o Product care instructions email
- o Upsell and cross-sell emails
- o Short-supply, re-order, and replenishment emails
- o Product review request email
- o Service satisfaction survey email
- o Purchase reward email
- o Purchase reward expiration warning email
- o Other post-purchase emails

☐ **Order fulfilled, shipped, delivered, etc. (related to delivery status of order)**

- o Purchase ready for in-store pickup email
- o Shipping confirmation email
- o Delivery confirmation email

☐ **Approaching or exceeding threshold**

- o Unlocking next level of loyalty program email
- o Goal met or achievement unlocked email
- o Almost out of stored value, credits, minutes, bandwidth, etc. or balance is zero email

☐ **Abandoning an item in a shopping cart**

- o Shopping cart abandonment email

☐ **Abandoning a checkout process**

- o Checkout abandonment email

☐ **Browsing product page without buying**

- o Browse abandonment email

- ○ Price-change notification email
- ○ Back-in-stock notification email (if that product was out-of-stock when browsed)

☐ **Downloading report, etc.**

- ○ Delivery of downloadable or thank you email

☐ **Creating a gift or wedding registry**

- ○ Registry welcome email

☐ **Registering for an event**

- ○ Registration confirmation email

☐ **Making/canceling an appointment**

- ○ Appointment/cancellation confirmation email

☐ **Crossing a geofence or approaching beacon**

- ○ Welcome to venue, conference, store, etc.

☐ **Signing a petition, taking a survey, etc.**

- ○ Thank you email
- ○ Donation request email

☐ **Entering a contest or sweepstakes**

- ○ Entry confirmation email

INACTION-TRIGGERED EMAILS

☐ **Not having made a purchase in a while**

- ○ Win-back email

☐ **Not having engaged with promotional emails in a while (or very long while)**

- ○ Reengagement or reactivation email
- ○ Re-permission email

☐ **Not having engaged with website or app**

or logged into web service in a while

- o Website, app, or service reengagement email

DATE-TRIGGERED EMAILS

☐ **Providing birth date of subscriber, spouse, children, pets, etc.; or date of wedding anniversary**

- o Birthday email

- o Wedding anniversary email

- o Email reminder about or discount for unpurchased items on wedding registry after the wedding date

☐ **Making a purchase**

- o Purchase anniversary email

- o Term of service or license expiring email

☐ **Date of event or appointment**

- o Appointment confirmation request email

- o Appointment reminder email

- o Appointment missed notification and reschedule appointment request email

- o Event or session feedback request email

- o Other post-event or -appointment messaging

☐ **An item is back in stock and subscriber requested to be notified**

- o Back-in-stock notification email

☐ **Signing up to receive email, join loyalty program**

- o Signup or membership anniversary email

MACHINE-TRIGGERED EMAILS

☐ **Wearable or other device's battery is low**

- o Low battery warning notification email

☐ **Printer or other device is low on ink or another consumable**

- o Refill needed notification email

☐ **Motion detector, door sensor, smoke detector, or other safety device is activated**

- o Safety alert notification email

☐ **Fault detected or service threshold reached**

- o Service needed notification email

And you can surely think up many other instances where a triggered email would help, educate, or reward your subscribers.

Although some triggered emails perform best when sent immediately, some perform better when sent after a delay. Some triggered messages are more effective as a series of emails rather than a single email. And personalization can greatly improve the effectiveness of some triggered emails.

Experiment to determine which elements, configurations, and timings work best for you.■

Bonus Resource:

Outstanding Email Marketing Examples
of Lifecycle Messaging

EmailMarketingRules.com/Examples

Targeting & Automation

110

When using behavior triggers, be careful not to cannibalize natural behaviors.

Subscriber behavior is wonderful for powering targeted messages, but be mindful of not interrupting natural browsing, shopping, and purchase behaviors.

For instance, abandoning shopping carts is a natural part of the shopping process for many consumers. Not every cart abandoner needs a cart abandonment email. Look at your organic return to purchase time, which is when the majority of customers return to their cart and check out on their own, and then set your cart abandonment email to launch shortly after that point. This way, you avoid sending emails to people who would have likely taken action without your email.

Also, consider setting a minimum shopping cart value to avoid triggering an email when there's very little revenue at stake. In that same vein, if a lot of revenue is at stake, consider sending more than one email.

Similarly, trigger your win-back emails to send just after your average purchase latency, which is your customers' natural time between purchases.■

Targeting & Automation

111

Be careful not to come across like Big Brother when using behavior triggers and personalization.

Some consumers are turned off by the idea that brands track their email and online activities. Be sensitive to these feelings by:

☐ Determining the optimal time to send each triggered email, recognizing that might not be immediately in some cases

☐ Crafting messaging that sometimes doesn't make it clear their action triggered the email

For instance, browse abandonment emails for high-consideration products could probably go out the next day. And that email could contain a buying guide or other helpful content without saying outright, *We noticed you looking at...* Although most people will connect the dots, make it seem plausible that the right content arriving at the right time is just a happy coincidence.

Of course, order confirmation emails should be sent immediately and have very direct messaging.■

"Creepy data is data the consumer doesn't know you have or you're not supposed to have."

—Ryan Phelan, Vice President of Marketing Insight at Adestra

Targeting & Automation

112

Avoid offering special incentives in messages triggered by a non-purchase.

Subscribers catch on very quickly. If you reward bad behavior, you'll only train recipients to behave badly.

For instance, if you send an incentive when a shopper leaves an item in their shopping cart, they will abandon their carts every time and wait for the email incentive to arrive before purchasing. You will have trained your subscribers to delay their purchases and will have given margin away needlessly.

It's now common behavior for many consumers to place items in their cart for consideration later—kind of like a wish list. Rather than offering an incentive, just email a reminder of the item(s) in their cart.

You can add urgency to these messages by mentioning sellout risks or highlighting the impending end of an existing sale. Depending on the product, you can also highlight reviews, educational material about the product category, or other informational content that might help the subscriber decide whether to purchase the product. These tactics are often enough to spur many subscribers to complete their purchase.

A subscriber abandoning the checkout process

mid-way through is certainly much more unusual behavior. It's also more directly addressable with an email that clarifies shipping, financing, and other available options. However, incentives in checkout abandonment emails encourage the same negative behaviors that incentives in cart abandonment emails do.

If you feel that you must include incentives in these emails, consider providing the incentive only to first-time abandoners and not serial abandoners.

However, it's best to save your triggered email incentives for when you really want to drive action, such as when you want a new subscriber to make their first purchase or win back a subscriber who hasn't made a purchase in a long time.■

Targeting & Automation

113

Maintain a minimum return on touch.

Most marketers would never dream of sending an email that asked subscribers to spend a dollar or less. They instinctively know that wouldn't generate a sufficient return—neither for the effort it took the marketer to create the email nor for the time asked of the subscriber to read and consider the email.

Yet, if we don't set the proper parameters, our marketing automation will happily send emails on our behalf with an insufficiently low return on touch.

For instance, if a subscriber abandons a shopping cart with a few dollars' worth of merchandise in it, will a cart abandonment email be triggered? Will a series of cart abandonment emails be triggered? If a subscriber buys a similarly low-value item, will a product review request email be triggered?

For both individual triggered emails and, especially, triggered email series, ask yourself if the resulting email touch is worthwhile in relation to the potential for email fatigue, unsubscribes, and spam complaints.■

Targeting & Automation

114

Place a cap on triggered email volume and establish a messaging hierarchy.

Triggered messages are one of the best ways to deliver more email to your most engaged subscribers. However, even the timeliest and most relevant emails can become excessive if too many messages arrive too often.

To keep this from happening, consider setting up the following controls:

Set conditions. Sometimes a simple behavior trigger is too blunt and it needs an additional level of detail. For example, if a customer browsed a product page for only a few seconds and then abandoned the page, they may not be a great candidate to get a browse abandonment email. In contrast, a person whose time on page was over a minute will have demonstrated much more intent and be a much better candidate to receive that email.

Similarly, make your triggered emails responsive to the circumstances of individual subscribers. For example, if a subscriber signed up for your emails via your Facebook page, then don't send the email in your welcome series about your Facebook presence.

Set a cap. Place a cap on how many triggered emails a subscriber can receive over the course of a day or week, and limit how frequently a subscriber can receive the same triggered email.

For instance, if a subscriber browsed one product category and then another an hour later, you probably shouldn't send them a browse abandonment email for each product category. You should pick one.

Establish a hierarchy. In addition to caps, establish a message hierarchy to give priority to the most effective triggered emails. For instance, if a subscriber left an item in their shopping cart after browsing several items, you'd probably want to send a shopping cart abandonment email instead of a browse abandonment email.

Similarly, you might want to delay a product review request email if it was scheduled to go out on the same day as a birthday email to avoid having the two messages compete with each other.

Moderate repetition. Additionally, you shouldn't send the same browse abandonment email again if the subscriber returns and browses the same product category the next day or perhaps even a few days later—although you'll probably want to do some testing to find out what the best minimum interval is between browse abandonment emails.

Putting this kind of logic in place makes your automated emails that much smarter.■

Targeting & Automation

115

Use segmentation, triggered emails, and other tactics to send your most engaged subscribers more email.

A small percentage of your subscribers drive the majority of your email marketing revenue. Increase the opportunity presented by these high-value subscribers by sending them additional targeted messages by:

☐ Using segmentation and suppression lists

☐ Setting up triggered emails that respond as they engage

☐ Presenting them with opportunities to opt up into additional mailstreams.

Those additional mailstreams could be for a loyalty program, offers from sister brands, or emails on other topics selected by the subscriber. When seeking these additional opt-ins, make the signup process as simple as possible and explain what's in it for the subscriber.■

Inactivity Management

"That email you're going to send next week? If you didn't send it, how many people would complain and wonder where it is? Because if they're not complaining when you don't show up, then you don't really have permission."

—Seth Godin, author of *Permission Marketing* and many other books

Sometimes subscribers aren't interested in your emails anymore but don't unsubscribe for some reason. Subscribers who haven't engaged with your emails in a long time represent a shrinking revenue opportunity and growing risk to your deliverability. They also dampen your performance metrics, making it more difficult to see trends and positive changes.

It's worth trying to get these subscribers engaged with your emails again, but realistically you'll end up letting most of them go. It's a small price to pay to say in the good graces of inbox providers.∎

WORDS TO KNOW

click-to-open rate: Percentage of subscribers who opened an email that also clicked the content inside, which is calculated by dividing clicks by opens

inactivity: A lack of action from a subscriber or customer over a period of time

post-click metrics: Browsing, carting, and other activities on your site that take place after someone clicks through one of your emails

reengage or reactivate: Getting a subscriber to open or click one of your emails after a long period of having not done so

total clicks: The number of times the links or linked images in an email were selected by subscribers, who then visited the associated landing page; a method of measuring clicks that includes repeat clicks by an individual subscriber

total opens: The number of times the images of an email were loaded or rendered; a method of measuring opens that includes repeat opens by an individual subscriber

unique clicks: The number of subscribers who selected a link or linked image in an email at least once and visited the associated landing page; a method of measuring clicks that only counts the first click made by individual subscribers, ignoring any subsequent clicks

unique opens: The number of subscribers who loaded or rendered the images of an email at least once; a method of measuring opens that only counts the first open made by individual subscribers, ignoring any subsequent opens

Inactivity Management

116

Recognize that inactive subscribers and inactive customers are different and require different remedies.

Managing inactivity typically requires a two-pronged strategy. That's because brands need to manage two kinds of inactivity via email:

☐ **Inactive subscribers**, email recipients who haven't opened or clicked any of your emails in a while, to maintain engagement and deliverability

☐ **Inactive customers**, subscribers who haven't converted in a while, to maintain sales and profitability

Each of those kinds of inactivity is unique, with different causes, risks, and remedies. (See Fig. 21 on next page.)

Address inactive subscribers by sending reengagement campaigns, with the goal of getting them to open or click. These campaigns tend toward non-promotional messaging such as:

☐ Asking the subscriber to update their preferences or take a poll, survey, or quiz

☐ Highlighting the social media activity of the brand or, better yet, its customers

☐ Promoting educational, instructive, or entertaining content, including events and webinars

Inactive Customer vs. Inactive Subscriber

Defined by...	
Lack of purchases	Lack of email opens and clicks
Risk of...	
Lost sales and lost customer	Poor deliverability and lost subscriber
Reduce risk by triggering...	
Win-back campaign	Reengagement and re-permission campaigns
Goal of that email is to get subscriber to...	
Purchase	Open or click email

FIGURE 21

If your reengagement efforts fail, then send a re-permission campaign, asking those subscribers to indicate if they're still interested in your emails.

Address inactive customers via email by sending win-back campaigns, with the goal of getting them to convert. These highly promotional campaigns almost always offer a brand's richest discounts.

We miss you is a common subject line phrase for both reengagement and win-back emails, which is perhaps an indication of the confusion between these two emails. For instance, it's not uncommon for brands to try to remedy inactive customers with reengagement campaigns and inactive subscribers with win-back campaigns.

However, sending reengagement campaigns to active subscribers who are inactive customers just gets you more engagement rather than the purchase that you want. And while a win-back can definitely reengage an inactive subscriber who's an active customer, you're likely unnecessarily giving away margin with a big discount and not necessarily addressing the relevancy issues causing the disinterest in the first place.

The worse misuse is sending win-back campaigns as a "purchase or else" re-permission campaign. This often means the loss of an engaged subscriber.

Why keep a subscriber who's engaged but not buying? There are a number of reasons:

- ☐ Every engaged subscriber helps your overall email engagement, which inbox providers factor in when deciding whether to deliver your emails to their users

- ☐ That subscriber may be converting indirectly through another email address or user account, such as that of a coworker or spouse

- ☐ That subscriber may be influencing others through word of mouth, a blog, social media, etc.

If you use the right inactivity remedies correctly, you'll reduce the number of inactive subscribers on your list—especially those who are also inactive customers—and you'll increase the number of engaged subscribers who are active customers.■

Inactivity Management

117

When defining inactive subscribers, take both their email and customer behaviors into consideration.

Email marketers sit uncomfortably between business owners and inbox providers, each of which has different agendas. On the one hand, business owners want to drive engagement, revenue, and profits among their customers. On the other, inbox providers want to protect their users from spam and other unwanted email. (See Fig. 22 on next page.)

For this reason, when defining what an inactive subscriber is, email marketers need to take both a brand's customer metrics and the inbox providers' email user metrics into account.

That said, always start with email user metrics. That's because inbox providers don't care if one of their users is one of your best customers. They only care if that user is engaging with your emails by opening them, scrolling through them, clicking in them, forwarding them, and taking other positive actions—many of which are only visible to inbox providers.

Email Marketers Have 2 Masters, 2 Sets of Success Metrics

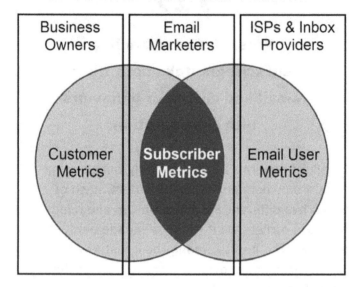

FIGURE 22

If your subscriber hasn't done any of those in a long while, inbox providers may start to junk or block your emails to that user. And if they see that too many of their users haven't engaged with your emails in a long time, they will begin junking or blocking all of your emails.

Needless to say, having one or more inbox providers block all of your emails is disastrous for an email program. This is why brands eventually need to stop mailing subscribers who don't show any activity by opening or clicking any of their emails.

Customer-Subscriber Activity Matrix

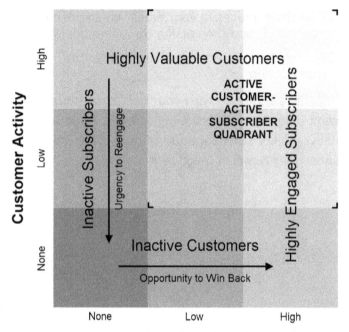

FIGURE 23

However, how quickly you try to reengage and ultimately re-permission inactive subscribers depends on their level of customer activity. (See Fig. 23 above.) You should swiftly address inactive subscribers who are also inactive customers.

But you should be more lenient toward inactive subscribers who are active customers, especially if they're high-value customers. That's because the subscriber may be:

- ☐ Engaging with envelope content, and then acting through other channels

- ☐ Blocking images in your emails so an open isn't recorded, and then acting through other channels

- ☐ Using another email address or identifier when converting

That said, even with your best customers, you can't delay re-permissioning forever, as your deliverability risks continue to mount the longer a subscriber remains inactive.■

Inactivity Management

118

Send your inactive subscribers different messaging at a lower frequency.

Once a subscriber has been inactive for many, many months, the chance of them becoming active again is small but definitely worth pursuing.

To try to reengage inactive subscribers, send them different emails than you send the rest of your list. The easiest way to do this is to take them off your active email list and put them on a reengagement list. This reengagement segment should receive any combination of:

☐ Your best, most compelling broadcast emails, such as your Black Friday or Cyber Monday campaign, if you're a retailer

☐ Win-back emails, which tout your richest offers with the goal of getting the subscriber to open, click, and convert again

☐ Preference update emails, which aim to get the subscriber to change the topic, frequency, and other options available to them in your preference center, if you have one

☐ Progressive profiling emails, which are polls, quizzes, surveys, or guided selling pathways that seek short-term information about a subscriber's needs or their interests

Those first two tactics address the chance that your offers just haven't been good enough to drive action. While the aim of the offer is to generate a conversion, for the purpose of reengagement, all you're looking for is the subscriber to open or click the email.

Those last two tactics acknowledge that it may not be the strength of the offers that's inadequate but that the offers or content are just wrong. Preference updates and survey results should give you information you can use to send them targeted email. Gaining additional insights for targeting is key because, otherwise, they're likely to go inactive again.

Whichever approach or combination of approaches you use, inactive subscribers should receive significantly fewer emails than your active subscribers. This is necessary because inbox providers use engagement metrics in their filtering algorithms, so having lots of inactive subscribers poses a risk to your deliverability.

You can reduce that risk by emailing inactives considerably less frequently. For instance, if you send daily emails, reduce that to weekly for inactives. Or if you send weekly emails, reduce that to once per month.

Doing so can have a dramatic effect on how engaged your subscribers look in the eyes of inbox providers. Generally, if a third to half of your list is inactive, reducing your mailings to inactive subscribers by 75% can increase the engagement

Increasing Engagement by Mailing Inactives Less Often

For an email list that's 50% active subscribers and 50% inactive subscribers

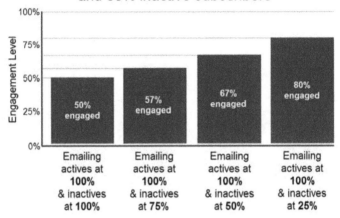

FIGURE 24

level profile of your sends by 30% to 60%. (See Fig. 24 above.)

In addition to protecting your deliverability, less frequent mailings to inactives can cause some of them to actually pay more attention to your emails and reengage.

In that same vein, sometimes withholding emails from inactives for a period of weeks can be effective, because some of them will notice the absence of your emails and then respond when you start sending again.

If you have the data and capabilities, you might also consider reaching out to inactive subscribers via other channels, such as direct mail, SMS, and targeted display ads online, in order to reactivate them. This approach might be particularly warranted for reaching customers who were high-value subscribers before becoming inactive.■

> *"If someone acts on your reengagement campaign, that's a great time to send a great offer because they're really paying attention."*
> —Holly Wright, Director of Digital Marketing at Appfire

Inactivity Management

119

Send a series of re-permission emails before you remove a chronically inactive subscriber from your email list.

If your reactivation efforts fail, then it's time to work toward removing a chronically inactive subscriber. However, don't just remove a subscriber from your list without warning.

Send a series of re-permission emails asking the subscriber to indicate either *Yes, I'd like to continue receiving special offers* or *No, please unsubscribe me*—or language along those lines.

Send up to three re-permission emails. Use different subject lines and send them on different days and at different times of the day to increase the response rate.

A *Yes* click in any of these emails puts the subscriber back on your active email list, as this action reconfirms their permission. Selecting *No* should take them to your preference center or opt-out page. And if the subscriber doesn't respond to any of the re-permission emails, then you should unsubscribe them.

Response rates for re-permission emails tend to

be very low, but they are worth the effort. Setting up an automated program to send these triggered emails takes relatively little work after you've set up a program to recognize chronically inactive subscribers.

Additionally, subscribers lost due to inactivity may react positively to your courteous efforts if they discover the re-permission emails later.■

Landing Pages

> *"When you neglect the landing page,*
> *the money you spend on acquisition and retention*
> *is largely wasted, flushed down the proverbial toilet."*
>
> —Tim Ash, Maura Ginty, and Rich Page,
> coauthors of *Landing Page Optimization*

The landing page is the final stage of email interaction. Until subscribers are able to perform a wide range of transactions entirely within an email, landing pages will be vital to finishing the conversation started by an email—and completing a conversion.∎

WORDS TO KNOW

landing page: Webpage, app, and any other digital destination that subscribers are directed to when they click a call-to-action in an email

Landing Pages

120

Choose the landing page that's going to provide the best subscriber experience while accomplishing your business goals efficiently.

The fledgling trends of email interactivity and native inbox functionality are very slowly allowing subscribers to complete more email calls-to-action without leaving the inbox. However, for the foreseeable future, emails will remain primarily a gateway that leads to a landing page where most of the engagement, purchase consideration, and sales conversions for an email campaign take place.

Most email marketers are responsible for designating or creating the landing pages for the calls-to-action used in the emails they create. While that's more responsibility, it's responsibility that email marketers should want because email campaigns can succeed or fail on the landing page.

For each of your calls-to-action, consider the following landing page options:

☐ Your homepage

☐ Internal page of your website, including product page, product category page, site search results page, etc.

☐ Dedicated, custom landing page on your website created just for the campaign

☐ Third-party sites, including social media sites like Facebook, Twitter, or Pinterest; ClickToTweet or another action facilitating site; partner's website, etc.

☐ Your mobile app

☐ Your store, restaurant, or other physical location

☐ Your call center

When choosing your landing pages, consider the following three concerns:

Expediency. Use landing pages that minimize the number of clicks or the amount of effort it takes for subscribers to convert. Extra effort translates into fewer conversions and higher website bounce rates. So take subscribers directly to the content they're expecting when they click through your email and make it easy to act.

For example, if they click a banner in your email promoting your clearance products, don't direct a subscriber to your homepage, even if there's a banner on your homepage promoting the clearance selection. If you want them to tweet something, provide a ClickToTweet link that at least pre-populates the designated hashtag. And if you're providing a discount that's good in a store, include a scannable barcode or some other method so it can be easily redeemed by a cashier or store rep.

Consider creating custom landing pages when there's no natural existing landing page for an email's call-to-action.

Conversion maximization. Some transactions require more handholding than others. So even if you've designed a simple landing page experience, sometimes customers will convert at a much higher rate if you provide a higher touch experience.

For example, consumers often want to speak a representative when buying life insurance, making large financial investment, and booking complex vacations. Make it easy for subscribers to reach your sales team or customer support when you promote these types of products.

Trackability. While it's sometimes possible to infer email's influence indirectly, always track the impact of your emails directly as much as possible. That's easily done when using website landing pages, but gets a little trickier when routing subscribers to offline destinations.

Barcodes in your emails can provide channel attribution, and individualized barcodes can provide attribution back to a unique subscriber. Using a unique phone number in your email campaigns can help you track which phone calls are being generated by your email campaigns, and it's even possible to dynamically insert phone numbers that are unique to individual subscribers into your emails, giving you subscriber-level tracking capabilities.

However, some campaign goals just aren't easily trackable. That said, don't let a lack of trackability cause you to add friction to or change a call-to-action if it's the right goal for your campaign.■

Landing Pages

121

Use language and images from the email on the landing page to create a smooth transition from email to landing page.

Give subscribers visual reassurances that they arrived on the right landing page after clicking through an email by using some of the same language, images, and other design elements.

Doing so creates continuity between the email and the landing page that's comforting to subscribers. Those who are unsure whether they've arrived at the right page might abandon your site or feel less certain about proceeding or converting.∎

"Maintain a consistent connection between your source ad and your landing page. Strong conversion scent ensures that visitors to your landing page get exactly what they expect to find. And that increases conversions."

—Unbounce

Landing Pages

122

Don't make subscribers hunt
for the items featured
in your emails.

If you use a product image in an email to promote a product category, position that featured product prominently on the landing page. Don't make subscribers scroll through page after page of products to find the one you featured.

If you can't reposition the product on the landing page, consider providing a separate link to the item's product page in the email—or at least include a caption in the email that includes the brand or name of the item so subscribers can search for it on your site.

Additionally, if you don't carry all the items in an image provided by the manufacturer, don't use the image. It erodes trust and frustrates subscribers when they can't find an item that you signaled you carried.■

Landing Pages

123

Design your website landing pages so they look good and function well across a wide range of platforms and devices.

Just as emails must display well on a variety of email clients and devices, website landing pages must also perform well in a variety of browsers, screen sizes, and devices.

For instance, having a mobile-friendly email design is considerably less effective if subscribers click through to a website that's not optimized for mobile. Subscribers should have a consistent, user-friendly experience when they move from an email to a landing page.

The good news is that web and mobile app rendering is much easier to master than email rendering.■

124

Design well-branded landing pages and email administration pages that offer a clear path forward after an interaction.

Imagine you're walking through a store and see signs for a product demonstration. If piques your interest, so you follow the signs to the back of the store and through a door that leads...into the back alley, where you see the product demonstration going on. It's not the best brand impression, so chances are you're not going to stick around.

This same scenario plays out in email programs when brands direct subscribers to barren pages with no branding, no navigation, and no path forward. I call it "Back Alley Syndrome."

This experience is most prevalent on pages that confirm an opt-out, a preference change, an email signup, and other administrative functions. However, it also occurs on email landing pages for videos, surveys, and other special, one-off content.

Often, these are the result of templates provided by email service providers and other vendors. In most cases, you can customize these pages to offer a better experience.

Dead-end pages such as these prematurely end brand interactions and make bad impressions. Always offer a path forward for subscribers to take once they've completed an interaction offered by an email.■

Landing Pages

125

Don't remove a landing page too quickly without providing an alternative.

Some subscribers will click through an email days or even weeks after receiving it, so removing email landing pages when a product sells out or a sale ends can generate *404 page not found* errors for subscribers. That frustrates and confuses subscribers, who might be unsure whether they've arrived at the right page or if a product is still available. It also fails to capitalize on their interest.

For product pages, if you plan on restocking the item, keep the page live. Consider offering visitors the option to sign up to receive a back-in-stock notification email when the item is available again. If the product was one-of-a-kind, consider redirecting visitors to similar items, while also notifying them that the item they originally sought is no longer available.

For sale event pages, consider redirecting visitors to a current sale page or posting a message that the sale has ended and suggesting other pages for them to visit.■

Workflows & Quality Assurance

"Every email deserves to be tested—even if you (or someone else) tested the template you're using yesterday. Email programs and apps are not only capable of breaking your design, but also butchering links, subject lines, images, and more."

—Lauren Smith, Enterprise & Partner Marketing Director at Litmus

Process predicts success. Having a solid process that takes you from pre-build ideation to post-send analytics dramatically increases your chances of producing high-performing emails.■

WORDS TO KNOW

email content calendar: A calendar indicating when you'll send or launch each of your emails, plus when you'll review or update your triggered and transactional campaigns

email marketing workflow: The people, process, and tools involved in conceiving, creating, testing, approving, sending, and analyzing the performance of an email

quality assurance: Ensuring that email content is error-free and functions properly and that the intended subscribers receive that content at the intended time

Workflows & Quality Assurance

126

Create brand guidelines specific to your email marketing program.

Every brand has guidelines that codify various design decisions to ensure that their brand has a consistent look in print, on the web, and elsewhere. Brand guidelines typically include approved logo designs, indicate which font faces can be used and in what situations, establish a color palette, and more.

However, not all of these design decisions smoothly translate to email because of limitations of the channel, such as limited HTML font support. Email also has some design considerations not present in other channels, such as the need for defensive design techniques like bulletproof buttons.

Create brand guidelines for your emails that recognize the limitations of the channel, as well as the special elements only found in email. For example, the need to use HTML text and the limited support for fonts means that you'll need to have button designs and font selections for your emails that differ slightly from your usual graphic designs.

Consider including the following elements in your email brand guidelines:

- ☐ Types of emails sent and template and styling used for each
- ☐ Content block templates
- ☐ Subject line and preview text guidelines
- ☐ Web font and HTML font families
- ☐ Call-to-action text guidelines
- ☐ Color palette
- ☐ Photographic style and image styling, formatting, etc.
- ☐ Button styling
- ☐ Defensive design elements, including *alt* text styling
- ☐ For both desktop and mobile versions:
  - ○ Header sizing, logo sizing, and logo placement
  - ○ Navigation bar content, styling, and sizing
  - ○ Font sizes for headlines, subheads, body text, and other content elements
- ☐ Footer elements
- ☐ Plain text version design elements, including spacing and dividers
- ☐ International or foreign language version considerations, including cultural sensitivities

Of course, depending on your industry or brand, you will probably have additional elements as well.■

Workflows & Quality Assurance

127

Minimize the number of email templates you use.

Creating numerous email templates invites errors and multiplies the effort it takes to maintain and optimize them. While it's tempting to create templates for every kind of email you send, limit yourself to just a few flexible, modular templates that allow you to swap different content block elements in and out as needed to make any email message you need.

Code snippets, partials, and other coding elements can also make it easy to update elements across multiple templates.

Many brands can make do with one template for their ecommerce, marketing, or newsletter email, and another template for their transactional and administrative emails. And some brands use just one master template, which further simplifies maintenance and reduces errors.∎

"Using an email template allows you to produce campaigns faster, since the underlying code is already written. Templates also keep your emails more consistent."

—Jason Rodriguez, author of *Professional Email Design* and *Modern HTML Email*

Workflows & Quality Assurance

128

Avoid email workflow processes that invite errors.

To help minimize errors, avoid problematic workflow processes.

For example, if you do work for multiple clients or have multiple brands in house, keep templates, email lists, and other email assets separate from each other. You can also use file naming conventions to help keep assets distinct from each other. If you have two clients or brands with similar names, consider making one of them all-caps in file names to better differentiate them.

Avoid overwriting previous emails or using placeholders you'll replace later. Sometimes those overwrites and replacements never happen. Moreover, copying an email sometimes also copies that email's audience targeting parameters and the plain-text portion of the email—elements that can be easily overlooked.

Copies of emails are extra difficult to proof and do quality assurance checks on because any unchanged copy and other elements appear valid.

Last-minute changes that are made after QA and approvals are also more likely to create errors.■

Workflows & Quality Assurance

129

Create an email content calendar to aid in resource allocation and content and design planning.

Many marketers start working on an email weeks or even months before the send date—especially those for peak season that involve extra design work, web or IT resources, or coordination with other teams.

An email content calendar helps you allocate time for planning and executing campaigns. It also ensures you retain an overview of your content, so you produce the right mix of content and put the appropriate focus on key selling periods. For instance, some retail brands start planning their holiday email promotions as early as July.

Having a content calendar also lets you plan for occasions when you need to have multiple content options available to respond to potential outcomes, such as promoting Super Bowl champion gear, albums of Grammy winners, or products pegged to whether the groundhog saw his shadow.

You can't plan for everything, however. Sometimes, news and other events provide great marketing opportunities. Give yourself the flexibility to participate in newsjacking and leverage current events to promote your products and engage customers.

Additionally, your email content calendar should include the review and update of triggered and transactional emails. It can take considerable time to optimize these messages for a new season with updated primary messaging and images and secondary content blocks. And that's on top of making potential changes to email signup forms and signup confirmation pages.

Having all of your email content needs listed in on one calendar can help you always see the big picture and prioritize. It will allow you to:

☐ Ensure you're getting critical tasks done

☐ Identify periods when you need to outsource tasks or call in extra help to achieve your marketing goals

☐ Recognize email content that's nice to have but not essential

If you're not already using an email content calendar, start by using one to plan out your peak seasons. Then consider expanding from there to using a year-round email content calendar.■

Workflows & Quality Assurance

130

Create an email brief for every message you send and refer to it throughout your workflow.

To maintain the focus of your emails throughout the production process, create a brief for each one at the beginning of the process that answers:

☐ **WHO should get this message?**

- All of your subscribers?

- If only a certain segment, how are you defining that segment? What's the list name?

- If subscribers only receive this email in certain circumstances, how are you defining that trigger for the email?

☐ **WHAT action do you want those subscribers to take?**

- Make a purchase? Watch a video? Register for an event? Tweet a hashtag?

- Do you have the best landing page set up to facilitate that action? Does the land page require extra setup time or special expertise?

- Are there any barriers or distractions you can eliminate to make it easier to take that action?

☐ **WHY will those subscribers be motivated to take that action?**

- What messaging, evidence, incentives, social proof, imagery, experiences, or interactivity will you use to convince them to take the desired action?

- What subject line(s) will you use?

- If the message includes personalization or dynamic content, have you set it up correctly? Do you have defaults in place?

- If your email includes new or advanced functionality, do you need extra time or outside expertise to implement it?

☐ **WHEN should those subscribers receive the message?**

- How long has it been since you last emailed those subscribers? How does this message fit into that cadence and the context of those previous emails?

- If there's an act-by deadline, are you giving those subscribers sufficient time to act?

- Should this message be segmented by time zone? Should it be segmented by average temperature or other regional characteristics?

- If it's a triggered email, how soon after the trigger should it be sent and are there any conditions under which it shouldn't be sent?

☐ **WHERE are those subscribers likely to read the message?**

- On what devices or in which email clients are they likely to read it? How should your email's design account for those environments? Will the functionality in your email be supported? Do you have fallbacks in place for when that functionality isn't supported?

- o In what physical location, circumstances, or context will your email be read? Does your email's design and copy need to factor that in?

- o Do you need to translate the message into a local or preferred language?

☐ **HOW will you measure this email's success?**

- o Opens? Clicks? Conversions? Revenue?

- o Do you have the correct tracking in place in the email and on the landing pages?

- o What messaging, image, or other element are you A/B testing in this email? Are you clear on the conditions for a conclusive and statistically significant test?

☐ **IS this email part of a series of messages or a subscriber or customer journey?**

- o Does this email fully reflect the trigger or circumstances under which the subscriber is receiving it?

- o How does this message build upon previous emails, if any, in the series or journey?

- o How does this email set up the next message, in any, in the series or journey to be successful?

☐ **DO you have any supplemental material that's important to answering the other questions?**

- o Were you inspired by an email, case study, article, or presentation that you saw? If so, attach that material to the brief.

- o Is there information that's important to understanding the goal, design, coding, etc. of this email? If so, include it in the brief.

Use this as a model to create your own list of questions that are suitable for your brand. If you can't adequately answer these questions, you should consider planning out the email better or perhaps not sending the email at all.

Once you've satisfactorily addressed each of those questions, then:

☐ Assign tasks and approval responsibilities

☐ Set deadlines for tasks and approvals, as well as limits on rounds of revisions

☐ Set a date for the review of the performance of the email and, if it's a triggered email, set a schedule for the ongoing review, update, and optimization of the email

When those are established, all the internal or external stakeholders should sign off on the brief. This confirms that everyone is on the same page about the email's goals and the responsibilities of everyone involved. If you're working with an agency, freelancers, or consultants, getting signoff on the brief is extra critical.

Make this brief easily accessible to everyone on the team, so they can use it as a single point of reference throughout the email production process.■

Workflows & Quality Assurance

131

Create a pre-send checklist to reduce the possibility of making a serious mistake.

The most common email errors involve incorrect subject lines, typos, broken personalization, misdirected links, and deployment mishaps like sending the same email twice or sending an email to the wrong segment.

To reduce mistakes, use the following checklist as a starting point for your own:

☐ Do you have the **right content** scheduled for the **right date**? Double-check sends that are based on holidays whose dates change from year to year, such as Thanksgiving and Easter. And read the content one last time to look for errors.

☐ Do you have the **right list (and suppression list) or trigger logic**? That's vital if you are segmenting the email, running an A/B test on a portion of your list, or operating multiple brands or working for multiple clients.

☐ Do you have the **right sender name**? This is particularly critical if you operate multiple brands.

☐ Do you have the **right subject line**? Avoid using placeholder text and don't leave subject line writing until the last moment.

☐ Do you have the **right rendering, functionality, and fallbacks**? Use a rendering preview tool or view a test send in all the major email client and browser combinations to make sure the message displays as intended—even when images and other functionality aren't supported.

☐ Do you have the **right personalization and defaults**? Check the logic (including substitutions strings and personalization strings and tags) and assets for your personalization and dynamic content—including what happens when you don't have data for a subscriber.

☐ Do you have the **right links and tracking**? Do all the links in the email lead to the correct landing pages, especially those for the key calls-to-action?

If content or other mistakes are routinely made, examine your production process to identify practices that invite errors and then set up additional safeguards.■

"One thing that does seem to prevent mistakes is having a system—a planned-out workflow that doesn't change."

—Pam Neely, freelance marketing content creator

Workflows & Quality Assurance

132

Preview every email you send in a wide range of email environments to ensure that they render and function as intended.

Support for HTML and CSS coding varies across email clients and browsers, and support can—and often does—change without notice. Because of that, it is important to use a rendering preview tool or manually view your emails in a wide range of email clients to check for inconsistencies.

Only testing your templates is not enough; you need to check every email you send. And if last-minute changes are made to a design, retest your email before sending it.

It's wise to pay extra attention to how your emails are rendering and functioning in the days and weeks after:

- ☐ You redesign an element of your emails, such as the header or footer sections

- ☐ You do a major email redesign or start using a new email template

- ☐ You switch email service providers

- ☐ An inbox provider or browser provider releases an update

While it can be tempting to only test the rendering and functionality of your emails when these major events happen, a lot of time can pass between these events. If you're not testing your emails on every send, small, unannounced changes to major email clients and significant changes at less popular email clients can have a lasting negative effect on a portion of your subscribers.∎

"This is email. We don't get the luxuries you web developers have. Email clients have no beta version, no docs, no release notes."

—Mark Robbins, Email Developer at Rebelmail

Workflows & Quality Assurance

133

Keep an inventory of your triggered email programs and regularly schedule time to update and fine-tune them.

Transactional and triggered emails have an unfortunate reputation as "set it and forget it" programs, which leads some brands to actually lose track of some of the most important emails that they send to customers and prospects.

Keep an eye on all of your triggered emails by keeping an inventory that includes:

☐ The name of the triggered email

☐ Where and in which email service provider or email platform the email can be found (particularly important if you use more than one ESP)

☐ The goal of the email

☐ The call-to-action and landing page of the email

☐ The intended audience of the email

☐ The trigger logic for the email

☐ Link to supplemental documentation, technical information, etc.

☐ Date the email was last updated

That last element is critical because transactional and triggered emails aren't "set it and forget it." They are "review and improve" programs. These emails need regular maintenance and optimization for the following reasons:

First, because inbox provider support for coding changes over time, checkups are necessary to ensure that triggered emails haven't developed rendering or functionality problems.

Second, your brand assets, messaging, and landing pages can become outdated. Promotions change, links become outdated, logos get redesigned, and executives and other staffers turn over, requiring that names and headshots used in emails to change.

Third, your brand strategy and messaging are constantly evolving. This provides opportunities to hone your copywriting, polish your design, and improve your targeting.

And fourth, the changing of the seasons, the approach of holidays, and the arrival of various deadlines provide opportunities to add seasonal content to triggered emails to make them more relevant. For instance, adding a content module about Christmas gifts to a shopping cart abandonment email can increase the effectiveness of those emails during the holiday season.

Because of all of those concerns, review your triggered emails quarterly. Reviews are also wise any time you change email templates, your website is significantly updated, or you change email service providers.■

Corrections & Apology Emails

"You shouldn't worry about when you will make an error. Instead, you should feel confident that you will be able to handle it when it happens to you."

—Jeanniey Mullen and David Daniels, coauthors of
Email Marketing an Hour a Day

Making mistakes in a channel that's high volume, high reach, and lightning fast is easy. In fact, it's practically inevitable. Therefore, in addition to putting checks in place to minimize the chance of making an error, prepare a disaster response plan.■

WORDS TO KNOW

apology email: Sent in response to an error, mishap, or bad press, this email apologizes, explains any action taking place in response, and tries to make amends

correction email: Sent in the wake of an email with one or more errors in it, this updated version of the email notes at the beginning of the subject line and/or body copy that the email is a "correction" or "update"

Corrections & Apology Emails

134

Don't draw undue attention to email mistakes by overreacting.

Very few email errors are serious enough to need correcting. Most are trivial and merely embarrassing, such as:

- ☐ Typos
- ☐ Image formatting and rendering issues
- ☐ One minor broken link among many
- ☐ Temporary issues such as an image server going down for a short period
- ☐ Broken personalization
- ☐ Minor deployment mistakes such as sending an email earlier than intended or sending it twice

Small errors are likely to go unnoticed or understood as errors if they are noticed. It's often better to move on.

That said, you'll need to address issues that are more serious.■

Corrections & Apology Emails

135

Take steps to reduce the impact of email marketing mistakes when they are discovered quickly.

When you discover a moderate to serious mistake in the content, links, targeting, or timing of an email that you've just sent, you can take a number of actions to limit the damage it causes.

First, stop the send if it hasn't completed. If your list is really large, a send could take hours, so you might have time to pause it, fix the error, and then resume the send. That way, you expose fewer subscribers to the error.

Second, you can fix some content errors post-send. For instance, if the mistake is in an image, correct it and then replace the hosted source file with the corrected image. If the mistake is with a link, see whether you can get the link redirected to the correct page.

Third, if the email contains incorrect, incomplete, or confusing information, use the landing page for the email to clarify the offer, timing of the event, or other details.

And finally, consider using social media and other channels to address any confusion caused by an email by emphasizing the correct information.

Along the way, check your email analytics to try to determine how large an impact the error made. Sometimes things aren't as bad as you think, which might influence how you proceed with damage control measures.■

Corrections & Apology Emails

136

Draft an apology email so you're prepared when the occasion arises.

Many brands don't send a single apology email over the course of a year. So to say that apology emails are rare is an understatement.

However, you want to be prepared in the event that misfortune befalls you so you can respond quickly—whether that misfortune is a serious email marketing error, a website outage, a PR issue, or a natural disaster. To that end, draft an apology email that you can update it with the necessary information.

As far as serious email marketing errors go, they come in a few different varieties, each of which deserves a different response.

First, for significant errors that only affect a small portion of your email subscribers, consider sending an apology email—or a resend of the original email with a message of explanation at the top—to only the affected segment.

For instance, if you send subscribers personalized discount codes and your website wasn't set up properly to accept those codes at the time of the send, then you could send an apology email to just those subscribers who tried to use their codes, telling them that the issue has been fixed and to please try again.

Second, for a serious mistake that only affects your email subscribers, an apology clears things up and mends the relationship. A good example of this kind of mistake would be a company that owns or services multiple brands accidently sending a message intended for the subscribers of one brand to the subscribers of another brand.

Permission is sacred. Accidently violating it is worth apologizing for and making it clear to subscribers that they won't receive any more messages from the brand—with the subtext being, "Please don't mark that email as spam."

And third, for particularly harmful or hurtful email mistakes—especially if a significant number of people are talking about it on social media—an apology email should be part of a full-spectrum apology that includes reaching out via social media and making statements to the media.

One last tip: If you send an apology email or resend an email, make certain that it is perfect. You don't want to follow one mistake with another.■

Corrections & Apology Emails

137

Keep a log of
email marketing errors.

Whether the error warranted an "all hands on deck" response or no response at all, be sure to take note of the mistake, cause, and your response. Keep a log that includes:

☐ Date of error

☐ Description of the error and its effect

☐ Which subscribers were affected

☐ Cause of the error

☐ Your response

You may want to note this information in your email brief and keep a separate log of mistakes that then link back to those briefs.

Why keep a log of mistakes? The pattern of errors can identify the need for changes in process and the need for more resources, whether human or technological. Hopefully you'll also see from your records that errors happen relatively infrequently in terms of errors per campaign created, making you feel a little bit better when accidents do happen.■

Unsubscribe Process

"Requiring subscribers to jump through hoops to be removed from your mailing list will either result in them clicking the Report Spam *button instead or finishing the process but leaving with a negative opinion of your company or brand."*

—Simms Jenkins, Founder & CEO of BrightWave; author of *The New Inbox* and *The Truth About Email Marketing*

Marketers tend to think of unsubscribes in very negative terms, but this negativity should be saved for spam complaints, which are an unequivocal form of failure. If a subscriber wants to leave your list, you'd much prefer they unsubscribe than resort to complaining for several reasons:

- ☐ Unsubscribes don't hurt your sender reputation, unlike spam complaints.

- ☐ If recipients unsubscribe, it indicates that they trust you to honor their opt-out, which is a positive sign from a brand perspective.

- ☐ If they click the unsubscribe link, you have an opportunity to potentially address the reason they're opting out or direct them to your other marketing channels, such as social media.

- ☐ You have a chance to honor their opt-out gracefully and have the last word, which should be one of thanks. ∎

WORDS TO KNOW

list churn: Subscribers lost to unsubscribes, spam complaints, and bounces from email addresses that no longer work

list-unsubscribe: Optional coding that marketers can add to the *<head>* of their emails to enable native unsubscribe links offered by inbox providers

opt down: When a subscriber chooses to receive a brand's emails less frequently

opt-out process: How subscribers remove themselves from your mailing list

opt over: When a subscriber opts into one of your other channels, such as social or mobile, during your email unsubscribe process

unsubscribe page: Webpage that is launched when subscribers click the unsubscribe link in your emails where subscribers complete the unsubscribe process

Unsubscribe Process

138

Recognize that list growth can also be boosted by reducing unsubscribes.

To grow your list on an absolute basis, the number of new subscribers that you add during a period of time has to exceed your list churn—that is, subscribers lost to unsubscribes, spam complaints, and hard bounces from email addresses that no longer work.

With most brands losing 25% or more of their subscribers each year, list churn drags down your list growth significantly. Developing strategies to reduce unsubscribes, as well as spam complaints, should be part of your list growth plans.■

Unsubscribe Process

139

Clearly identify the subscriber on the opt-out page and in the preference center.

Give the subscriber assurances that they've arrived at their opt-out page or preference center by showing at least their email address prominently, if not other information, such as their name.

Doing this also helps to prevent recipients of a forwarded email from unintentionally unsubscribing the subscriber who sent it to them.■

Unsubscribe Process

140

Give subscribers options in addition to completely opting out.

You absolutely don't want to impede a subscriber from opting out, but recognize that you might be able to address the issue that's driving them to unsubscribe.

A common reason subscribers opt out is that they feel they receive too many emails. Providing the ability to opt down and receive fewer emails can retain some subscribers who feel this way. Once a month and once a week are common opt-down email frequency choices.

Another reason subscribers give for opting out is that the emails were not relevant. Letting subscribers select or change content or product preferences can correct that problem.

Some subscribers simply want to change their email address and think they need to unsubscribe and then re-subscribe. Providing a *Change Your Email Address* link in your emails, and a similar option in your preference center or on your unsubscribe page, simplifies this process and eliminates the risk that they never get around to re-subscribing after opting out.

This option also keeps your customer and subscriber records clean by ensuring that you attribute both the subscriber's old and new email address—and their associated activity—to a single customer file. Otherwise, you'd likely create a second file for the same customer and lose the ability to act on that past behavior.

Other subscribers might still want to receive messages from you, but would prefer to get them via another channel. You might be losing an email subscriber, but if you give them the ability to opt over to direct mail, a social network, or some other touchpoint, you'll keep the lines of communication open, which should be a business priority.

If you have sister brands, giving outgoing subscribers the option to sign up for emails from those brands might also pay off.

During the holiday season, when email volume spikes, you might also consider giving subscribers the option to pause or "snooze" their subscription until after Christmas or the New Year.

And lastly, when given the option to *Stay Subscribed*, a surprising number of subscribers do so, which indicates that some are just exploring their options. Use your unsubscribe page or preference center to remind subscribers of the benefits of receiving your emails and give them the chance to re-affirm their subscription.■

Unsubscribe Process

141

Be gracious when subscribers opt out to avoid brand damage.

Just because a subscriber doesn't want to receive any more emails from you doesn't necessarily mean they won't buy from you again or interact with you via other channels. So be polite and gracious for the sake of your brand relationship.

For instance, in your messaging, say you're sorry to see them go and hope that they'll re-subscribe in the future. If your business is a restaurant, thank the patron for being a subscriber and say you hope to see them in one of your restaurants soon. If you're running a nonprofit, reiterate the importance of your mission and show your appreciation for the subscriber's support.

Whatever you do, don't act as if the relationship is over, because it most likely isn't. And even if the relationship is over for the time being, nothing is permanent.■

Unsubscribe Process

142

Confirm an unsubscribe request via the channel through which it was requested.

Most unsubscribe requests will occur through your website, via your unsubscribe page or preference center. Confirm those opt-outs on your website.

Sending an opt-out confirmation email to someone who has just said not to send them any more email might irritate them—perhaps to the point that they hit the *Report Spam* button or bad mouth you on social media. The negative risks associated with these emails usually outweigh any benefits, such as helping protect against the rare cases of malicious opt-outs, when a person uses your opt-out page to unsubscribe someone else, or cases of recipients of a forwarded email unintentionally opting out a subscriber.

That said, if subscribers can opt out by replying to one of your emails with *unsubscribe* or some other word in the subject line, then sending them an opt-out confirmation email is completely appropriate.

Following that same logic, unsubscribe requests that come through your call center can be verbally confirmed on the spot, and requests that come through the mail should be confirmed in a letter.■

Unsubscribe Process

143

Enable the native unsubscribe functionality where supported by inbox providers.

A number of inbox providers will display an unsubscribe link for your emails as part of their interface if you include list-unsubscribe code in the *<head>* of your email. This code is optional, but the vast majority of brands include it—with many email service providers adding it automatically.

The downside of this opt-out mechanism is that it can circumvent your unsubscribe page or preference center. That means those opt-outs skip any retention messaging and opt-down, opt-up, opt-over, and profiling options you've created.

However, the upside is that some subscribers trust it more than the unsubscribe links provided by senders. So instead of using the *report spam* button as an opt-out method, some subscribers will use the native unsubscribe link.

This is a highly favorable trade because spam complaints hurt your deliverability while unsubscribes do not; and highly visible opt-out links reassure subscribers that they'll be able to easily unsubscribe in the future if they want to.■

Unsubscribe Process

144

Routinely audit your opt-out processes to make sure they are working properly.

Consumers expect you to honor unsubscribe requests immediately and often report any additional emails they receive afterward as spam. The U.S.'s CAN-SPAM Act and anti-spam legislation in other countries also require that you honor unsubscribe requests swiftly, so taking care of opt-outs is a matter of quality assurance, good customer service, and legal responsibility.

Even if you use an email service provider to handle opt-outs through the unsubscribe link in your emails, periodically check to make sure they're working as expected. Check other opt-out pathways as well, such as those via email replies, call center calls, and postal mail.∎

Testing & Optimization

> *"For marketers, testing is at the heart of improving conversion, measuring is at the heart of holding these conversion improvements to an increasing standard, and optimization is at the heart of persuasion."*
>
> —Bryan Eisenberg, author of *Always Be Testing*

A vigorous testing program is one of the hallmarks of a great email program. It is a critical form of listening and helps your program to be more user-friendly. Testing different subject lines, email designs, content, and landing pages helps you understand what motivates, interests, and appeals to your subscribers, so you can serve them better.

In the absence of A/B testing, you're just making changes, rather than making improvements.

Every brand has a different image, voice, and audience, so testing is necessary to see if you can translate tactics and strategies inspired by other brands into success for your brand.

Although uncovering huge performance differences is rare, keep in mind that small improvements add up to big results over time.∎

WORDS TO KNOW

A/B testing: Exposing a portion of your subscribers to one version of an email or landing page and another portion of your subscribers to another version to see which version performs better

challenger: In an A/B test, the design or process you are testing against your existing champion, hoping to see an improvement in performance

champion: During an A/B test, your existing design or process

50/50 split test: A type of A/B test exposing half your subscribers to one version of an email or landing page and the other half of your subscribers to another version and seeing which version performs better to inform future decisions

multivariate testing: Similar to A/B testing, except multiple variations in an email or landing page are tested simultaneously, which requires lots of data to do accurately

statistically relevant or significant: Having enough data from a test that the results are meaningful rather than simply the result of chance

10/10/80 split test: A type of A/B test exposing 10% of your subscribers to one version of an email or landing page and another 10% of your subscribers to another version, seeing which version performs better, and then exposing the remaining 80% of your subscribers to that winning version

Testing & Optimization

145

Use your email metrics to identify areas for improvement and future testing.

The results of your email campaigns help you understand what's working and what's not, and can inform your decisions about what to test.

For instance, if for a particular campaign, your open rate was near your average but your click rate was below average, then it would indicate that the content of your email wasn't compelling enough.

If your click rate was about average but your conversion rate was below average, either the email content set the wrong expectations or there are problems on the landing pages for that email. Perhaps the messaging on the landing page wasn't compelling enough, or perhaps the landing page didn't provide a smooth transition from the email, causing subscribers to believe they arrived at the wrong page and then abandon your site.

If your click-to-open rate is low—that is, a high open rate with a low click rate—then it would indicate a disconnect between the expectations set by your subject line and the content of the email.

If you wanted recipients to share your message but your total opens were nearly identical to your unique opens, then subscribers didn't find the content worth sharing—at least not by forwarding the email.

Mapping your click-to-open rate across the various calls-to-action within your email can tell you which CTAs subscribers found most compelling. It can also give you insights into how far subscribers were scrolling, which might inform future positioning of content.

That's just a sampling of the ways your email metrics can direct you toward tests that are more likely to yield actionable insights.■

"Just because it's popular doesn't mean it's right for you."
—Mike Nelson, Co-Founder of Really Good Emails

Testing & Optimization

146

Create a calendar or list of tests to run so you can methodically build on your findings.

Take the time to plan out your testing schedule to ensure that you're strategically focusing your efforts on the pain points where you have the most to gain, rather than just doing random ad hoc testing. In addition, use your calendar to help build on and further validate what you learned from previous tests and periodically re-validate those.

Take your A/B testing up another level by creating a profit and loss (P&L) statement for all of your testing efforts. This will help communicate the value of your testing efforts to your executives.

Analytics, customer surveys, diary studies, and focus groups can help you identify which elements of your email program to test and can give you ideas for challenger designs and processes.

Everything big and small is open to testing, but here are some common A/B tests to get you started:

EMAIL DESIGN
Subject lines, preview text, and preheader text

☐ Different lengths

☐ Number of components (e.g., highlighting one

offer vs. two)

- ☐ Different offers (e.g., percent vs. dollar discount)
- ☐ Statement vs. question
- ☐ Value vs. lifestyle appeal
- ☐ First-name personalization vs. generic address or none
- ☐ Different capitalization, punctuation, special characters, and emojis

Headline

- ☐ Different wording
- ☐ Different lengths
- ☐ Different sizes
- ☐ Different fonts or styling

Images

- ☐ Different sizes
- ☐ Different position
- ☐ Model vs. product
- ☐ Positioning of model (e.g., looking straight vs. looking toward key copy or call-to-action vs. looking away from it)
- ☐ Live shot vs. illustration
- ☐ Static image vs. animation vs. video
- ☐ Manufacturer image vs. your image vs. customer image

Copy

- ☐ Different position relative to images
- ☐ Different copy lengths

☐ Different benefits or features highlighted

☐ Promotional vs. non-promotional copy

☐ Including social proof (e.g., testimonials, Likes on Pinterest or Instagram, etc.)

Calls-to-action

☐ Different sizes

☐ Button vs. link

☐ Different button shape

☐ Different wording

☐ Different colors

☐ Different positions

☐ Different landing pages

☐ High commitment vs. low commitment (e.g., *Buy Now* vs. *Learn More*)

Product grid

☐ Number of columns in grid (e.g., two vs. three)

☐ Which product elements to include (e.g. product name, brand, price, etc.)

Secondary messages

☐ Number of secondary messages, including none

☐ Order of secondary messages

☐ Related to primary message vs. not

PROCESSES
Subscription process

☐ Different signup language

☐ Different form elements (e.g., just email address vs. more fields)

- ☐ Making fields optional vs. required
- ☐ Showing or linking to sample emails vs. not

Unsubscribe process

- ☐ Different language on opt-out page
- ☐ Different alternatives made available

AUTOMATION

Triggered messages

- ☐ Different trigger logic
- ☐ How quickly to send the message after it's triggered
- ☐ Whether to send a series of triggered emails
- ☐ The delay between triggered emails in a series
- ☐ Under what conditions an email in a series is skipped
- ☐ Under what conditions an email series ends

Inactivity

- ☐ Different lengths of inactivity
- ☐ Different content tactics to reengage (e.g., rich offer, different subject lines, etc.)
- ☐ Different re-permission messaging

"Design like you are absolutely right, then optimize like you were wrong from the start."

—Jordie van Rijn, Founder of Email Monday

Testing & Optimization

147

Perform tests on groups of active, unbiased, random subscribers.

Choosing a poor sample of subscribers for your A/B tests can significantly skew the results, making them potentially unreliable.

First, make sure you perform tests with active subscribers. Including inactive subscribers in your testing sample weakens results, in addition to directing your focus away from the subscribers who drive the performance of your email program.

Of course, the one exception to this is if your testing is specifically aimed at inactives, such as a test of win-back messaging.

Second, when testing email design changes, choose sample groups composed of new subscribers. Existing subscribers will likely resist design changes initially and it can take a while to change their expectations and retrain how they interact with your emails. New subscribers aren't biased by interactions with your previous designs, so they are the ideal candidates for these tests.

And third, the subscribers involved in the test should be randomly selected from whatever audience you've identified as most appropriate for the test.■

Testing & Optimization

148

Make sure the results of your email tests are statistically significant.

If your test groups are too small, then the results won't be reliable. So use large, randomized groups—of, say, several thousand active subscribers—and aim for at least 150 conversions for each variation. Doing so ensures that the results are statistically significant.

Whether results are statistically significant is measured in terms of confidence. Your goal is to reach 95% confidence that the results didn't happen by chance before calling the test complete.

Email service providers often provide at least simple testing functionality that includes confidence measures. If not, testing tool providers exist.

In regards to email testing, if your email list is small, then you'll likely be able to do only 50/50 split tests. That's where you send one version of an email to half your list and another version to the other half of your list. You then see which version performs better and use the learnings from the test to inform future email content and design decisions.

If your email list is large, you might be able to do 10/10/80 split tests. That's where you create two versions of an email, send each version to

10% of your list, and then later send the winning version to the remaining 80% of your list.

With 50/50 and 10/10/80 splits, it's often best to have only one variation between the two versions that you send so that it's clear exactly what element caused the difference in response. For instance, the two versions of an email would be exactly the same except that one would have a red CTA button and the other a blue button. That way, if the email with the red button performs better, you know it's because of the button color, which would inform your future design decisions.

If your email list is truly huge, you might be able to do multivariate testing, where multiple variations in an email are tested simultaneously. This flavor of A/B testing is trickier to set up and requires a lot of data to get meaningful results, but the advantage is that you get better information about how each of the variations interact with each another. That data can help you identify the variations that have the most impact on your goal.

Similar math would apply to the testing of landing pages, signup forms, preference centers, unsubscribe pages, and other email-related webpages.

Be prepared for some—perhaps many—of your tests to be inconclusive because the difference in performance between the two versions is small. You'll also uncover some hidden gems, however, where the performance difference is 25%, 50%, or even more than 100%.

As a reminder, make sure that you're using the

appropriate success metrics for your test. Focus on deep metrics, such as clicks and conversions, even when judging subject lines and other elements early in an email interaction.■

"Most tests will fail. Failing less is winning."
—Catalin Bridinel, Senior Designer at Booking.com

Testing & Optimization

149

Challenge your new champions in order to verify wins and uncover new gains.

Finding a new champion doesn't mean you're done testing. Sometimes you only see fleeting improvements from a change because they're driven by novelty, so it's important to re-test the same element or process periodically to confirm the results or to uncover additional improvements.

Also, keep in mind changes in production and technology costs as they can have a significant effect on calculations. For instance, a drastic drop in production costs associated with a tactic can turn it from a failed challenger into a new champion.∎

"Successful and astute e-mailers quickly see the value of testing... They quickly implement the results of their research, constantly alert to changing market conditions that might dictate a change in course."

—Herschell Gordon Lewis, author of *Effective E-mail Marketing*

Testing & Optimization

150

Use A/B testing to settle disputes.

Disagreements in email marketing are inevitable—whether it's between email marketing teammates, between email marketers and leadership, or between the brand and any agencies and freelancers employed.

If the stakes are small, executive decisions can settle debates so everyone can move on. But if the stakes aren't so small, an A/B test can be a relatively easy way to definitively settle a disagreement in a data-driven fashion.

Nowadays, email service providers and other tools make A/B tests fairly easy to do—and you should be doing these tests routinely anyway. If you settle debates this way regularly, it will make this process less emotional and everyone involved will see that sometimes they're right, and sometimes they're wrong. Using A/B testing in this way will also foster a data-driven approach within your email program, and that's essential for future success.■

"At Google, every dispute is settled by testing."
—Perry Marshall, Keith Krance, and Thomas Meloche, coauthors of *Ultimate Guide to Facebook Advertising*

The Last Word on Recommended Best Practices

The Tested Rule

Because brands and their subscribers are different and sometimes face unique circumstances, you may occasionally find an advantage in selectively, temporarily, or even permanently bending or breaking a Recommended Best Practice. Recognizing that gives us our second Power Rule, *The Tested Rule:*

Break the rules, but only if

you can prove that doing so leads to

superior long-term performance.

Don't break the rules just to break the rules. Do so with purpose and with a full realization of the potential benefits and the potential risks.

It's not difficult to find celebrated anomalies of brands breaking the rules successfully, but you won't find many, because usually the results just aren't that impressive. Moreover, you'll rarely hear about all the brands that broke the rules and lost.■

PART II

The Frameworks

Having broken email marketing down into individual components, let's now put the pieces back together with some frameworks so you can see how different groups of components function as one.

Understanding the following concepts allows you to coordinate your efforts, work toward a particular goal, and create an effective, cohesive experience for your subscribers.■

Permission

"While the power of permission is what makes email a true powerhouse in the digital world (without permission, email is a mere mortal form of direct marketing), the 'what about this' scenarios that many ask show a big divide."

—Simms Jenkins, Founder & CEO of BrightWave; author of *The New Inbox* and *The Truth About Email Marketing*

Although permission standards in some other countries are much higher and very much a black-or-white proposition, permission has always had plenty of gray areas in the U.S. That grayness begins with the strength of the permission grant and continues all the way through to the end of the relationship, forcing marketers to continually assess the point-by-point risks to their sender reputation.

THE 3 COMPONENTS OF PERMISSION

Email marketers typically talk about permission as being single opt-in (SOI) or double opt-in (DOI). However, that only speaks to whether the opt-in was confirmed, or verified.

However, confirmation is just one of three parts of an opt-in consent that is the start of every email relationship. The three components of permission are signup, context, and confirmation.

A permission grant's strength is the sum of the strength of the signup, that signup's context, and the opt-in confirmation.

1. STRENGTH OF SIGNUP

Whether the signup was made actively, passively, or not at all determines signup strength. Active signups are the strongest and include requiring people to check an unchecked opt-in box or complete a form that's solely for signing up to receive a brand's promotional emails.

Passive signups are weaker and include not unchecking a pre-checked opt-in box during an interaction. In these cases, the person is automatically subscribed unless they take an action to avoid it.

And signups are absent or unwillingly made when the notice of opt-in is hidden in terms and conditions, privacy policies, or entry rules—or when email addresses are harvested, bought, bartered for, or otherwise procured as spammers do.

2. STRENGTH OF CONTEXT

The strength of the context of the signup depends on the subscriber's proximity to purchase at the time of signup, which has a significant impact on the value and risk profile of a new subscriber. It may be helpful to think of context as whether the signup happened in an active customer setting, a prospective or passive customer setting, or a noncustomer setting.

A signup context is strongest when a signup occurs during checkout, the creation of an account, or similar transactional interaction. Essentially, a subscriber demonstrates a higher level of interest in the brand when they are willing to buy something from them and provide information beyond their email address.

> **Subscriber acquisition sources near your conversion and customer service touchpoints preselect valuable subscribers.**

The context is weaker when signups occur as part of a non-transactional interaction with a brand, particularly if that interaction is highly incentivized. For example, some people will agree to receive emails in order to enter a sweepstakes or to get access to a report that they want, but that doesn't mean they will actually be receptive to your emails.

And context is the weakest when there hasn't been any kind of interaction with the email address holder—or the interaction was long ago, such as the email address belonging to a former customer.

3. STRENGTH OF CONFIRMATION

Whether the subscriber takes a definitive action to confirm the subscription, passively confirms their subscription indirectly, or doesn't confirm their opt-in in any manner determines the strength of the opt-in confirmation.

Active confirmations use the confirmed opt-in (COI) or double opt-in (DOI) process, which considers an opt-in unconfirmed until the subscriber indicates that they truly intended to opt in by clicking a link in a subscription activation request email or opt-in confirmation request email.

Passive opt-in confirmations use a confirmed opt-in lite (COIL) approach, which looks for subscriber engagement as proof that they want to continue receiving emails. For example, if a subscriber doesn't open or click any of the first 10 emails you send (including your welcome emails) or any of your emails sent during their first 4 months on your list—whichever comes first—then you should see this as a major red flag and cease mailing them. At that point, the email address represents more of a risk to your deliverability than an opportunity to grow sales.

COIL reduces spam complaints from those subscribers who never intended to sign up or immediately regretted doing so, and limits the effects of reaching inactive accounts intentionally or accidently provided by people. Although COIL doesn't eliminate the risks posed by typo spam traps and malicious signups, it does lower the risks posed by them by reducing the number of times you email them.

While COIL provides less protection than DOI, COIL doesn't slow list growth like DOI does, since at least 20% of people who signup tend not to complete an active confirmation process.

All signups should be confirmed
actively via opt-in confirmation emails
or passively through
near-term engagement.

It's not recommended, but a sender could also forego the protection of any kind of confirmation and just send an opt-in notification in the form of a welcome email or simply the next email in a mailstream without engagement-based confirmation.

COMMON COMBINATIONS

Looking at all three components of an opt-in, the strongest permission grant would be an active signup occurring during a customer transaction that is then actively confirmed using DOI. However, relying solely on that combination of opt-in components would seriously constrain the growth of your email list.

Instead, brands generally balance list growth and list quality by maximizing one of these factors. (See Fig. 25 on next page.)

A Goldilocks permission grant
is not so strong it overly constrains
list growth nor so weak
it harms deliverability.

For instance, here are two common scenarios where a single opt-in (passive or no confirmation) would suffice for most brands:

Components of an Email Opt-In

	Context	Signup	Confirmation
Active	During customer transaction During registration or account creation	Unchecked opt-in box Completion of email signup form	Double opt-in confirmation
Passive	During interaction with brand On lead generation form On brand's social media pages During highly incentivized interaction with brand	Pre-checked opt-in box Clear and conspicuous notification	Notification + engagement-based confirmation Engagement-based confirmation
None	On third-party's site Long past interaction or transaction No previous interactions	Hidden notification No signup	Notification without confirmation No confirmation

FIGURE 25

☐ When a person completes an email signup form (active signup) on the brand's website (passive context)

☐ When a person checks an opt-in box (active signup) during checkout (active context)

And here are two common scenarios where a double opt-in (active confirmation) would be advised:

☐ When a person enters a contest (passive context) and all entrants are clearly notified on the entry form that they'll be subscribed by entering (passive signup)

☐ When a person completes a lead generation form to download a report (passive context) and the opt-in box on the form is pre-checked (passive signup)

In each of those cases, active consent is given—either through an active signup or an active confirmation. That said, of the two, active confirmation is viewed by some inbox providers, blacklist operators, and courts as the stronger proof of signup, since only the email address holder can confirm a signup.

RELYING ON CONTEXT ALONE

Some brands also find success with customers (active context) without using active consent or active confirmation.

For example, in the retail industry, some brands use a pre-checked opt-in box (passive consent) during checkout or a registration process without active confirmation. Consumers have been well trained to look for these opt-out opportunities, but the risks to quality are higher because the marketer is only securing implied or passive consent.

Some brands will use hidden consent notifications (no consent) during checkout without active confirmation. This kind of permission, which is sometimes referred to as an assumed or soft opt-in, is much more common in B2B industries where customers generally expect to occasionally receive emails about new features, new products, and educational content from their vendors.

Even riskier is implicit opt-in, where a person who provides their email address for some other purpose—like receiving a whitepaper or report—is then opted in to receive additional emails without active confirmation.

In all of these scenarios where the marketer is relying on context and securing neither an active signup nor an active confirmation, be extra diligent about monitoring spam complaints, engagement, and deliverability. Marketers should also give considerable thought to the kind of content that they send and how frequently they send it, as that can significantly affect subscriber tolerances.

Marketers operating outside of the U.S. should be particularly mindful of the components of the opt-in processes they use in different regions and countries, as the legal requirements can differ dramatically. For instance, proof of signup will likely be necessary in any legal dispute over permission practices, so implicit opt-ins and other passive opt-ins are risky.

Most anti-spam laws outside of the U.S. stress active signups, contexts, and confirmation.

Regardless of your permission practices, maintain a list of all the sources through which you collect email opt-ins and routinely track the performance of your subscribers that join your list through each of those acquisition sources.

BEYOND THE OPT-IN

Of course, the permission grant is just the beginning of a subscriber's time on your email list. Over the course of an email relationship, each subscriber's permission exists in one of six states. (See Fig. 26 on next page.)

The six subscriber statuses are: unconfirmed, subscribed, actively unsubscribed, undeliverable, inactive, and passively unsubscribed.

The introduction of engagement metrics into inbox providers' filtering algorithms and the risks posed by spam traps require that all opt-ins should now be considered ***unconfirmed*** at their inception. After a subscriber takes the appropriate action to confirm their opt-in, consider them ***subscribed***. Subscribers stay in this state until they unsubscribe actively or passively, or their email address becomes undeliverable.

Subscriber Status

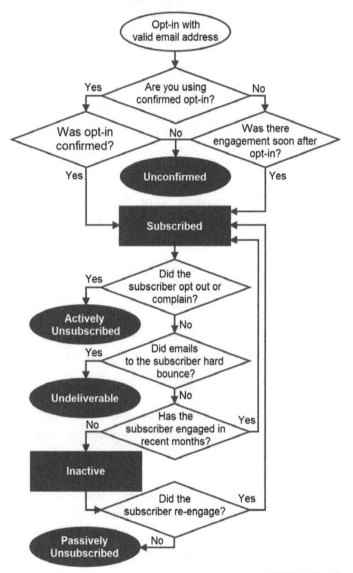

FIGURE 26

Subscribers become **actively unsubscribed** through a variety of mechanisms. A subscriber can opt out via your unsubscribe page or preference center—or, if you empower them to, via email reply, letter, call center rep, or native unsubscribe links provided by an email client. They can also opt out with a spam complaint, but you hope the other routes you offer are more appealing.

Subscribers become **passively unsubscribed** when they have been **inactive** for a long time and attempts to reengage them have failed—with more effort and greater deference given to inactive subscribers who are customers or were customers at one time. (See Fig. 27 on next page.) For these subscribers, accept that permission has expired rather than to risk damage to your sender reputation by pursuing the increasingly remote possibility that they'll tune in to your emails again. Although marketers need to define their own deliverability risks around sending email to inactives, when an email address becomes **undeliverable** and hard bounces because the inbox provider doesn't recognize the account, then you must stop emailing the address immediately. Becoming undeliverable is a form of passively unsubscribing, but it carries much more serious deliverability risks. Inbox providers have a low tolerance for hard bounces and penalize you if have too many, just like they do when you have too many complaints.

Permission is the foundation of email marketing.

Managing Inactive Subscribers

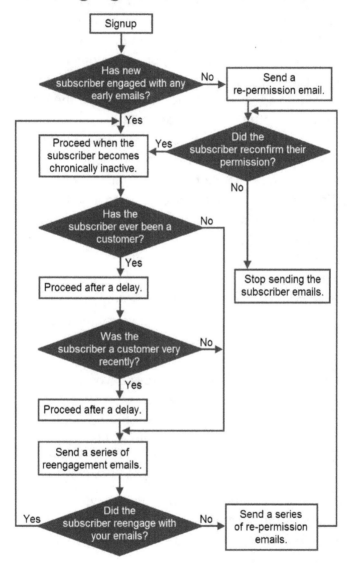

FIGURE 27

Finding the optimal permission grants allows you to grow your list quickly and safely, and understanding the different states of permission allows you to manage your risks during the lifespan of a subscriber.■

———————————————

"Many...understand that the inbox is the holiest of places on the internet. They understand that when a person asks to receive an email they are letting someone into their lives and giving them access to that most powerful of things: their attention."

—Jason Rodriguez, author of *Professional Email Design* and *Modern HTML Email*

List Growth

"Having a large list sounds ideal, but it guarantees nothing—except, perhaps, potential deliverability challenges. It certainly doesn't ensure the high ROI for which email is famous."

—Loren McDonald, Marketing Evangelist at IBM Watson Marketing

The way list growth is often talked about, you might think that it is synonymous with acquisition—that is, adding more email addresses to your list. However, that's only one of three factors that create meaningful list growth.

List growth is composed of new subscribers added, subscribers lost, and the productivity of your subscribers.

Clearly, adding new subscribers is key to list growth. Ways to achieve this include:

☐ Making your existing signup forms and opt-in calls-to-action more prominent

☐ Simplifying your signup process to boost completion rates

☐ Training store, call center, and event staff to better promote the channel and facilitate opt-ins

☐ Auditing your acquisition sources to ensure that glitches and malfunctions aren't leading to subscriber loss

☐ Using your other marketing channels—paid, owned, leased, granted, and earned media—to promote your email program

☐ Adding new acquisition sources, particularly those close to your sales and service operations

ABSOLUTE LIST GROWTH

Although subscriber acquisition is essential, you can't calculate your absolute list growth without considering subscribers lost, too. List churn, which is the number of subscribers lost over a period, directly reduces list growth because a portion of your new subscribers just replaces lost subscribers.

If your acquisition rate is higher than your list churn, then your list size increases. However, if your list churn is higher than your acquisition rate, then your list size shrinks.

This might seem obvious, but acknowledging this reality means you can boost your absolute list growth by lowering your list churn or subscriber replacement rate.

A number of activities can reduce your list churn:

☐ Improve your permission practices and expectation setting so fewer subscribers are lost through spam complaints and unsubscribes early in the email relationship

☐ Identify the sources of subscribers that churn the least and focus on increasing acquisitions through those sources

☐ Make your messaging more compelling and relevant by sending more segmented emails, triggered emails, and emails with personalized content

☐ Give subscribers other options besides unsubscribing, such as reducing the frequency at which they receive emails

With most B2C brands sending 150 to 200 broadcast emails a year, even with a good unsubscribe rate of 0.25%, you're seeing more than a third and as much as half of your list churn—and that's not including subscribers that go inactive or become undeliverable.

Because opt-out rates compound with every campaign you send, reducing them even a little has a big effect annually.

REAL LIST GROWTH

But even absolute list growth doesn't give you the full picture. The best measure is to look at real list growth, which factors in subscriber productivity. This is essential because replacing high-value subscribers with low-value ones degrades the power of your list, whereas the inverse builds it.

One way to measure real list growth is to factor in subscriber lifetime value (SLV) when looking at your subscriber gains and losses. For instance, if in a month you lost 1,000 subscribers that had an average SLV of $100 and you gained 1,000 subscribers through an acquisition channel that tends to attract subscribers with a SLV of $10, then your real list growth fell significantly even though your absolute list growth was zero.

Expressed in dollars, real list growth measures changes in the overall value of your email list.

Modelling overall list value involves a mix of actual SLVs based on lost subscribers plus the estimated SLVs based on the acquisition sources of new subscribers and the average historical SLVs of subscribers from those acquisition sources.

ENGAGED LIST GROWTH

Alternatively, for simpler math, you could track engaged list growth, which measures the number of subscribers who have engaged with at least one of your emails over a period. For instance, you could look at the number of subscribers each month that have clicked in at least one email. Although this method isn't as good as measuring real list growth, it is a good proxy because most engaged subscribers eventually convert.

Conveniently, many of the actions that reduce list churn will also increase engagement and SLV, particularly sending more personalized and targeted messaging. Other activities that grow engagement and SLV include:

- ☐ Paying attention to how your email campaigns affect your most valuable subscribers

- ☐ Identifying the behaviors that differentiate high-value subscribers from less valuable ones and encouraging those behaviors

To get the full picture on the health of your list growth, you need to look at how many subscribers you're adding and how many subscribers you're losing—while factoring in the actual and potential productivity of both groups. Doing so puts the appropriate focus on list quality and ensures you're building an email list that's growing in power, not just in size.■

"You're way better off with a highly engaged list of 200,000 people as opposed to an unengaged list of 2 million."

—Jacob Hansen, Deliverability Consultant at SendGrid

Inbox Placement

Email marketers rightfully obsess over inbox placement, which is their ability to have their emails arrive in subscribers' inboxes rather than being blocked or routed to junk folders. After all, if your subscribers don't receive your emails, then your efforts are all for naught.

However, there's sometimes confusion over what exactly determines a brand's deliverability and who's responsible for it.

Your infrastructure, sender reputation,
email content and frequency,
and send volumes determine
your deliverability.

INFRASTRUCTURE

Having properly configured infrastructure demonstrates to inbox providers that you're not a spammer or part of a bot network, which are rarely configured properly. This means publishing WHOIS contact information, setting up a reverse DNS for your IP address, and authenticating your domains.

You should also think of infrastructure more broadly to include the throttling or rate limiting of your email volume to stay within thresholds established by inbox providers, as well as bounce management. The latter involves the immediate removal of email addresses that hard bounce because the inbox provider doesn't recognize the address—often referred to as reaching unknown users. It also includes the removal of email addresses that soft bounce many times because the user's inbox is full, which is a sign the account is likely abandoned.

> **Infrastructure is where your email service provider plays the largest role in the deliverability of your emails.**

Although infrastructure is an important component of deliverability, the components that you control—your sender reputation and email content and frequency—have a much greater influence on whether your emails reach your subscribers' inboxes.

SENDER REPUTATION

Your permission practices and the reactions from the recipients of your emails determine your sender reputation. The foundation is your permission practices and processes, which should aim to add subscribers to your email list that want to hear from you and avoid adding spam trap addresses and the email addresses of people who don't want to hear from you.

Inbox providers and spam watchdogs see spam traps on your email list as a strong sign that you're buying email lists, mailing subscribers that have been inactive for years, and being reckless with your acquisition processes. There are different kinds of spam traps associated with each of those activities—including pristine, recycled, and typo spam traps—all of which can lead to serious deliverability problems.

Negative reactions by recipients also affect your sender reputation. Spam complaints are the most dreaded because they can start to cause problems after your complaint rate exceeds 0.1%. However, inbox providers also pay attention to softer indications that mail is unwanted by a user, such as unread emails being deleted. (See Fig. 28 on next page.)

In part because marketers used to bloat their email lists with inactive subscribers to drive down their complaint rates, inbox providers now put considerable emphasis on the positive reactions or engagement of subscribers. Inbox providers track dozens of user behaviors in some cases, including scrolling, starring, forwards, and other actions that demonstrate interest in the emails their users receive. However, marketers can't see or can't easily see the vast majority of those user signals.

Subcriber Engagement Signals that Affect Deliverability

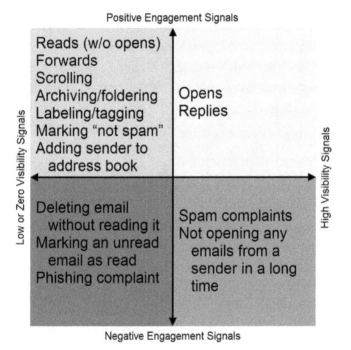

Positive Engagement Signals

Reads (w/o opens)
Forwards
Scrolling
Archiving/foldering
Labeling/tagging
Marking "not spam"
Adding sender to
    address book

Opens
Replies

Low or Zero Visibility Signals

High Visibility Signals

Deleting email
    without reading it
Marking an unread
    email as read
Phishing complaint

Spam complaints
Not opening any
    emails from a
    sender in a long
    time

Negative Engagement Signals

FIGURE 28

Marketers generally measure engagement with just three metrics:

☐ Opens, which are positive when they happen at least occasionally and negative when they don't

☐ Replies, which are of little use since marketers have trained subscribers not to reply

☐ Clicks, which are a proxy for some of the positive signals that marketers can't see

Because inbox providers insist that subscribers engage with—not just tolerate—marketing emails, it's dangerous for brands to hold onto chronically inactive subscribers.

> **Low engagement rates are nearly as dangerous to your deliverability as high spam complaints.**

The emphasis on both complaints and engagement rates by inbox providers makes it impossible for marketers to game the system, which now favors a quality over quantity approach to list growth.

EMAIL CONTENT & FREQUENCY

Email content and frequency still play a role in deliverability, but it's not as large as in the past. Many years ago, content filters scrutinized the words used in subject lines and body copy, looking for "spammy" words, such as *free* and *offer*.

Although word choice is still given a little weight, today content filtering is much less about the words you use and more about where your emails link to and how you code your emails.

Linking to sites with poor reputations or using URL shorteners, which are favored by spammers to obscure the destinations of their links, can have a dramatic effect on deliverability. And including JavaScript, Flash, and other coding capable of carrying malicious payloads will also do serious damage to your deliverability.

However, if your sender reputation is good and you're linking to only reputable sites, there's no need to censor your word choices in your emails or worry about image-to-text ratios, which was once a major consideration.

An erratic email frequency can also get you in trouble because spammers often operate in random bursts. Seasonal variations that increase volume are okay if they aren't extreme, but long quiet periods followed by short periods of high activity will raise red flags with inbox providers. Generally, inbox providers like to see consistency in a sender's email volume.

Note that how subscribers react to the frequency at which you email them is an entirely separate issue from the sending patterns that inbox providers like to see.

One way smaller brands and brands with uneven mailing patterns can get around frequency issues and some of the hassles of sender reputation management is by using a shared IP address to send email. This is when several companies send email from the same IP address, which means they are at least partially affecting each other's sender reputation.

ESPs that specialize in serving smaller senders typically offer shared IP addresses that they manage, smoothing out sending patterns and monitoring the sender reputation of each of their IP addresses to ensure high deliverability.

They also generally require their users to use

confirmed opt-ins in order to protect the sender reputation of these shared IP addresses. These ESPs also handle warming up IP addresses, where email volumes going through a new IP address are slowly increased, which gives inbox providers an opportunity to get used to this new source of email volume and ascribe it a sender reputation.

Larger senders manage enough volume to have their own dedicated IP addresses, where they control all aspects of their sender reputation.

SEND VOLUMES

While that's an advantage of being a large sender, a drawback is that inbox providers scrutinize brands with high volume sends more. So big email marketers are a bit more likely to have their emails blocked or junked by inbox providers.

That makes it even more important for high-volume senders to pay attention to the health of their email list in terms of unknown users, spam complaints, engagement, inactivity, and other factors.

THE KEYS TO DELIVERABILTY

The critical takeaway here is that...

> **The responsibility for
> and power over deliverability
> resides with senders.**

To minimize your risks, embrace this responsibility by:

☐ Choosing an experienced, reputable email service provider with solid infrastructure

☐ Actively managing your sender reputation

☐ Crafting relevant email content and sending it at an effective frequency.

DELIVERABILITY STATUS

Depending on how well you manage all of those factors, your emails that don't bounce could be:

☐ Blocked globally, so that none of the users at one or more inbox provider receive your emails

☐ Blocked locally, so that some individual users at one or more inbox provider don't receive your emails

☐ Junked, so that some users at one or more inbox provider have your emails delivered to their junk or spam folder

Or, if your emails don't encounter any of those problems, they will be delivered to the intended inboxes. The goal of deliverability management is to maximize that inbox placement.

TAB PLACEMENT

One element that's outside of the scope of deliverability is tab placement. While a number of inbox providers now have tabbed inboxes that sort emails by type and other factors, which tab an email lands under is of no consequence when it comes to deliverability. All tabs are considered part of the inbox.

You should try to see tab placement as of no

consequence as well and refrain from asking subscribers to re-tab your emails or move your messages from one tab to another. You should also refrain from trying to game your tab placement, as you risk angering inbox providers, many of whom can penalize your brand's performance in search results and other areas, in addition to in the inbox.

Tab placement has proven to have little impact on email performance. So let your subscribers worry about how best to manage their inboxes. Instead, you should focus on sending highly relevant messages that your subscribers eagerly anticipate receiving. If you do that, your subscribers will give your emails the attention they deserve, regardless of how they organize their inboxes.■

Email Audience Funnel

"It's a moment where marketing happens, where information happens, and where consumers make choices that affect the success or failure of nearly every brand in the world."

—Jim Lecinksi, author of
Winning the Zero Moment of Truth

Successful email marketing is a series of smart choices about who you want to take action. These audience-selection decisions start with how you grow and manage your email list and continue all the way through the funnel to conversion.

The Email Audience Funnel details the tactics and metrics used to measure audience selection from list building and messaging strategy at the program level to email targeting and email interactions at the email level. (See Fig. 29 on next page.)

The key is recognizing that...

A successful Email Audience Funnel
is one where each stage maximizes
the effectiveness of the lowest stages
by selecting the right audience
members to continue on.

Email Audience Funnel

TACTICS	LIST BUILDING	METRICS
Acquisition sources, permission practices, list hygiene	**Subscribers**	List growth, deliverability, subscriber lifetime value
	MESSAGING STRATEGY	
Message mix, frequency, preferences, time-optimization, reengagement	**Engaged Subscribers**	Open and click reach
	EMAIL TARGETING	
Segmentation, automation, time-optimization	**Email Recipients**	Engagement rate, unsubscribe rate, and spam complaint rate
	EMAIL INTERACTIONS	
Sender name, subject line, preview text	Openers	Open rates
Email design, defensive design, messaging, personalization, interactivity, call-to-action	Clickers	Click rates
Landing page selection, design, content, and optimization; conversion process and options	Converters	Conversion rates and revenue
	EMAIL SHARING	
Focused and targeted messages, share-with-your-network (SWYN) calls-to-action	**Recipients of Shared Emails**	Forwards and social shares

FIGURE 29

It's tempting to want to optimize each stage in isolation—to focus your list building on maximizing subscriber growth and to focus your envelope content on maximizing opens.

However, that's an overly simplified view of how audience selection works. It assumes that all subscribers are equal and that all opens are equal—and they're not.

You don't want just anybody on your email list; you want subscribers who are going to engage and convert. And you don't just want anyone to open that email; you want openers who are the most receptive to your call-to-action to open that email.

Each stage of the Email
Audience Funnel has one job,
which is to maximize converters
at the bottom of the funnel.

If you don't have quality subscribers, it's difficult to have engaged subscribers. If you don't have engaged subscribers, it's difficult to have enough behavior to target well. If you don't target subscribers well, it's difficult to get the right openers. If you don't have the right openers, it's difficult to get the right clickers. And if you don't have the right clickers, it's difficult to get the right converters.

Each stage depends on all the ones that preceded it, which is why optimizing any single stage in isolation tends to result in underperformance.

Let's look at each stage in turn...

LIST BUILDING

The top-most level of the Email Audience Funnel is your subscriber base. How and where you acquire them and the expectations you set with them when they sign up directly impacts your success.

Growing your list using subscriber acquisition sources close to your conversion and customer service touchpoints generally results in subscribers with high lifetime values, while those far from these operations tend to generate little value and hurt your deliverability.

Your permission practices go hand-in-hand with your acquisition sources. The context of a strong acquisition source allows you to have more relaxed signup and confirmation practices, while weak contexts require stronger practices.

List hygiene is also a critical part of list management. That not only involves keeping bad email addresses and role-based email addresses off your list, but also purging chronically inactive subscribers who couldn't be re-permissioned.

MESSAGING STRATEGY

The next level of the Email Audience Funnel is your engaged subscribers. The frequency at which you send emails, the content and calls-to-action of those messages, and how well those all align with subscribers' expressed and implied preferences will determine which if your subscribers stay engaged.

If you send lots of broadcast emails with one-size-fits-all messaging, then your program will have a narrow appeal and engagement will likely suffer. However, if you have a healthy mix of broadcast, seasonal, segmented, and triggered emails, and use personalization wisely, then your program's appeal will be much wider.

> **Engaged subscribers are a measurement of how well you're succeeding at the zero moment of truth.**

If you've created positive experiences for a subscriber recently, then that bodes well for obtaining your next open, click, and conversion sooner rather than later. On the other hand, if you've created negative experiences, then that increases the chance that the subscriber will tune you out, unsubscribe, or, in an act of vengeance, mark your emails as spam.

Together, list building and messaging strategy are the two program-level elements of the funnel. Next are the audience selection elements of individual emails, with a look first at email targeting.

EMAIL TARGETING

To state the obvious, when you send an email, it goes to your subscribers, with your engaged subscribers effectively being the vast majority of that audience. However, every email you send doesn't—and indeed shouldn't—go to every one of your subscribers.

Many of the messages you send are best received by only a portion of your subscribers because of their expressed interests or past actions. And other messages are best received only by certain subscribers at a certain time based on past actions or a lack of action.

Segmented and triggered emails narrow the audience of a message, increasing engagement and reducing the email fatigue caused by receiving irrelevant messages. And time-optimized emails are also a component of audience selection, as the time of day, day of week, and point in season can influence subscriber action.

So email targeting focuses your audience by speaking to a particular portion of your subscribers—again, with your engaged subscribers typically making up the vast majority of those likely to respond.

The second email-level of the Email Audience Funnel is email interactions, which has three stages.

EMAIL INTERACTIONS

The audience selection that takes place within an email is accomplished through the messaging. The right messaging at each of the three stages of an email interaction allows recipients to self-qualify or self-select themselves to proceed to the next stage.

Email interactions happen in three semi-connected stages: envelope content, body content, and landing page.

Envelope content. Before they open an email, subscribers see the envelope content, which always consists of the sender name and subject line, and sometimes also includes the preview text, sender email address, and reply-to email address.

The sender name, the text that says who sent the email, has the greatest impact on whether your emails are opened, deleted, or reported as spam because email is a permission-based channel. So your sender name should be instantly recognizable by subscribers. Usually, this name is the brand the subscriber signed up to hear from.

The subject line tells subscribers what your email is about. Although creativity has its place, the most effective subject lines are straightforward and predispose those who open the email to engage with its content.

The goal of subject lines isn't to generate opens; it's to generate openers who are likely to convert.

The preview text appears right after or below the subject line in many email clients and is comprised of the first HTML text in the email. Most often pulled from the preheader text, preview text should extend or reinforce the subject line, giving subscribers more information about the content of the email.

The sender's email address sometimes is displayed beside the sender name, and the reply-to email address only appears in some email clients when someone replies to your email. Both email addresses should be well-branded to avoid raising doubts about the validity of the sender.

Successful envelope content generates high click-to-open and conversion-to-open rates. But, equally important, it reduces opener's remorse, which leaves subscribers feeling like you wasted their time and makes them less likely to open future emails from you.

Body content. When subscribers open an email, they see the body content. Most marketing emails are a mix of text and images. B2C brands, lifestyle brands, and promotional messages rely more on images, while B2B brands, value brands, and transactional messaging relying more on text.

Keep in mind that subscribers don't read emails; they scan them. So pay extra attention to headlines; use bullet points and sentence fragments to communicate quickly; and make call-to-action links and buttons clear and obvious.

Whatever the design and messaging, the body content should help the subscriber determine if they are a good match for the call-to-action of your email and whether they should become a clicker.

Landing pages are the web pages, apps, and other destinations subscribers arrive at after clicking the calls-to-action in your emails. A strong connection between the email content and the landing page reassures subscribers that they've arrived at the right place. For instance, consider repeating headlines and images from the email on the landing page.

From there, your checkout, registration, and other processes hopefully turn your email clickers into converters—which is the ultimate goal of most email interactions and, indeed, the ultimate goal of email programs.

Increasingly, this traditional linear model of email interactions is being disrupted.

Tracking progression and influence at each stage is becoming more difficult because of the growing number of ways that subscribers can bypass one or more stages of an email interaction. (See Fig. 30 on next page.)

For instance, a subscriber could read the envelope content about a sale you're holding and, rather than clicking through, open a new browser window and type in your website's URL. Or they could hop in their car and drive to your store, if you're promoting a store sale. Or they might search for a hashtag in your subject line on social media and join the conversation there. Or they might call your call center and make a purchase that way. Or they could tell a spouse, friend, or co-worker, who might convert.

All are positive, desirable actions, but they're difficult to measure because the subscriber deviated from the traditional linear interaction path. Unfortunately, that's just small sample of

Email Interaction Flow

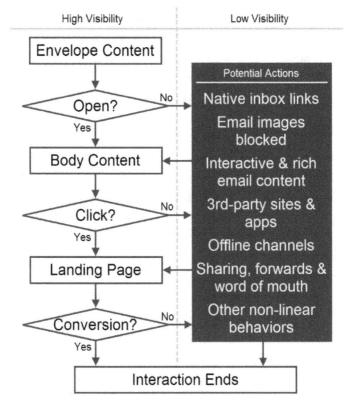

FIGURE 30

how tracking can be short-circuited.

Additionally, body content can lead subscribers to skip the landing page associated with your email's calls-to-action. They can forego clicking through and instead search for your brand or product in a search engine, visit your brand on social media, or open your mobile app to take action.

Moreover, rich email content, such as HTML5 video, pulls content into emails that previously would have been on a landing page. Such capabilities are good for inbox providers because they keep their users in the inbox, and they're good for marketers because they lower the barriers to taking the desired action—although they do effectively limit the response to a single action.

Native inbox links are also disrupting the traditional flow of email interactions. Enabled by marketers, these links appear as part of the email client interface and perform a variety of actions. These include subject line quick links that let subscribers click through to the landing page for the primary call-to-action of the email without opening the email.

These also include native unsubscribe links, which can allow subscribers to opt out without visiting the sender's unsubscribe page or preference center. Generally more trusted than the unsubscribe links offered by senders, these links promise the efficiency of a *Report Spam* button, but without harming the sender reputation of the sender.

All of this is to say that email interactions are getting trickier to follow and therefore...

Whatever return on investment you think your email program is generating, it's likely significantly higher.

Withhold studies and other tests can help you develop a fairly accurate ROI model, but ultimately returns are a spectrum that goes from easy-to–measure soft ROI to difficult-to-measure hard ROI.

The third and final email-level of the Email Audience Funnel is email sharing.

EMAIL SHARING

Unlike every other stage of the Email Audience Funnel, subscribers do the audience selection in the Email Sharing stage instead of marketers. And the audience selection they do is highly targeted, with forwards acting like triggered 1-to-1 emails and social sharing acting like segmented emails.

Just like during the Email Interaction stages, marketers influence email sharing through their email messaging. To spur forwards and social sharing, email marketers should:

☐ Periodically create exceptional email content or experiences worth sharing and talking about, and use a deviation in email design to make it clear that the message is special

☐ Keep the email design simple and clean and focus your email on a single message, as this allows subscribers to forward the message without needing to explain to the forward recipient what in it they're sharing

☐ Personalize and target the message, as pointed messages encourage subscribers to share it with people who are just like them, whereas broad, generic messaging tends not to inspire much sharing

☐ Include prominent share-with-your-network (SWYN) links, as nothing spurs email sharing like asking subscribers to share your email

How you build your list, strategize your messaging, target your messages, and design your message all impact the kind of audience you're building. Don't build an impressive-looking list; build one that's impressively productive by always choosing quality over quantity.■

_____

"Conversions are the only metric that truly matter."
—Mike Le, COO at CB/I Digital

Subject Line & Preview Text Writing

"The best subject lines tell what's inside, and the worst subject lines sell what's inside."

—MailChimp

Email subject lines are the most tested element of email marketing. That's because they're incredibly important and marketers' guts are frequently wrong about what makes a good subject line.

Complicating matters is the fact that the goal of subject lines is often misunderstood; its influence underestimated; and its relationship with preview text ignored.

First, the goal of your subject line isn't to generate an open (unless that's the sole goal of your campaign). Its goal is to generate openers who are predisposed to click and convert. That's why the winner of a subject line A/B test should be the one that creates more bottom of the funnel activity.

Second, subject lines influence subscribers even when they don't open the email. A good subject line can spur a subscriber to visit your store or website, open your mobile app, mention your brand on social media, call your call center, tell a friend or colleague about your brand, and even make a purchase—all without them having to open the email.

The dark side of a subject line's influence is that a misleading or overly vague subject line that doesn't match up well with the content of the email can make subscribers feel tricked and manipulated, similar to how they feel when falling prey to click-bait. "Open-bait" subject lines have a similarly negative effect on subscribers, giving them opener's remorse and reducing the chance they'll open future emails from you.

And third, while subject lines are the most tested email element, preview text is tested infrequently and is often completely unoptimized. Since many of the most popular email clients support preview text, it should be seen as a "second subject line" and marketers should spend nearly as much time writing them as they do their subject lines.

CUE-DIVE METHOD

Even when you firmly understand the goal of envelope content and appreciate its influence, there's no secret formula for subject line and preview text success. However, there is a list of ingredients that are easily remembered as the CUE-DIVE Method.

Subject line and preview text content can be Contextual, Urgent, Emotional, Detailed, Intriguing, Visual, and Earned.

Scoring your subject lines and preview text against those seven attributes and tracking the response of your subscribers over time allows you to determine which to use, how frequently to use each, and in what circumstances. In other words, you'll learn which attributes cue your subscribers to dive into your emails and convert.

Here's a breakdown of each attribute:

CONTEXTUAL

This subject line and preview text content pertains to the subscriber and their context—whether it's their location, recent behavior, or circumstances. It includes content that is...

☐ Personalized   ☐ Relevant

☐ Localized   ☐ Requested

☐ Behavior-based   ☐ Anticipated

☐ Segmented

This attribute helps explain the high open, click, and sales conversion rates of transactional, triggered, segmented, and highly personalized emails when the subject line is closely aligned with the content and purpose of those emails.

For example, it explains the performance difference when the subject line "Buyer's Guide to SLR Cameras" is used for a broadcast email to everyone on a retailer's list and when it is used for a browse abandonment email sent of subscribers who browsed SLR cameras but didn't buy one.

URGENT

This content is time-dependent or time-sensitive. This attribute describes content that is or involves...

☐ Deadlines   ☐ Events

☐ Limited quantities   ☐ Alerts

☐ New   ☐ Topical

☐ Seasonal   ☐ Newsjacking

☐ Holidays

Urgency is a key messaging tactic across all channels because it answers the question: Why should I give you my attention now?

EMOTIONAL

This content suggests how people should feel or appeals to subscribers' emotions to motivate them. It involves or appeals to subscribers'...

☐ Lifestyle messaging   ☐ Activism

☐ Pop culture references   ☐ Competitiveness

☐ Aspirations   ☐ Greed

☐ Happiness   ☐ Guilt

☐ Responsibility   ☐ Vanity

☐ Gratitude   ☐ Anxiety

☐ Generosity   ☐ Shame

☐ Compassion   ☐ Fear

☐ Charity   ☐ Slang

☐ Duty   ☐ Profanity

    ☐ Shock

Emotion can motivate when logic does not. It's a key messaging tactic of lifestyle brands, political groups, nonprofits, and other organizations.

DETAILED

This content describes the primary call-to-action of the email in a straightforward manner. It provides details about or entails...

☐ Offers   ☐ Exclusives

☐ Value   ☐ Uniqueness

☐ News   ☐ Branding

☐ Information   ☐ Brand Positioning

☐ Content

Detailed content answers the question: What is this email about? And it helps the subscriber decide whether they'll be interested in the email's content.

INTRIGUING

This attribute relies on creating questions in the subscriber's mind, questions they're compelled to find out the answer to by opening the email. Often, this is referred to as creating a "curiosity gap," as described by psychologist George Loewenstein. This approach involves or includes content that is...

☐ Questions   ☐ Strange

☐ Curiosity   ☐ Pop culture

☐ Mysterious   ☐ Humor

☐ Chance   ☐ Puns

☐ Surprise   ☐ Weird

While this content can be effective, it's also among the riskiest because it encourages marketers to play games with their subscribers' time. If the content of the email ends up being disappointing, that can make subscribers feel manipulated and lead to opener's remorse.

Sometimes we focus too much on grabbing our subscribers' attention and not enough on not wasting their time.

So while this tactic might boost the opens of the campaign it's used for, it might suppress opens for subsequent campaigns, creating a net loss of engagement. Use this tactic thoughtfully and sparingly.

VISUAL

This subject line and preview text content draws the eye and has an impact before any words are read. It includes or entails using...

- ☐ Very short subject lines (and to a lesser extent very long subject lines)
- ☐ Abbreviations and all-caps
- ☐ Unusual spellings
- ☐ Unusual or heavy punctuation
- ☐ Special and Unicode characters
- ☐ Emoticons
- ☐ Emojis

Emojis are the fresh, new face when it comes to visual subject line and preview text elements, but don't underestimate the power of typography to create visual interest. The artful and judicious use of all-caps, dashes, asterisks, plus-signs, and other characters can be eye-catching.

As with intriguing envelope content, there can be higher risks associated with visual elements. Overuse or going too far can make your brand seem desperate for attention. Plus, some of these elements, particularly emojis, can be too casual or off-brand for some companies.

EARNED

This attribute pertains to content related to earned media—that is, what other people are saying about you. It includes content from or involving…

- ☐ Reviews
- ☐ Testimonials
- ☐ Endorsements
- ☐ Media coverage
- ☐ Community activity
- ☐ User-generated content
- ☐ Hashtags

Consumers give more weight to what others say about you than what you say about yourself. That's the power of earned media and why you should look for opportunities to use this content in your envelope content.

MIX & MATCH

Subject lines generally incorporate two, maybe three, of those attributes. Preview text incorporates another one or two, which may or may not overlap with the attributes used in the subject line.

Detailed, contextual, intriguing, and earned tend to be primary attributes, while urgent, emotional, and visual tend to be secondary attributes that pair well with any of the primary ones.

A couple of interesting combinations to be aware of include using:

☐ An intriguing subject line to grab attention, but then using a detailed preview text to close the curiosity gap immediately and reduce opener's remorse

☐ Highly visual preview text or white space, perhaps with some branding, to create emphasis on the subject line content

Experiment with different combinations across your subject lines and preview text to see what your subscribers respond to in various situations.

BE WARY OF TRUNCATION

Many email clients cut off subject lines after about 40 characters, so if your subject line is longer than that, it could be negatively affected. Be careful that a critical attribute or bit of content isn't lost.

For instance, depending on how your subject line is worded, truncation can potentially turn an emotional and detailed subject line into an emotional and intriguing subject line because some vital details were lost.

Truncation doesn't have to be lethal to a subject line. If you don't want to change the wording of your subject line, consider using your preview text to clarify the details or other attribute or content that is being truncated in certain email clients.∎

———————————————

Bonus Resource:

Outstanding Email Marketing Examples
of Subject Lines

EmailMarketingRules.com/Examples

Rendering & Defensive Design

"Building great emails that perform across the myriad of clients and devices is difficult and, oftentimes, extraordinarily frustrating. It involves working with markup at which most designers would cringe and hacking your way to success."

—Jason Rodriguez, author of *Professional Email Design* and *Modern HTML Email*

Website developers have it hard. They deal with a number of environments equal to the number of operating systems times the number of browsers times the number of devices and screen sizes. But...

Email rendering is

exponentially more complex

than website rendering.

That's because email developers have three additional rendering layers to contend with:

☐ Email service providers

☐ Email clients

☐ Image blocking

Let's look at each rendering layer in turn...

EMAIL SERVICE PROVIDERS

Before you even send an email, your email service provider alters them. Alterations can include:

☐ Adding tracking pixels to measure opens

☐ Replacing links with redirects for tracking clicks

☐ Changing your email's DOCTYPE

☐ Stripping out certain kinds of code

Most of the time, these changes don't affect the rendering of an email, but sometimes they do. Often there are ways to circumvent this, but it's wise to ask your ESP if and how their platform modifies your email code.

OPERATING SYSTEMS

Whether on a desktop, tablet, smartphone, smartwatch, or another device, the operating system (OS) affects the rendering of an email through the functionality it supports for web- and app-based email clients.

WEB BROWSERS

If a subscriber views an email in a webmail client, then the web browser they're using can also affect the rendering of that email. Web browsers are like a secondary operating system layer for webmail.

EMAIL CLIENTS

After the ESP, operating system, and browser layers of rendering, marketers' emails are then affected by webmail and app-based email clients— of which there are an increasing number.

Email clients don't all support the same code, with each one stripping out unsupported code before rendering the email. This can lead to significantly different email rendering across email clients.

This rendering layer is complicated further by the fact that it's not stable. Updates to email clients are made regularly, tend not to be announced, and changes affecting email rendering are almost never documented. Of course, that's on top of the updates to OSs and browsers.

Past email client changes like this have led to images in emails suddenly having a 1-pixel border; inbox display preferences overriding the default styling of background, text, and link colors; and special characters like ™, ©, and ♥ being converted into 16x16-pixel emoji images. In those instances—and many others—email marketers were left to scramble for workarounds to regain control over how their emails looked.

Webmail clients have yet another layer to contend with. Rendering may be affected by whether the message is imported from another email service using...

IMAP/POP

In webmail clients, whether an email is native to that email platform can affect rendering. For example, emails viewed in Gmail may display differently if the person has a gmail.com email address than if they import emails into Gmail from their aol.com address.

In that first case, the emails are "delivered" via HyperText Transfer Protocol (HTTP). In the second case, the emails are imported using either Internet Message Access Protocol (IMAP) or Post Office Protocol (POP)—both of which can affect email rendering in rare instances.

The next layer affecting email rendering is...

DEVICE/SCREEN SIZE

While screen size considerations aren't unique to email development, it has been more challenging for email developers. That's because support for media queries, which enables responsive design, has been less than universal across email clients.

Because of that uneven support, email marketers have embraced a range of mobile-friendly design approaches—some of which employ hacks—as they migrate away from the desktop-centric design that dominated prior to this decade.

> **The Age of Mobile has fundamentally and forever changed email design.**

This shift sees various flavors of mobile-aware design and responsive design replacing desktop-centric email design, which is characterized by multi-column layouts, small text, and high link densities.

Mobile-aware design uses basic techniques to create a single email that functions well across a range of screen sizes but is deferential to smartphones. Responsive design uses a variety of advanced techniques to serve up versions or renderings of an email that are optimized for particular screen resolutions or email clients.

Responsive design holds the most promise because the number of screen sizes and the spread between the smallest and largest screen sizes is likely to continue to grow.

IMAGE BLOCKING

The final rendering layer that marketers have to deal with is image blocking. A significant number of inbox providers still block the images in emails by default. For the images in your emails to be displayed, subscribers have to enable or turn on images, which they can do for individual emails or for all emails from a particular sender.

Even if images are turned on by default, subscribers are sometimes able to turn off images, either through their email client or browser.

As long as this is the case, you'll need to use *alt* text, HTML text, and background colors to preserve the integrity of your messages.

THE BIG PICTURE

In total, installed app-based email environments like Outlook and the native iPhone email app have five layers, while webmail environments like Gmail have seven. That's a lot of possible combinations across each of those layers. (See Fig. 31 on next page.)

This massive level of rendering variability is due to the fact that...

Email is an open platform with
no universal coding standards.

The fact that email can be sent from and read on so many platforms is what makes email so ubiquitous and its reach so powerful. However, rendering issues remain a major negative consequence of this open platform.

Because of how fluid the email rendering environment is, it's highly recommended that you use a rendering preview tool for every send—or at the very least set up a variety of test accounts to check the rendering of your emails.

Paying attention to every possible OS-app-

FIGURE 31

browser-client-device combination is nearly impossible—and a poor use of your time. Analyze your subscriber base and focus your attention on the most popular combinations among your subscribers, while only occasionally auditing how your emails render in the other environments.

Beyond being vigilant about previewing email rendering, marketers need to embrace a broadly defensive approach to email design.

DEFENSIVE DESIGN

The concept of defensive design originally came about as a way to deal with a fairly likely and very disruptive rendering issue: image blocking. Because of the devastating effect this could have on a message, marketers developed a three-prong system of fallbacks to preserve message integrity that consisted of using *alt* text, HTML text, and background colors.

However, marketers also used fallbacks to safeguard their email designs from poor support for everything from animated GIFs to HTML.

Today, fallbacks are even more vital as smartphones, smartwatches, and an ever-growing range of email clients with inconsistent support for HTML and CSS threaten message integrity.

So rather than just thinking of defensive design as a way of coping with image blocking, it's wise to think of it much more broadly as a system of fallbacks to address the full range of threats to the rendering of your emails.

Defensive design consists of design and coding fallbacks that allow an email to communicate its message effectively when images, HTML, CSS, and other enhancements aren't supported.

'PLATFORM-PERFECT' EMAILS

The idea of creating email designs that are "pixel-perfect" everywhere was recognized long ago as an exercise in futility. It's not only impossible, but you wouldn't strive for such consistency because it would mean that you were designing down to the lowest common denominator, and it's impossible to create widely compelling email experiences under those circumstances.

Instead, email marketers have embraced progressive enhancement, which is the idea of creating "platform-perfect" emails that maximize the email experience made possible by an email client or device. Those enhanced experiences are backed up by fallbacks that ensure the graceful degradation of your emails when they're viewed on platforms that don't support those enhancements.

This parallels other email marketing developments such as personalization, segmentation, and triggered emails, all of which reject a "one size fits all" approach in favor of creating tailored email experiences.

ENHANCEMENTS & FALLBACKS

The available enhancements and corresponding

fallbacks range widely. They also fall into two buckets: ones for email elements and ones for the entirety of the email. (See Fig. 32 below.)

For example, an email element enhancement would include using Google fonts and web fonts but listing a web standard font in your font family coding as a fallback.

And an email structure enhancement would include using multipart MIME and including an

Defensive Design

Fallback	Enhancement
HTML text, alt text & background colors	images
first frame of animation	animated gif
image or animated gif	HTML5 video
web safe fonts	Google & web fonts
none	emojis
default rendering & client-specific enhancements	media queries
plain-text part or watch-html part of multipart MIME	HTML

FIGURE 32

HTML part and a plain-text part as a fallback for devices like smartwatches that can't handle HTML.

Of course, when enhancements aren't supported, your default design is the fallback. And for some email elements and structures, there simply are no fallbacks at all. They're either supported or they're not and the element is just gone.

For example, that's the case with emojis in subject lines. Support varies and they might not be displayed, which can leave your subject line impaired if you're using them as substitutes for words. For that reason, it's best to use them as visual enhancers or as a form of punctuation to separate subject line message components. Otherwise, you should be very confident in your ability to segment your list and send emoji-filled subject lines only to those subscribers who tend to open your emails in email clients that support them.

Instead of playing down to the lowest common denominator and creating mediocre email experiences for all of your subscribers, use progressive enhancements to play up to the widest reasonable diversity and create the most compelling email experiences feasibly possible for each of your subscribers.∎

Email Frequency

"The key to establishing the right email frequency with your customers, as in every aspect of email marketing, is to plan, test, adapt, analyze, and refine. Each marketer will find that different rules apply to different customers."

—Simms Jenkins, Founder & CEO of BrightWave; author of *The New Inbox* and *The Truth About Email Marketing*

How many emails do you send your subscribers each month? Answering this question used to be pretty straightforward because nearly all your subscribers received the same number of emails from you.

Now this question prompts many more questions:

☐ What month is it?

☐ Do you mean new subscribers or existing subscribers?

☐ Are you referring to active subscribers, or all subscribers including inactives?

☐ Do you mean loyalty program subscribers or the ones in my core promotional program?

☐ Should I exclude transactional and post-purchase emails from that count?

You ask these questions because marketers now send many targeted emails in addition to broadcast emails. (See Fig. 33 on next page.) And

Value-Risk Profile of Email Targeting-Frequency Mix

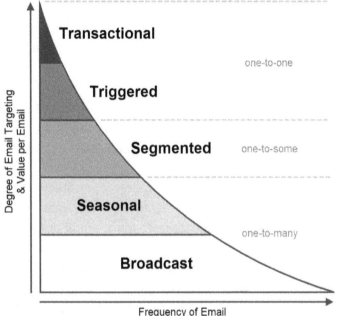

FIGURE 33

that means that there no single ideal email frequency anymore.

Brands have as many ideal email frequencies as they have subscribers.

And each of those subscriber's email frequency is the sum of the broadcast, seasonal, segmented, triggered, and transactional emails they receive.

ONE-TO-MANY EMAILS

Each subscriber's baseline email frequency is determined by their selections when they sign up. If no options are offered, then everyone starts with the same baseline. However, if you offer different topic selections or different newsletter mailstreams, those picks will decide a subscriber's baseline broadcast email frequency.

You can experiment to find the optimal baseline email frequency for your program by seeing how your subscribers respond in aggregate to increases in email volume.

Seasonality is the first variable that affects the baseline email frequency throughout the year. You should be sending subscribers more email during your most active periods—whether it's the holiday season for retailers, the run up to Valentine's Day and Mother's Day for florists, the winter months for travel companies, or the end of year for nonprofits, for example.

Model your seasonal variations in email frequency on your seasonal variations in sales. Seasonal emails should enhance existing natural seasonal increases in sales.

As you determine your ideal baseline frequency and your seasonal variations, keep in mind that your risk of causing email fatigue, unsubscribes, spam complaints, and deliverability problems are greatest with these broadcast and seasonal emails. You don't want those emails to undermine the effectiveness of your segmented, triggered, and transactional emails.

After you find that sweet spot for your broadcast and seasonal volume, it's then all about the individual.

ONE-TO-SOME & ONE-TO-ONE EMAILS

Just like seasonal email volume should mirror swings in purchase patterns...

The frequency at which individual subscribers receive emails should mirror their level of engagement.

Put another way, a subscriber's engagement is a feedback loop that tells you "I really enjoy getting your emails, so feel free to email me more often" or "I'm not enjoying the emails you're sending me that much so send me something else or email me less often."

The safest ways to respond to your subscribers' positive feedback is to send them segmented and triggered messages, in addition to using personalized and dynamic content in your broadcast and seasonal emails.

Use browsing and purchase patterns, in addition to preferences that your subscribers directly stated through a preference center or progressive profiling, to send segmented emails. Use those same data points to create targeted dynamic content within broadcast, seasonal, and other messages.

**Smart targeting naturally
sends more email to only
those subscribers who will be
the most receptive to it.**

These one-to-some email tactics send more messages and more personalized messages to subscribers who:

☐ Have indicated their preferences

☐ Are clicking in your emails, on your website, and in your mobile app

☐ Are responding to progressive profiling done via email, your website, your mobile app, or some other channel

Additionally, set up an array of events that trigger one-to-one emails that arrive when subscribers are the most responsive. If all that is successful, then you'll also be sending transactional emails, which can themselves generate additional sales.

As with one-to-some messages, your one-to-one emails naturally go to your most engaged subscribers. In addition to being low-risk, one-to-one emails are critical because these very relevant messages convert at a high rate.

**Sophisticated email marketers
generate most of their
revenue from triggered
and transactional emails.**

Subscriber Personas by Email Volume & Type

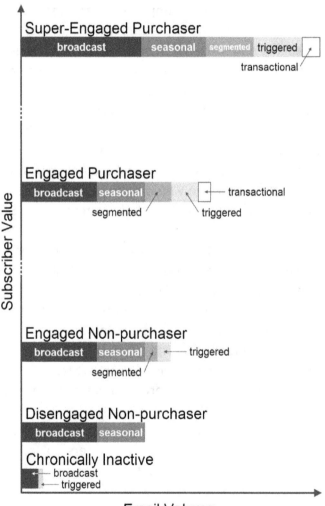

FIGURE 34

When coupled with good inactivity management, this approach results in different subscriber personas receiving different volumes and types of email messages. For example, a super-engaged purchaser would have opted up into additional broadcast and seasonal mailstreams, would receive many segmented and triggered emails because of their high engagement level, and would get transactional emails from their purchases.

At the other end of the spectrum, a chronically inactive subscriber would receive a reduced number of broadcast emails and the only triggered emails they'd receive would be inaction-triggered messages aimed at getting them to reengage. (See Fig. 34 on previous page.)

Catering to and optimizing your messaging and message volume for those personas—and all the variations in between—is key to serving them well and maximizing their value as a subscriber and customer.

Measure how well you're serving these subscriber personas by the strength of your persona mix and how well you convert less valuable personas into more valuable ones through triggered interventions.

Although elevating subscribers from one level to the next is not easy, when marketers do so, the rewards grow exponentially.■

The Subscriber Lifecycle

*"The customers are the assets;
not the store and not the ecommerce sites."*

—Michael Brown, Partner at A.T. Kearney

To maximize the value of an email relationship, you need to cater to your subscribers' needs and wants throughout their entire subscriber lifecycle—from the time they sign up to the time they unsubscribe. To do that, you have to develop tactics that address the major subscriber moments from beginning to end.

The subscriber lifecycle has six stages: Acquisition, Onboarding, Engagement, Reengagement, Super-Engagement, and Transition.

The acquisition and onboarding stages are at the start of the email relationship. The three engagement stages are in the middle. And the transition stage is at the end of the lifecycle. (See Fig. 35 on next page.) Many brands don't have programs in place to address subscribers during each of these stages, but every brand should.

The Subscriber Lifecycle

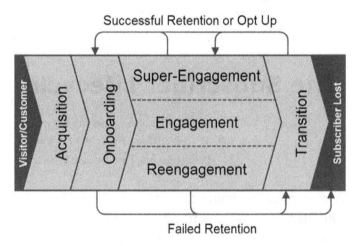

FIGURE 35

---

1. ACQUISITION STAGE

The acquisition stage consists of the methods you use to get consumers to opt in to your email program, as well as the entirety of a confirmed opt-in process. This is where you answer the "What's in it for me?" question would-be subscribers ask themselves and where you set expectations around the content of your email and the frequency at which you'll send them.

Depending on the acquisition source, consumers will need a different level of convincing and of explanation. In general, sources farther from your sales and service operations will require stronger messaging, just as they tend to require a higher level of permission to avoid deliverability risks.

2. ONBOARDING STAGE

The onboarding stage consists of your opt-in confirmation page and your welcome email or welcome email series. This stage starts immediately after the acquisition stage and could last many weeks.

Again, you'll want to address new subscribers differently depending on their acquisition source and customer history.

3. ENGAGEMENT STAGE

The engagement stage consists of your baseline promotional mailstream. For most brands, these will be your regularly scheduled broadcast emails, plus the increases in seasonal messaging that occur around your key selling seasons.

4. REENGAGEMENT STAGE

Supplementing or replacing the engagement stage, the reengagement stage consists of messaging tactics designed to address inactive subscribers and those in danger of soon becoming inactive. These tactics include:

☐ Sending win-back, reengagement, and other inaction-triggered emails

☐ Sending different messages and using different envelope or body content than what engaged subscribers receive

☐ Withholding emails for a number of weeks

☐ Drastically reducing email frequency to minimize the risk to your sender reputation posed by inactive subscribers

The purpose of the reengagement stage is to return disengaged subscribers to the engagement stage rather than having them progress to the transition stage.

5. SUPER-ENGAGEMENT STAGE

Supplementing or replacing the engagement stage, the super-engagement stage consists of tactics that further engage your most engaged subscribers.

These tactics, all of which result in these subscribers receiving additional emails, include:

☐ Setting up an array of action-triggered messages, including browse and cart abandonment emails, back-in-stock notification emails, replenishment emails, and other post-purchase emails

☐ Sending segmented messages based on browse and purchase behavior, expressed preferences, and progressive profiling

☐ Giving subscribers opportunities to give you more information through your preference center and progressive profiling and then using that information to power segmentation and personalization

☐ Offering a loyalty program with a supplemental mailstream or a higher-volume mailstream that replaces the one that non-loyalty members receive

☐ Getting subscribers to opt up into additional mailstreams, whether offered by your brand or by your sister brands

While reengagement reduces

the risks posed by inactives,

super-engagement fosters more opportunities with active subscribers.

6. TRANSITION STAGE

And lastly, the transition stage consists of your unsubscribe page, preference center, opt-out confirmation page, and re-permission emails. The purpose of the transition stage is two-fold.

First, you want to avoid unnecessary damage to your sender reputation. Making it very easy for subscribers to withdraw their permission helps you minimize spam complaints, and letting go of chronically inactive subscribers increases the engagement level of your subscriber base.

And second, you want to attempt to retain the subscriber by giving them alternatives to opting out, such as reducing how often they receive messages or changing their content preferences so the emails they receive are more relevant. In the best possible scenario, a subscriber might adjust their preferences and suddenly be super-engaged.

If none of that can be achieved, then you want to try to get them to opt over to another channel that will serve them better and allow your brand to continue to communicate with the customer. That will lessen the loss of them as an email subscriber.

That said, unsubscribes aren't necessarily forever. People do occasionally re-subscribe later, sometimes through a different email address. And even if that doesn't happen, it's important to recognize that...

The end of an email relationship doesn't mean the end of a business relationship.

So be courteous and gracious during the unsubscribe process to avoid brand damage. Your customers' experiences with your email program are just one facet of their overall impression of your brand.

Although subscribers generally progress though each stage of the lifecycle in a linear fashion—moving from acquisition to onboarding to engagement and finally to transition—that won't always be the case. Depending on what your email program offers, there could be opportunities at each stage to move back to another stage.

For instance, during the transition stage, a subscriber could opt out of the mailstream they were in and then opt into a new one, putting them back at the onboarding stage with the new mailstream. And during the reengagement stage, an email asking the subscriber to update their preferences could lead to the same change of mailstream.

Of course, there are always opportunities for subscribers to skip ahead as well, usually resulting in the abrupt end of the email relationship. For instance, a subscriber could opt out during onboarding, skipping right to the transition stage. And during the engagement stages, they could report your emails as spam or your emails to them could hard bounce, meaning an immediate loss of the subscriber.

So, just as a subscriber can move up and down through the three engagement stages, they might also jump around through the other stages, too. A subscriber's lifecycle is not always a predictable straight line.■

Subscriber Journeys

*"The customer's journey—from behaviors before
they've even opted in to your marketing messages,
all the way through repeat purchases as a loyal buyer—
is critical to not only initial marketing success, but also
to generating long-term revenue from repeat customers."*

—Ellen Valentine, Global Head of Customer Experience
Watson Customer Engagement, IBM

Customer journey maps involve detailing all the different sequences of touchpoints each of your customer personas might use for every action during each of the six components of the customer lifecycle: Awareness, Consideration, Purchase, Usage, Retention, and Evangelism. Mapping all of that out takes a lot of time and the involvement of many departments.

While that's tremendously valuable, let's instead focus on the much more manageable and email-centric activity of creating subscriber journeys.

**Turn a moment into a journey
by turning one email into a series.**

While a subscriber journey can be cut short to just a single email, the objective is to engage subscribers with a series of complementary emails that build upon each other. Subscriber journeys generally start with and rely heavily on triggered or transactional emails, but they can also involve segmented emails. And while subscriber journeys play a role in the onboarding, reengagement, and transition stages of the Subscriber Lifecycle, they really shine in the super-engagement stage.

Creating a subscriber journey involves three major steps:

1. DEFINE PROBLEM OR OBJECTIVE

It all starts with identifying an area of the business that could be improved through an email intervention. Your goal could be expressed in terms of sales, satisfaction, retention, evangelism, or another aspect.

2. FIND MOMENTS THAT MATTER

Next, identify those moments when reaching out to a subscriber with the right message can have a sizable, positive impact. As previously discussed, some common moments that matter involve signups, registrations, purchases, and inactivity.

But to turn that moment into a journey, think about the moment as just the starting point. Many journeys involve interactions over time, so it may be helpful to think about 90-day customer retention, time to first purchase, email engagement during first 30 days as a subscriber, and similar time-delimited metrics.

For example, if you're trying to create greater satisfaction and engagement among your conference attendees, the journey would start with someone registering for the event, which would trigger an initial transactional email and also add that person to a list of attendees that would receive emails before, during, and after the conference.

3. CREATE THE JOURNEY

With the goal defined and the starting point of the intervention identified, now you can start to craft a journey, by answering these questions:

The journey trigger

- ☐ What triggers the journey? Is the first email action-, inaction-, date-, or machine-triggered?

- ☐ Is the first email in the journey sent immediately? If not, how long is the send delayed?

The first email

- ☐ Are there multiple versions of this email based on personas, subscriber geolocation, or other factors?

- ☐ What is the content of each version of the email? Do they include any personalization or dynamic content?

- ☐ What is the primary call-to-action? What are the secondary calls-to-action, if any?

Subsequent emails

- ☐ Is the next email in the journey conditional on anything? Continued action? Further inaction? The value of past actions in the journey, such as the value of a shopping cart or purchase?

- ☐ How long should the delay be between this email and the previous email in the journey?

- ☐ Are there multiple versions of this email?

☐ What is the content of each version?

☐ What are the calls-to-action?

As you determine the logic, timing, and messaging of subsequent emails in the journey, also ask yourself:

☐ What is the journey-ending action, the action that stops subsequent emails in this journey from being sent?

☐ How long will the journey last? Days? Months?

☐ Does this journey scale to the opportunity? Do subscribers receive more or fewer emails based on the value of their actions, profile, etc.?

☐ If all conditions are met, what's the maximum number of messages in this journey?

☐ While a subscriber is on this journey, should other emails be completely or partially suppressed?

As you build out a journey, think about the Customer Lifecycle. Some journeys will be focused on one component of the lifecycle. For instance, a shopping cart abandonment journey might include emails reminding the subscriber what's in their cart and suggesting alternative products, both of which are forms of Consideration.

However, other journeys involve multiple components. That's why I prefer a nested model of the Customer Lifecycle rather than a linear one. (See Fig. 36 on next page.)

For instance, a new email subscriber welcome journey might include emails asking subscribers to

The Customer Lifecycle
Nested Model

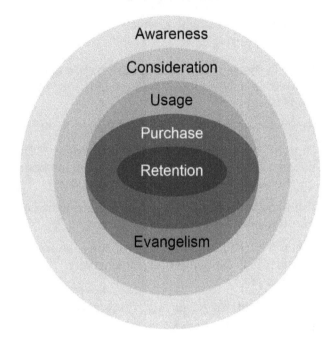

FIGURE 36

---

refer their friends in exchange for an incentive (Evangelism), tell you their favorite brands (Consideration), and follow your brand on social media (Awareness).

A consumable product purchase journey might include emails that confirm the order (Purchase) and provide a subscription offer to deliver more of the product every month (Retention).

A durable goods purchase journey might

include emails that confirm the purchase (Purchase), provide setup or installation instructions (Usage), offer supplemental warranty coverage (Consideration), and ask the subscriber to review the product (Evangelism).

A software trial journey might include emails providing instructions and tips (Usage) and end-of-trial notifications that try to get them to become a customer (Consideration).

An event journey might include emails confirming registration (Purchase), trying to upsell the attendee on a workshop (Consideration), detailing keynote speakers and breakout sessions (Usage), listing recommendations of things to bring to the conference (Usage), and soliciting feedback on the conference after it's over (Evangelism).

And a reengagement journey might include emails asking the subscriber to update their preferences (Consideration), offering them a big discount on their next purchase (Consideration), and telling them about other channels through which they can hear from your brand (Awareness).

This nested model also helps you focus on personas, recognizing that people can advocate for your brand without purchasing it or even using it, and that people can be users of your product without being purchasers. The latter is often the case with B2B products and services, for examples, where executives and other stakeholders sign off on products that others throughout the organization then use.

MAPPING OUT MULTIPLE JOURNEYS

Once you have one journey set up, look for opportunities to set up additional ones. Start by exploring the possibility of expanding existing single-email triggered campaigns. Then try to leverage other moments that matter to create more journeys.

As you do this, continually try to scale the journey to the opportunity. Bigger opportunities deserve longer journeys, while small opportunities deserve short ones—or perhaps just a single triggered email. Use conditional triggers and dynamic content to ensure that every email in a journey is relevant to all of the personas that go on that journey.

Keep track of all of your journeys using a subscriber journey map. (See Fig. 37 on next page.) Consider listing out each of your journeys, noting the number of emails and the goal of each one in terms of building Awareness, Consideration, Purchase, Usage, Retention, or Evangelism. For shorthand, consider using "1A" to denote that the first email in the journey aims to build awareness, for example.

To illustrate what this would look like, Fig. 37 includes mappings of all of the journeys discussed on the past three pages.

After you've done the big picture view of all of your subscriber journeys, then create an email brief for each email in a journey, being sure to note the delay between triggers, any conditions on

Subscriber Journey Map
Unspooled Hub and Spoke Model

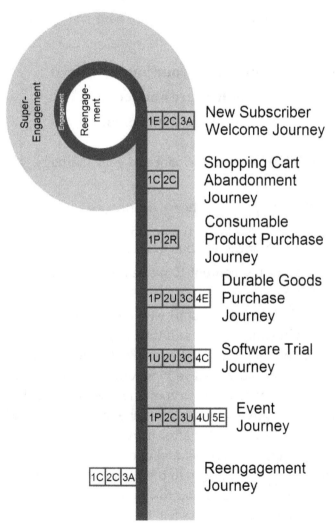

Super-Engagement

Engagement

Reengage-ment

1E 2C 3A — New Subscriber Welcome Journey

1C 2C — Shopping Cart Abandonment Journey

1P 2R — Consumable Product Purchase Journey

1P 2U 3C 4E — Durable Goods Purchase Journey

1U 2U 3C 4C — Software Trial Journey

1P 2C 3U 4U 5E — Event Journey

1C 2C 3A — Reengagement Journey

FIGURE 37

whether a particular email in the journey should be sent, and what the journey-ending action is.

NURTURING EXISTING JOURNEYS

Unlike broadcast emails that are sent and never touched again...

The emails in your journeys need regular care and feeding. These are living emails.

To maximize performance of your journeys, you should:

☐ Routinely review their performance

☐ A/B test the logic, timing, messaging, and other aspects of the various emails in the journey

☐ Update the content to make it seasonally relevant

Don't be afraid to start with minimum viable emails in your journey and then improve them over time. That approach is the topic of the next chapter.

Also, because we live in an omnichannel world, look for opportunities to coordinate your subscriber journeys with actions in other channels. That is the subject of the chapter after next.

Subscriber journeys and one-off triggered and transactional emails drive the majority of email marketing revenue at a growing number of brands. In the years ahead, this will be a vital way that brands use email.

But it's already a growing area of competitive advantage for the brands that have made early investments in journeys, because these take time to set up, build out, and optimize.

Catching up to the leaders will take extra effort. And if you're one of the leaders, continue to press your advantage.■

"A well-designed customer journey map can be priceless. If your resources are scarce, a customer journey map will help you distinguish the critical touchpoints— where certain actions must be taken— from the ones that can be handled later on."

—Irek Klimczak, Content Marketing Expert at GetResponse

The Minimum Viable Email & Incremental Improvements

"The strength and power of anything—whether it is a business, an individual fitness plan, or event—has its foundation in an accumulation of small, incremental improvements that all either fit together or build on each other. To sum it up: small improvement x consistency = substance."

—Nicole Larrauri, President of The EGC Group

Email marketing can seem at times dauntingly complicated. As a consequence, sometimes new projects never get off the ground and big improvements never become a reality because getting from point A to point P or from point J to point T just seems unachievable.

Rather than trying to make an impossible leap, try breaking your email project down into much smaller and much more manageable steps.

MINIMUM VIABLE EMAILS

For new emails, embrace the minimum viable email—the absolute simplest version of an on-brand email that fulfills the intended goal.

For example, if you're creating a shopping cart abandonment email for the first time, build a one-time triggered email with simple logic. And have that email contain simple messaging that tells the subscriber that they left something in their cart and that they can return to their cart to complete their purchase by clicking the included link.

Is that going to be a great execution of a cart abandonment email? No, but it will likely start generating positive returns and, more importantly, it will give you a foundation on which to build.

INCREMENTAL IMPROVEMENTS

Once you have created an email, strive for incremental improvements—small changes or additions in terms of content, design, and other aspects that make the experience better.

One of email marketing's strengths is that email frequencies and volumes are high enough that marketers have plenty of opportunities to make improvements and tests quickly reach statistical significance.

Consider these potential improvements:

Content of email
- ☐ A/B testing of messaging, images, call-to-action, layout, number of content blocks, etc.
- ☐ Including personalization or dynamic content based on stated preferences, behavior, demographics, location, acquisition source, etc.
- ☐ Including live content
- ☐ Including AI-driven content suggestions and

other predictive intelligence
- ☐ Including seasonal messaging

Design of email
- ☐ A/B testing of fonts, styling, colors, layout, etc.
- ☐ Improving legibility
- ☐ Clarifying content hierarchy
- ☐ Emphasizing calls-to-action
- ☐ Removing distractions and adding white space

Rendering of email
- ☐ Improving mobile rendering
- ☐ Improving images-off rendering
- ☐ Improving plain text version
- ☐ Improving other fallbacks

Interactivity of email
- ☐ Including animated GIFs, HTML5 video, and other rich media content
- ☐ Including email carousels, hamburger menus, and other interactive features

Audience of email
- ☐ Improving segmentation by behavior, demographic, psychographic, or other data
- ☐ Improving email's trigger logic

Timing of email
- ☐ Improving time zone optimization
- ☐ Improving seasonal, regional, or temperature-based optimization

Series messaging of email
- ☐ Optimizing number of messages in series

☐ Optimizing timing of each message in series

☐ Setting the optimal conditions under which the next message in the series is sent

Cross-channel coordination of email

☐ Improving coordination with direct mail

☐ Improving coordination with social media

☐ Improving coordination with push messaging

☐ Improving coordination with in-store messaging

☐ Improving coordination with advertising

☐ Improving coordination with other channels

Landing page(s) of email

☐ Improving messaging, design, or functionality of existing landing page(s)

☐ Creating custom landing page(s)

Returning to the example of the minimum viable shopping cart abandonment email: Over time, you could make that email dynamic so it shows the items that were abandoned, add suggestions of alternative products, expand it into a series of emails, and then make those additional emails conditional based on the value of the cart.

Don't be afraid to start small and then gradually make improvements.■

Cross-Channel Synergies

*"Email will be seen as not just a high-ROI channel by itself
but rather a platform that integrates with and
makes other channels more successful."*

—Loren McDonald, Marketing Evangelist at
IBM Watson Marketing

Email marketing is good as a standalone channel,
but it's amazing when it's de-siloed and integrated
with other channels.

There are four primary cross-channel
opportunities to consider when looking at your
channel mix and your marketing priorities:

1. MULTICHANNEL CUSTOMERS

Customers are significantly more valuable and more
engaged when they engage with your brand through
multiple channels. So use email marketing to expose
your customers to other channels. And conversely,
use other channels to grow your email marketing list.

2. MULTI-TOUCH INTERACTIONS

While marketers would love for consumers to
convert after just one exposure to their message,
the vast majority only convert after many

exposures, if they convert at all.

Email marketing can be a valuable part of a multi-touch marketing campaign, echoing the messages that you're using in other channels and drive action and move consumers down the path to sales conversion.

In most cases, the message you use in your email campaigns won't be exactly the same message you use elsewhere, because adapting your message to each channel is important. However, it will reinforce the same overarching message with the same theme, key message, and images, creating a critical mass of messaging that tips the subscriber into converting.

3. CONTENT SYNERGIES

Email is much quicker than some channels like direct mail. It's also more trackable than slower channels like radio. Plus, it's typically less expensive. For all those reasons, email marketing a good testbed for messages to use in those other channels.

The converse is also true: Email marketing can be informed by faster and more dynamic channels, such as site search and social media.

4. UNIQUE IDENTIFIER & PROFILING

Since email addresses are powerful unique identifiers, data from your customers' email marketing interactions can be extremely helpful in building out customer profiles. That data can then be used to power targeted ads and messaging in other channels using the customer's email address.

Email marketing is the perfect companion for all the channels it has supposedly killed or been killed by over the years.

Here are examples of how you can apply these strategies:

Email + Website
- ☐ Include a prominent email signup form on homepage, one in the footer of every page of your site, and one integrated into your checkout process

- ☐ Chose the best landing pages on your website for the calls-to-action in your emails

- ☐ Use browse, carting, and purchase behavior to trigger browse abandonment, cart abandonment, and transactional emails, respectively—as well as to build the subscriber's profile for future segmentation, personalization, dynamic content, and predictive intelligence

- ☐ Use elements of the titles of successful blog posts as subject lines and preview text

Email + Site Search
- ☐ Use trending searches to inform what to promote in your emails and highlight in your subject lines

- ☐ Use trending searches to inform when to send or start including seasonal messaging

- ☐ Include "Top Searches" in emails

Email + Paid Search

☐ Use high-performing paid search terms in your email subject lines and in body copy

☐ Use paid search to A/B test and optimize potential email landing pages, as vice versa

☐ Use paid search to drive visitors to email signup and lead generation pages

Email + Mobile

☐ Use responsive design to target mobile users with mobile-specific calls-to-actions such as a CTA to download your mobile app or sign up to receive text messages

☐ Provide click-to-call phone numbers in your mobile-friendly emails

☐ Use email to reengage subscribers who haven't used your mobile app in a long time

☐ Promote SMS signup to your email subscribers

☐ Allow people to sign up for email by texting you their email address

Email + Social Media

☐ Link to your social media pages in your emails

☐ Include "share with your network" calls-to-actions to spur social sharing of your email content

☐ Use activity, especially trending activity, on your social media pages to inform or determine email content (i.e., highlight most-pinned products)

☐ Use a Facebook tab, Twitter cards, and other social media mechanisms to collect email signups

☐ Use your email list to target subscribers and lookalikes with social media ads

Email + Direct Mail

☐ A/B test images or messaging in emails and use the winners in your direct mail or catalog

☐ Coordinate arrival of email with arrival of direct mail or catalog to attract more attention

☐ Ask subscribers to sign up to receive catalog for more targeted and efficient distribution

☐ Use email and web behavior to power personalized direct mail promotions

☐ Use direct mail to try to reengage inactive subscribers

Email + Stores

☐ Offer e-receipts

☐ Allow store customers to opt in to promotional emails, preferably through kiosk, POS tablet, or pin pad

☐ Set up a geofence around stores during special events that triggers a mobile app push message offering an incentive to users who sign up for email

☐ Use email messaging to recruit seasonal workers, since your subscribers are likely quite familiar with your brand and offerings

☐ Have stores, sales associates, and call center reps report negative customer interactions so promotional emails to those customers might be paused to prevent unsubscribes and spam complaints in response to the bad experience

Email + TV

☐ Tell subscribers about news coverage or other TV attention your products and services get

- ☐ Tell subscribers about upcoming TV specials or appearances on TV shows and encourage them to watch it

- ☐ Give subscribers sneak peeks of major TV commercials such as Super Bowl ad or Super Bowl teaser ads

Consumers don't separate your brand into different channels. They see one brand, and expect organizations to treat them as one person, no matter how many channels they're using to interact with your brand.

With companies shifting from email marketing as a standalone channel to email marketing as an integrated part of an omnichannel experience, make sure that each of your channel teams coordinates their activities and shares insights with the others.■

"Remember: A customer doesn't know there are different teams managing different aspects of their journey—and frankly they don't care. Their expectation is for it to be a seamless experience."

—Jenna Tiffany, Founder & Strategy Director at Let'sTalk Strategy

Recovering from Mistakes

"F**kups are learning opportunities."

—Russell Patton, Senior Email Deployment Specialist at Archer>Malmo

First, let's acknowledge that email marketing mistakes are inevitable. Email is too dynamic, too complex, and too quick of a medium to avoid mistakes completely. The best you can hope for is to keep mistakes infrequent and small, and then to manage them quickly and recover with a degree of grace when they do happen.

Next, let's dispel the idea that every mistake you make deserves a response. By the time you recognize you've made a mistake, behind-the-scenes fixes may not be worth the effort. And if you send a correction or apology email, you run the risk of drawing more attention to the mistake, as well as driving more unsubscribes and spam complaints simply from sending the additional email. So before you do anything, ask yourself...

Is the error minor or easily understood by subscribers as an error?

Minor errors are often overlooked, ignored, and quickly forgotten, so it's best to let these go. These kinds of mistakes might include:

- ☐ Blank subject lines or ones composed of placeholder text
- ☐ Typos in subject lines or body copy
- ☐ Broken first-name personalization
- ☐ Minor rendering issues, such as misaligned images
- ☐ Temporary rendering issues, such as an image server outage
- ☐ Emails that went out a little too early or late
- ☐ Sending the same email to the same recipients multiple times

Subject lines are hotspots for email errors because they are so often left until the last minute to write. I've seen blank subject lines; placeholder text like "To Be Added" and "Postcard Optin"; broken first-name personalization; and tons of misspellings including "Chistmas," "Miniumum," and "Hiliarous." As cringe-inducing as those are, none deserve action.

Image misalignment and unanticipated image borders have also been quite common over the years, in part because of the ever-changing code support at all the various inbox providers. For that reason, it continues to be important to check the rendering of your emails across a wide range of email clients.

Some temporary issues, such as your image

server going down for a while, may also fall into the category of minor errors.

While deployment errors often qualify as significant, sometimes they too can be relatively minor. For example, pet supplies online retailer Drs. Foster & Smith sent out their 2007 "Happy Thanksgiving" season's greeting email a full week early. While some subscribers surely scratched their heads at the timing, it was close enough that it wasn't a big deal. Drs. Foster & Smith wisely refrained from sending any kind of correction or apology and just moved on.

Similarly, sending two or three copies of the same email one right after the other isn't worthy of action either. While the recipients are likely to be a little annoyed by it, everyone will assume it was an error. So sending an apology email may be perceived by some as yet another unnecessary email, exacerbating the problem.

That said, if you accidently sent five or more copies of the same email within a short span of time, then an apology is probably justified because of the magnitude of repetitive emails. For instance, on Aug. 24, 2016, restaurant chain Applebee's sent six emails over 16 minutes. They sent an apology explaining that they "experienced a glitch" in their email service and would be keeping subscribers up to date "in a responsible way" going forward.

If you're unsure if an error is truly minor, check your email metrics. You can also check the buzz about your brand on social media and monitor replies to your emails to help determine if an error is more than minor. Sometimes things aren't as bad as you imagine them to be.

> **Action is needed when an error significantly impairs subscribers' ability to act on the email or causes significant brand damage by annoying, angering, or offending subscribers.**

If you've determined that the error is significant, then ask yourself...

Has the send completed?

Email isn't instantaneous, especially if you're sending to a list of tens or hundreds of thousands or more. If you catch the mistake soon enough, you can pause the send, limiting the number of subscribers exposed to the error and giving you time to find a fix.

At Litmus, thanks to feedback via social media, we recognized a major error breaking the live Twitter feed that we had embedded in our "Save the Date" email promoting our Litmus Live conference in 2015. We were able to pause the send 10 minutes after it started so only 53,000 of our subscribers received the broken email. We then resumed the send an hour later after fixing the issue, and also resent the email to those who received the broken one.

Regardless of whether you're able to pause the

send or not, a fix still may not involve sending another email. Ask yourself...

Can you fix the error or eliminate most of the resulting confusion post-send?

While you can't edit the code of an email after you've sent it, you can take a number of actions that can change the content of the email or clarify the content of the email post-click. Some of these steps include:

☐ Updating image files

☐ Redirecting links

☐ Clarify messaging on the landing page

☐ Changing external CSS style sheets, if used

☐ Updating live content

Gmail's move to cache images has made this tactic less effective, but updating image files is still an effective way to alter email content. The hero image can be replaced. Any graphical text can be changed. And in certain situations, you may be able to overwrite most of the content of an email, as OfficeMax did in a June 15, 2012 email when they discovered they'd accidentally resent an email from the previous week.

In some situations, you might be able to redirect links included in the email. For instance, if you linked to a page on your site that doesn't exist, producing a 404 "page not found" error, you could put a redirect in place to shunt visitors to the correct page. Plus, many email service providers replace all the links in your emails with ESP-hosted links that include tracking. Some ESPs now allow you to change the destination of those tracking links.

You can also use landing page copy to clarify an offer made in an email. For example, on Jan. 6, 2013, Amazon.com accidently sent out an email promoting BCS championship gear 24 hours before the game was to take place. This was obviously an error to anyone who was interested in the game, but Amazon decided to send an apology email, which only drew more attention to the mistake and caused the incident to become overblown.

An alternative would have been to use the landing page to clarify that the products would become available "tomorrow after the game," to respond to social chatter about the error in that channel, and then to re-send the BCS championship gear email after the game as originally planned.

If you're using more advanced functionality like live content that's served up at the time of open and external CSS style sheets, you may be able to make changes to the email so that future opens display the correct content.

If you can't do enough post-send to mitigate a serious error, you should re-send the email with a correction notice or send an apology email.

However, before you send that email to everyone, ask yourself...

Does the error only affect subscribers who click or try to convert?

Some email errors don't affect everyone. In those cases, targeted efforts can fix the situation without drawing undue attention to the mistake. Some subscriber groups that might deserve attention might include subscribers who:

☐ Enabled the email's images to display

☐ Clicked on a broken link or a link to an incorrect landing page

☐ Tried to use a personalized discount code

In these cases, you can use your email analytics to send a corrected email or an apology email only to those who were affected by the mistake.

If the error affects all of your subscribers who received the email, then send a corrected version or an apology email to everyone.

To help minimize the scrambling that's likely to occur in the aftermath of a mistake, draft a generic apology email ahead of time so you can quickly drop new messaging into it when the need arises.

For instance, on July 15, 2013, email marketing agency Alchemy Worx accidentally emailed a rendering test send for one of its clients to the subscribers of the agency's newsletter. Permission is sacred, so it was wise to make it clear to their subscribers that it was a one-time mistake and that they wouldn't be receiving any more emails from the client. Being veteran email marketers,

Alchemy Worx responded quickly, sending a simple email signed by the CEO that succinctly explained the error and apologized.

However, in most cases, you'll be correcting the details of an offer or event. So rather than a dedicated apology email, you'll want to send a corrected version of the email with a brief explanation of what was wrong. Most often brands accomplish this by prefacing their subject line with "Oops:" or "Correction:" and then including a one sentence explanation in the preheader text at the very top of the body copy. Sometimes brands will also alter the hero image to include an apology.

On the upside, using a subject line that makes it clear that you're apologizing generally translates into higher open rates. Schadenfreude gets the best of us all.

Some brands seem to be very prone to apologizing, and that might be on purpose. However, since it's difficult to measure the long-term brand damage done by overly frequent apologies, it's best to spend your goodwill when you actually make a mistake.

While speed is of the essence, it's critical to avoid compounding the situation by making mistakes in your correction or apology email.

That may seem obvious, but this has happened on numerous occasions. For instance, on Mar. 30,

2007, MLB Shop sent an email that contained no body copy at all. The next day they resent the email, using the same subject line, and the body copy was completely missing again. Your response to a mistake should help you regain the confidence of your subscribers, not lose more of it.

Once you've sent your correction or apology email, you may not be done. Ask yourself…

Does the mistake warrant wider damage control?

Sometimes email mistakes have an impact that goes well beyond your subscribers. In these cases, you may need to get your public relations, legal, call center, social media, and other teams involved.

Such ill fortune struck Shutterfly when a May 14, 2014 email congratulating new moms was accidently sent to a "large group of customers" who didn't recently have a child. For the recipients who'd had miscarriages or difficulties conceiving, the email caused them genuine pain—and some of them made their feelings known via social media, where the story took off. In response, Shutterfly wisely sent an email apologizing, tweeted an apology, and responded to media inquiries about the issue with more apologies.

Over the years, numerous universities including Carnegie Mellon, Johns Hopkins University, and Fordham University have erroneously sent acceptance emails to students who weren't supposed to receive them. In each of those cases, the response involved emailed apologies as well as social media and PR interventions.

Even if the mistake doesn't warrant wider damage control, consider giving customer service reps and social media managers a heads up in case they get questions about it.

Keep in mind that your email audience and your social audience aren't exactly the same, and that only a fraction of your email subscribers will likely be aware of any kind of email marketing mistake you've made. So be wary of broadcasting any apologies or corrections via social media unless you're doing wider damage control.

Replying directly to people who comment about the mistake is generally a better strategy for eliminating any confusion, and has the added benefit of not drawing more attention to the matter.

AFTER THE DUST SETTLES

Whether the error warranted no response or an "all hands on deck" response, be sure to take note of the date, mistake, the cause of the error, and your response for your records. Then ask yourself the final question in this overall process... (See Fig. 38 on next page.)

Can I change my process to reduce the chance of this mistake recurring in the future?

Sometimes errors are simply unavoidable. On

How to Recover from a Mistake

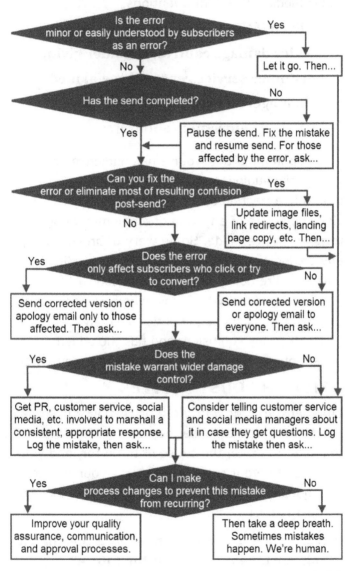

FIGURE 38

occasion, unique, unusual, and even extraordinary circumstances intervene and mess things up. But you can usually avoid these mistakes by putting the right safeguards in place.

So anytime your organization suffers a significant email marketing mistake—or a string of minor ones—it's worth reviewing what went wrong and figuring out whether any changes in process are needed. Some process changes to consider might be:

☐ Creating a brief for every email to ensure that the goals, messaging, audience, and timing are all clear—and then double-checking the final email against this brief

☐ Eliminating production processes that invite errors

☐ Restricting access to certain tools or tool functions for some team members

☐ Improving copyediting

☐ Using an email rendering tool to ensure emails display and function as intended across all email client and browser combinations

☐ Ensuring all links function, lead to the correct destinations, and have the correct tracking

☐ Running the final email through spam filter tests

☐ Strengthening the approval process

☐ Adding other checks to your pre-send checklist

Having a rigorous email production workflow with clear lines of responsibility and good lines of communication can go a long way toward keeping mistakes rare and small.■

Email Marketing Workflows

"Every designer has a different workflow when it comes to designing emails."

—Lee Monroe, Designer at Mesosphere

Every email you create should contribute to your overarching strategy and be informed by the regular monitoring of the industry and the programs of your peers and competitors. And in creating each of those emails, you should follow a clear, documented, and consistent email production workflow.

A basic email workflow has eight steps: Conception, Copywriting, Design, Development, Audience Selection, Approval, Send, and Analysis.

Let's discuss each of these steps in more detail:

1. CONCEPTION

☐ Brainstorm and strategize email

☐ Create email brief

☐ Make assignments and set deadlines

☐ Get signoffs on brief

In this critical first step, you hash out the idea and reasoning behind the email—and then thoroughly document the goal, audience, messaging, key performance indicators, and other elements of the email in a brief.

Keep assignments and deadlines in the brief and have all key stakeholders sign off on it so that it becomes a single point of reference.

If you work with an agency, freelancers, or consultants, this step is extra critical and can take on a contractual quality.

2. COPYWRITING

- ☐ Write subject line and preview text
- ☐ Write body copy
- ☐ Acquire images and conceptualize art
- ☐ Write alt text
- ☐ Write plain text version of email
- ☐ Review, revise, and finalize all content

The second step is to work on the text of the email, including the envelope content and the HTML and plain text parts of the body content.

If you have images that you know will be used in the email, consider going ahead and writing *alt* text for them—although some may find it more natural to write this during either the design or development steps.

If you don't have existing images to use, spend a little time brainstorming visual concepts, themes, and elements.

3. DESIGN

☐ Create wireframe or choose template

☐ Review, revise, and finalize wireframe

☐ Create images

☐ Design email

☐ Review, revise, and finalize design

The third step is to decide the layout and graphics for the email. If you're creating an email design from scratch, you'll want to finalize a wireframe or sketch of the overall design before spending too much time on graphics. However, if you're using a template, then the layout will be largely predetermined.

When creating images, consider image file formats and sizes to ensure that your email's load time will be reasonable. Be extra mindful of load times if you're using any animated GIFs.

4. DEVELOPMENT

☐ Code email

☐ Add Google Analytics and other tracking and analytics coding

☐ Check personalization, dynamic content, and other data logic, including defaults

☐ Import email into email service provider

☐ Test email rendering, load time, links, spam filtering, progressive enhancements, interactivity, etc.

☐ Review, revise, and finalize coding

The fourth step is to code the email, including

tracking and any data merges needed for personalization and other content.

While the copywriting and design steps included review phases, testing and review is extra important during development because email client environments are inconsistent and can change without notice.

5. AUDIENCE SELECTION

☐ Select list, define segmentation, or set up trigger logic

☐ Set up A/B testing, including sample sizes, winner selection criteria, etc.

With the email written, designed, and coded, the next step is to select the audience, whether that's selecting an existing list, creating a segmented list, or defining a trigger for the email. Audience selection is also a critical step in running any A/B test on an email.

6. APPROVAL

☐ Check email against brief

☐ Seek approvals

☐ Revise email until all approvals obtained

The sixth step is to present the final draft to your stakeholders so you can get approval. But before you do that, it's best to do a final check against the brief to make sure that there wasn't scope creep or any drift in the message or goals.

Note that all of the previous steps also included some level of review and approval, which should have also entailed looking at the brief for guidance, but this step is where final approval of the entire email is sought.

7. SEND

- ☐ Complete pre-send checklist
- ☐ Schedule send or enable triggered email
- ☐ Monitor send—halting send and sending a correction or apology email, if necessary

Once full approval is secured, you're ready to send the broadcast or segmented email, or launch the triggered or transactional email.

However, before you do, it's highly advised that you run through a pre-send checklist. Yours may already have items checked off from the completion of earlier steps, and that's fine.

But you'll want your checklist to include final checks of all the critical elements that ensures the email displays and functions as intended, and that you're sending this email to the right people at the right time.

And after you send the email, you'll want to do some monitoring to ensure that all went as planned and that no interventions are necessary.

8. ANALYSIS

- ☐ Post-send email and subscriber analytics
- ☐ Examine A/B testing results
- ☐ Document learnings and opportunities, and make any necessary adjustments to your workflow for the future

The final step is to follow up on the performance of the email at an appropriate time. For a broadcast or segmented email, that might be five or so days post-send; for triggered and transactional emails, maybe a few weeks post-launch.

Email marketing is an iterative process. With every send, look for lessons learned to apply to future emails. And with every month or two of triggered activity, uncover potential improvements that you can make—and perhaps even apply those improvements to your other triggered emails. But you can only do that if you monitor performance.

These ongoing learnings, along with the continual monitoring of industry trends and competitors and peers for inspiration, constitute a growing foundation or zero step to your workflow.

MODEL YOUR OWN PROCESS

Adapt these steps to your own email creation process. For instance, if one person both writes and codes your emails, then consider merging those two steps. The same may be true if the same person both designs and codes your emails.

Also, if you work with an agency on one of more of these steps, then you may have additional phases of a step that involve the presentation of work and formal rounds of revisions.

Whatever your circumstances, constructing a clear process helps establish expectations and clarifies roles, both of which will help your organization create better emails.∎

Email Attribution

"Attribution is hard. Prospects and customers engage with brands across so many touchpoints along the path-to-purchase, and marketers struggle with effectively assigning influence to their various investments."

—Tom Lee, Group Product Manager at LinkedIn

Attribution for every marketing channel is tough. Email marketing is no different.

Email marketing has a reputation of being a highly measurable channel. That reputation is only half-deserved, a fact that creates additional problems because marketers often think they're seeing the whole picture when they're not.

LINEAR & NON-LINEAR INTERACTIONS

Linear email interactions are very trackable—where a subscriber receives an email, opens it, clicks a call-to-action, and then converts on the landing page. So long as you use tracking UTMs for Google Analytics and your email service provider is tracking clicks appropriately, you can easily connect the dots from email to conversion.

This is especially true if you're using a last touch attribution model, where all credit is given to the final touchpoint that precedes a conversion.

But consumers are routinely non-linear creatures. Subscribers will see an email, not open it, and then go and convert because of it anyway. Or they could open it, not click, and convert. Or see the email and tweet about it, causing several other people to convert.

While advancements in analytics and tracking are helping marketers connect the dots on consumer behavior better than ever, that progress is racing against the proliferation of dots to connect. That's a race that technology may eventually win, but for the foreseeable future we should acknowledge that:

> **Whatever revenue or activity**
>
> **you can attribute to email marketing**
>
> **is simply a proxy for what's**
>
> **actually happening.**

That said, marketers can use a variety of tactics and measurement approaches to get a more accurate picture of how email marketing is contributing to your business.

BETTER TRACKING

Standard tracking can miss non-linear behaviors, as well as pass-along behavior. Here are a few ways to better connect email content to action:

☐ Unique online and in-store discount codes for the email channel—or, better yet, unique discount codes for each subscriber, and then encourage or incentivize sharing of that code to identify influencers

☐ Email channel–exclusive discounts that can only be redeemed by clicking through an email

☐ A unique telephone number for the email channel (even subscriber-specific phone numbers for individual-level tracking are possible)

These techniques let you trace activity back to the email channel, and can start to give you better visibility into the indirect influence of email. They can increase the accuracy of metrics like email campaign revenue, revenue per email campaign, email and sales conversion rates, email marketing revenue, and email marketing profit.

SEEING THE INVISIBLE

But even with better tracking, email's influence can be elusive because subscriber actions can be so incredibly varied, widespread, and non-linear. Here are a number of ways to take a more holistic approach to measuring email's influence:

Revenue/activity on email send days. Look at what happens to your sales, website traffic, social media mentions, app downloads, call center activity, and other channels on days that you send an email. Chances are that you'll see spikes, even if the email didn't direct subscribers to those channels. That's because—opened or not—

Emails prompt brand activity,

not just email activity.

The upside of this approach is that it's easy to calculate and captures both subscriber's direct and indirect action, plus word-of-mouth, social buzz, and forwards that started with your subscribers.

The downside is that email's influence will be hard to see if you're emailing more than every third day. This approach doesn't capture the impact of targeted campaigns very well, if at all, so it's best for examining the influence of broadcast email campaigns.

Total revenue per active subscriber over a period of time like a month, quarter, or year. While you can do a separate calculation just looking at email revenue per subscriber, for this metric, look at all the revenue you get from your subscribers regardless of channel origin. Include all subscribers who haven't been deemed chronically inactive and removed from your active mailing list. Divide that total by the average number of active subscribers you had during that time period.

This metric has a few advantages. First, it recognizes that the giving of an email address is a sign of trust and signals greater intent. Even if a subscriber doesn't engage with your emails very often, the sheer fact that they're a subscriber will generally increase the amount they spend or donate to your brand.

Second, it captures all indirect personal activity. So if seeing an email's subject line drives them to convert in another channel, this metric captures that.

And third, if your brand is using email addresses to target customers and prospects via social media or other channels, the metric captures any success in other channels that is due to getting that email address as an identifier.

The downside of this approach is that it only captures subscriber activity, not any passalong or word-of-mouth influence. It also captures all activity by the subscriber, not just actions driven by email messaging.

Incremental lift filters out activity that would have occurred naturally in the absence of email's influence. Measuring incremental lift is done by doing a withhold study, which involves stopping sending all email (except transactional emails) to a group of subscribers for a period of time, and then comparing the activity of those subscribers to the activity of a control group of similar subscribers who received emails normally.

Use a statistical significance calculator to determine the appropriate size of your withhold and control groups. Plan to run withhold tests during off-peak and peak seasons to get the most accurate results.

The downside of this approach is that it's difficult to execute, reduces your email revenue because you're not sending to some subscribers, doesn't capture passalong or word-of-mouth influence from email, and potentially confuses or irritates subscribers who had their email withheld.

To mitigate the risks around that last downside,

make customer service reps aware of who is in a withhold group and allow them to add back in any subscribers who reach out to complain that they haven't been receiving emails from your brand.

Value of an email address. Each of those three metrics can give you a way to calculate the value of an email address by comparing subscribers to non-subscribers. Alone or in combination, they can help you determine the productivity of your email list, which is a deep metric that's superior to a surface metric like list size.

Knowing the value of an email address to your brand is powerful not only because it helps put a value on your email program, but because it informs how much you should be spending to acquire subscribers in terms of advertising, incentives, events, and other list-building tactics.

PIECEMEAL VIEW

For high-consideration and long-lifespan goods and services, sales conversions may be so far between that revenue-oriented metrics need to be heavily augmented with activity-oriented metrics to see progress down the sales funnel.

The best metric here is **average cost per action**. How much do you spend on advertising, incentives, events, and other channel activities to get your customers and prospects to:

☐ Download an ebook or report

☐ Register for a webinar or other event

- ☐ Download your mobile app
- ☐ Take a survey, quiz, or other progressive profiling device
- ☐ Read a blog post or article
- ☐ Apply for a credit card or financing

When you have an average cost per action calculated, you can then attribute that value to your email program every time it drives that action.

NO SINGLE METRIC

You'll likely discover that there's no one metric that tells you everything you want to know about the topline success of your email program. Just like it's foolish to rely solely on first-, last-, or any-touch attribution to get the big picture of how your email marketing program is doing, you'll likely want to use a mix of key performance indicators.

It's worth noting as you analyze your KPIs, see what's moving the needle, and devise changes that while data-driven decisions are great, staying true to your brand is also important. Don't let your dashboard vectors replace your brand compass.■

"The most important things don't show up in analytics. I want a graph of hand-written thank you notes received and karma earned."

—Andy Crestodina, Co-Founder & Strategic Director of Orbit Media Studios; author of *Content Chemistry*

The Last Word on the Frameworks

The Team Rule

Depending on the size of your organization and the industry that you're in, the responsibilities for email marketing might fall entirely on you or a small group of coworkers. Don't let yourself get siloed and isolated.

Email marketing works best as part of a comprehensive cross-channel strategy that receives input from multiple sources—including the web, store, merchandising, social, customer service, management, and broader marketing teams.

That fact gives us our third Power Rule, *The Team Rule:*

Email marketing is a team sport,

where you have to collaborate with

and understand other teams,

and vice versa.

The *vice versa* in this rule is particularly critical. Not only do you need to educate yourself about the concerns and goals of your colleagues, you need to educate them about email marketing best practices so they understand your issues and objectives.

I hope this book helps you to do that—particularly with executives, who can take your email program to new heights with their support.■

"Email marketers have to successfully 'manage up' to executives with excellent analytical skills and storytelling skills. And it's an absolute imperative to be networking and building connections within your organization and not operating as a silo."

—Melissa Shaw, Co-Founder & Co-CEO of Shaw + Scott

PART III

The Future

Email marketing is a living machine that's always changing and evolving. In this final part, let's look at some of the developments likely to occur in the coming years.■

The Only Constant

11 Ways Email Marketing Will Change
in the Decade Ahead

"As a company, you need to get to the future first,
ahead of your customers, and be ready to
greet them when they arrive."

—Marc Benioff, Founder, Chairman, & CEO of Salesforce

Because it's well established among consumers and the vendor community, people like to refer to the email channel as *mature*. However, don't mistake that to mean it's static. It's far from it. (See Fig. 39 on next page.)

Over the past decade:

☐ The definition of *spam* has been completely redefined because of inbox providers successfully blocking malicious, unwanted email

☐ Social media gave marketers new content for their emails and gave subscribers new ways to share email content

☐ Inbox providers began factoring engagement rates into their filtering algorithms, forcing marketers to overhaul their list building and list hygiene practices

☐ Email automation tools allowed brands to

respond quickly to subscriber actions with the right triggered message

☐ The iPhone and all the mobile devices that followed radically reshaped email design and brought a newfound immediacy to email

☐ The emergence of Big Data allowed brands to take personalization and targeting to the next level

The next decade of email marketing will surely be just as dynamic. Here are some of the ways that email marketing is likely to evolve in the years ahead:

_____

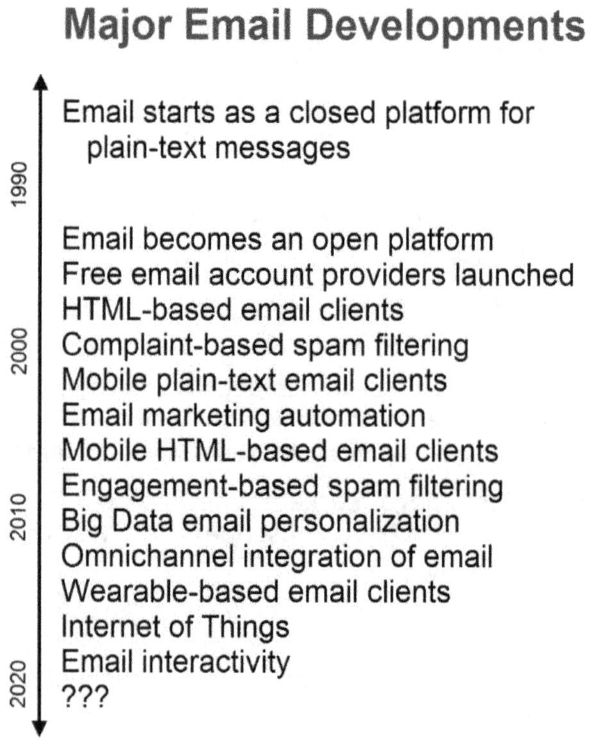

Major Email Developments

1990
Email starts as a closed platform for
   plain-text messages

2000
Email becomes an open platform
Free email account providers launched
HTML-based email clients
Complaint-based spam filtering
Mobile plain-text email clients
Email marketing automation
Mobile HTML-based email clients

2010
Engagement-based spam filtering
Big Data email personalization
Omnichannel integration of email
Wearable-based email clients
Internet of Things

2020
Email interactivity
???

FIGURE 39

Email rendering will become even more complex as the market for wearables and the Internet of Things take off. Some devices will be able to display full emails, whereas others will show only subject lines, making clarity within envelope copy even more important.

Because of shrinking device sizes, the voice- and gesture-based navigation of inboxes and the **audio transcription** of emails will become issues at some point. Email design concerns will then include determining which content is read out and picking the appropriate voice "fonts" and intonation "styles." Voice interfaces may empower brands to create voice-optimized emails by introducing a voice-html part of multipart MIME emails.

> **Responsive design will take on entirely new dimensions because of the rise of wearables and voice-driven interfaces.**

Image blocking will cease to be an issue. Inbox providers won't see it as a security issue and their ability to block spam will make it unnecessary.

The trend toward **inboxes within inboxes** will continue, primarily through the further rollout of tabbed inboxes that partition inboxes into sub-inboxes. Consumers can manage their email more easily when similar messages are grouped.

This allows email users get in a shopping or social frame of mind, for instance, and then deal with all the emails of that sort. Better organized and more logical inboxes are good for email users, email marketers, and inbox providers.

Relatedly, email inboxes will slowly continue to take on more communication functionality, creeping toward becoming a **unified inbox**, where emails, texts, social updates, voicemails, and other messages will comingle just one click away from each other. Mobile devices have provided a template for how to do this, with alerts and notifications all appearing on lockout screens.

Along with mixing of media types, the inbox will gain more **rich content and interactivity**. People will be able to play videos, browse product assortments, and eventually even make purchases—all without leaving their inboxes. Moreover, all content will be up to date at the time it's opened.

> **The emails of the future will be much more like sending subscribers a microsite than a static message.**

Personalization, segmentation, and triggered emails will be used at much higher levels than they are today thanks to marketers' ability to tap **Big Data**, harness cross-channel integration, and leverage sophisticated digital marketing platforms. As a result, email marketing will become even more profitable—even after taking into account rising production and platform costs.

Artificial intelligence and automation will make acting on Big Data much easier and make data-driven marketing much more pervasive. AI will take over some email marketing tasks completely, particularly those that require instant action. Automation will become more fluid and adaptive, shifting from being prescriptive to principle-based sense and respond.

However, in most cases, machine learning will simply provide email marketers with suggestions for triggers, segmentation, offers, copy, subject lines, and more.

Going hand in hand with Big Data, the collection of personal data will likely become much more transparent and permission-based. Email preference centers will morph into **communication preference and profile centers**, where consumers can modify their cross-channel messaging preferences and edit personal information collected about themselves.

This will largely come about because of changes in **consumer attitudes toward privacy**. More companies will incorporate privacy protections into products. In fact, device and software companies will eventually compete on their default privacy features.

Along the way, it seems inevitable that new **privacy and data security legislation and regulations** will come into effect. As has been the trend in recent years, these advancements will be driven by Europe, with the U.S. quietly resisting.

Underlying all of this is the fact that...

The single most disruptive force affecting email marketing is the rising expectations of subscribers.

Because there's always a small number of leading brands that are delivering exceptional email and omnichannel experiences. These brands gradually raise subscribers' expectations, making it more challenging for all other brands.

Given the constant change in our industry, especially on the technology front, it pays to be proactive. If you wait until there are five case studies in hand before implementing or even testing a particular change or tactic, you will have guaranteed that you're a year or more behind some of your competitors.

As an email marketer, if you're not living at least six months in the future, you're in trouble.

Content schedules, testing schedules, and technology upgrade and rollout schedules are all critical to competing effectively in the email marketing industry. The future of email is always in motion, so you always have to be chasing it. Thankfully, the velocity of email marketing is so fast you have nearly unparalleled opportunities to fail small and then quickly recover and improve.

Despite all of these possible changes, the one

thing that won't happen anytime soon is email being disrupted and overtaken by another channel. Despite claims that social and mobile were the new kings of communication, those channels only made email more relevant and more entrenched in the end.

Email hasn't been dethroned because no other channel can match its scale, richness of message, one-to-one capabilities, or open platform. That last point is critical and why Facebook, a closed platform, will never become large enough to threaten email in any meaningful way.

The only thing that could threaten email would be another open platform—possibly an open platform social network with email at its core. Email's core technologies are more than a decade old, so this new platform might come from a major refresh of the underlying technology driven by Google or Microsoft.

Similar to the way open standards forced AOL (the market leading inbox provider in the 1990s) to eventually allow its users to email non-AOL users, the same thing might happen with social media. If this happens, you can expect a new edition of *Email Marketing Rules* to follow shortly thereafter.∎

"Email is the new email."

—Jordie van Rijn, Founder of Email Monday

The Last Word on the Future

The Evolving Rule

Books are a great way to appreciate the big picture, understand the general state of the industry, and get a firm grasp on the fundamentals. However, because email marketing is a dynamic and rapidly changing channel, books are not the ideal way to stay up to date.

That fact brings us to our fourth and final Power Rule, *The Evolving Rule:*

> **Be constantly learning and**
>
> **experimenting because**
>
> **email marketing**
>
> **is always evolving.**

This is only the beginning of your email marketing journey—a journey that frankly never ends. I've been doing email marketing research for more than a decade and I can honestly say there's no shortage of new trends, tactics, and tools to explore.

I hope that *Email Marketing Rules* has helped propel you on your journey by giving you new perspectives, sparking your imagination, and getting you excited about improving your program.

Before you do that, however, here are three final steps you should take:

1st

If you enjoyed this book and think others would benefit from reading it, please submit a short review on Amazon.com. Reviews have a huge impact on the visibility of a book, and are especially meaningful for independent authors like me.

2nd

Visit EmailMarketingRules.com and sign up to receive updates via email to get my latest thoughts on everything email marketing—including new email marketing research, current examples of inspiring email campaigns, and timely discussions about the issues affecting our industry.

You'll also find links to follow me on social media.

3rd

Connect with others in the email marketing community, starting with some of the wonderful experts who regularly inspire me, who I list along with their Twitter handles in the Acknowledgments on the page after next. You can also find this list at

EmailMarketingRules.com/Experts/.

Follow them. And follow the people that they interact with.

If you're not on Twitter, track them down on LinkedIn and connect with them there.

The email marketing community is very active, surprisingly open, and extremely welcoming, so I wholeheartedly encourage you to jump in and join the conversation.

And although social networks are wonderful, attending conferences can be even more rewarding. Conferences offer educational content and great networking opportunities, allowing you to meet face-to-face and shake hands with the folks you've connected with online.

I wish you all the best with your email efforts and hope to see you online or at an event soon.∎

Acknowledgments

Brilliant People to Whom I'm Grateful

This book is the culmination of a thousand conversations. Some of those were live, via email, on Twitter, or through comments on my blog posts. Others were silent conversations I had by reading the articles, whitepapers, and blog posts of my peers.

I am grateful for all the conversations I've had over the years, but I am especially grateful for those I've had with...

Justine Jordan (@meladorri)
Jeffrey K. Rohrs (@jkrohrs)
Joel Book (@joelbook)
Jay Baer (@jaybaer)
Loren McDonald (@LorenMcDonald)
Simms Jenkins (@SimmsJenkins)
John Caldwell (@jacaldwell)
Ryan Phelan (@ryanpphelan)
Dave Chaffey (@davechaffey)
Tim Watson (@tawatson)
Jordan Cohen (@jcohen808)
Jeanne Jennings (@jeajen)
Scott Hardigree (@indiescott)

Len Shneyder (@LenShneyder)

Kevin Mandeville (@KevinMandeville)

Jason Rodriguez (@RodriguezCommaJ)

Elliot Ross (@iamelliot)

Jordie van Rijn (@jvanrijn)

Dela Quist (@DelaQuist)

Derek Harding (@innovyx)

Morgan Stewart (@trendlinei)

Andrew Kordek (@andrewkordek)

Laura Atkins (@wise_laura)

George Bilbrey (@returnpath)

Alex Williams (@alexcwilliams)

Ben Chestnut (@benchestnut)

Kara Trivunovic (@ktrivunovic)

Kristina Huffman (@krudz)

Andrea Smith (@andreasmith77)

David Daniels (@EmailDaniels)

James Koons (@Email_Privacy)

Andrew Bonar (@andrewbonar)

Ros Hodgekiss (@yarrcat)

Matthew Vernhout (@emailkarma)

Al Iverson (@aliverson)

Spencer Kollas (@spencerkollas)

Heather Goff (@HPGchatting)

Dennis Dayman (@ddayman)

...as well as Jay Brangiforte, Mark Brownlow, Aaron Smith, Lisa Harmon, DJ Waldow, Dylan Boyd, Jeanniey Mullen, and the late, great Stefan Pollard. Thank you all for shaping, confirming, and challenging my views.

For helping me complete this book, I'm indebted to my amazing editors—Jeffrey K. Rohrs, Joel Book, and Jay Brangiforte. Their insights, guidance, and suggestions were invaluable.

For designing a fantastic book cover, my thanks go to my colleague and fellow email marketing book author Jason Rodriguez.

And for making all my thoughts and sentences a little more succinct and clearer, I'm grateful for my colleague Kayla Lewkowicz and her keen copyediting.

I'd also like to acknowledge Michael Pollan, whose book *Food Rules* strongly influenced the format and style of my book (and perhaps influenced my choice of title as well).

On a more personal note, I'd like to thank my mother, who passed away from cancer during the writing of this edition. She was endlessly supportive of all of my endeavors, because she had endless faith in me. She was a nurse and a serial entrepreneur who reinvented herself several times—and the profound impact she had on my views as a man, father, and husband wasn't clear to me until much later in life. I miss you, Mom.

And finally, my most heartfelt thanks go to my wonderful wife, Kate, who supported and encouraged me during all the late nights and weekends I spent writing this book and the previous two editions, who knows more about email marketing than any doctor should, and who inspired me to write *Email Marketing Rules* in the first place. Thanks, Love. You're the best!■

Index

Where to Find Definitions & Details

Figures

Charts, Diagrams, and Illustrations